Sunny Memories of Foreign Lands
(Volume 1)

Harriet Beecher Stowe

Alpha Editions

This edition published in 2024

ISBN : 9789364731294

Design and Setting By
Alpha Editions
www.alphaedis.com
Email - info@alphaedis.com

As per information held with us this book is in Public Domain.
This book is a reproduction of an important historical work. Alpha Editions uses the best technology to reproduce historical work in the same manner it was first published to preserve its original nature. Any marks or number seen are left intentionally to preserve its true form.

CONTENTS

Preface..- 1 -

Introductory...- 3 -

   Breakfast In Liverpool—April 11............................- 5 -

   Public Meeting In Liverpool—April 13. ....- 8 -

   Public Meeting In Glasgow—April 15. ....- 15 -

   Public Meeting In Edinburgh—April 20. ....- 20 -

   Public Meeting In Aberdeen—April 21. Address Of The Citizens....................................- 29 -

   Public Meeting In Dundee—April 22................- 32 -

   Address Of The Students Of Glasgow University—April 25. ....- 36 -

   Loud Mayor's Dinner At The Mansion House, London—May 2...................................- 38 -

   Stafford House Reception—May 7....................- 39 -

   Congregational Union—May 13........................- 41 -

   Royal Highland School Society Dinner, At The Freemason's Tavern, London— May 14. ....- 51 -

Antislavery Society, Exeter Hall—May 16 .... - 53 -

Soirée At Willis's Rooms—May 25 .... - 59 -

Concluding Note. .... - 66 -

Sunny Memories of Foreign Lands Letter I .... - 67 -

Letter II .... - 76 -

Letter III .... - 94 -

Letter IV .... - 102 -

Letter V .... - 115 -

Letter VI. .... - 123 -

Letter VII .... - 140 -

Letter VIII .... - 155 -

Letter IX .... - 182 -

Letter X .... - 197 -

Letter XI .... - 219 -

Letter XII .... - 234 -

Letter XIII .... - 241 -

Letter XIV .... - 247 -

Letter XV .... - 253 -

Letter XVI ....- 260 -

Letter XVII ....- 269 -

Letter XVIII .... - 278 -

Notes ....- 286 -

PREFACE

THIS book will be found to be truly what its name denotes, "Sunny Memories."

If the criticism be made that every thing is given *couleur de rose*, the answer is, Why not? They are the impressions, as they arose, of a most agreeable visit. How could they be otherwise?

If there be characters and scenes that seem drawn with too bright a pencil, the reader will consider that, after all, there are many worse sins than a disposition to think and speak well of one's neighbors. To admire and to love may now and then be tolerated, as a variety, as well as to carp and criticize. America and England have heretofore abounded towards each other in illiberal criticisms. There is not an unfavorable aspect of things in the old world which has not become perfectly familiar to us; and a little of the other side may have a useful influence.

The writer has been decided to issue these letters principally, however, by the persevering and deliberate attempts, in certain quarters, to misrepresent the circumstances which, are here given. So long as these misrepresentations affected only those who were predetermined to believe unfavorably, they were not regarded. But as they have had some influence, in certain cases, upon really excellent and honest people, it is desirable that the truth should be plainly told.

The object of publishing these letters is, therefore, to give to those who are true-hearted and honest the same agreeable picture of life and manners which met the writer's own, eyes. She had in view a wide circle of friends throughout her own country, between whose hearts and her own there has been an acquaintance and sympathy of years, and who, loving excellence, and feeling the reality of it in themselves, are sincerely pleased to have their sphere of hopefulness and charity enlarged. For such this is written; and if those who are not such begin to read, let them treat the book as a letter not addressed to them, which, having opened by mistake, they close and pass to the true owner.

The English reader is requested to bear in mind that the book has not been prepared in reference to an English but an American public, and to make due allowance for that fact. It would have placed the writer far more at ease had there been no prospect of publication in England. As this, however, was unavoidable, in some form, the writer has chosen to issue it there under her own sanction.

There is one acknowledgment which the author feels happy to make, and that is, to those publishers in England, Scotland, France, and Germany who have shown a liberality beyond the requirements of legal obligation. The author hopes that the day is not far distant when America will reciprocate the liberality of other nations by granting to foreign authors those rights which her own receive from them.

The *Journal* which appears in the continental tour is from the pen of the Rev. C. Beecher. The *Letters* were, for the most part, compiled from what was written at the time and on the spot. Some few were entirely written after the author's return.

It is an affecting thought that several of the persons who appear in these letters as among the living, have now passed to the great future. The Earl of Warwick, Lord Cockburn, Judge Talfourd, and Dr. Wardlaw are no more among the ways of men. Thus, while we read, while we write, the shadowy procession is passing; the good are being gathered into life, and heaven enriched by the garnered treasures of earth.

H.B.S.

INTRODUCTORY

THE following letters were written by Mrs. Stowe for her own personal friends, particularly the members of her own family, and mainly as the transactions referred to in them occurred. During the tour in England and Scotland, frequent allusions are made to public meetings held on her account; but no report is made of the meetings, because that information, was given fully in the newspapers sent to her friends with the letters. Some knowledge of the general tone and spirit of the meetings seems necessary, in order to put the readers of the letters in as favorable a position to appreciate them as her friends were when they were received. Such knowledge it is the object of this introductory chapter to furnish.

One or two of the addresses at each of several meetings I have given, and generally without alteration, as they appeared in the public journals at the time. Only a very few could be published without occupying altogether too much space; and those selected are for the most part the shortest, and chosen mainly on account of their brevity. This is certainly a surer method of giving a true idea, of the spirit which actually pervaded the meetings than could be accomplished by any selection of mere extracts from the several speeches. In that case, there might be supposed to exist a temptation to garble and make unfair representations; but in the method pursued, such a suspicion is scarcely possible. In relation to my own addresses, I have sometimes taken the liberty to correct the reporters by my own recollections and notes. I have also, in some cases, somewhat abridged them, (a liberty which I have not, to any considerable extent, ventured to take with others,) though without changing the sentiment, or even essentially the form, of expression. What I have here related is substantially what I actually said, and what I am willing to be held responsible for. Many and bitter, during the tour, were the misrepresentations and misstatements of a hostile press; to which I offer no other reply than the plain facts of the following pages. These were the sentiments uttered, this was the manner of their utterance; and I cheerfully submit them to the judgment of a candid public.

I went to Europe without the least anticipation of the kind of reception which awaited us; it was all a surprise and an embarrassment to me. I went with the strongest love of my country, and the highest veneration for her institutions; I every where in Britain found the most cordial sympathy with this love and veneration; and I returned with both greatly increased. But slavery I do not recognize as an institution of my country; it is an excrescence, a vile usurpation, hated of God, and abhorred by man; I am under no obligation either to love or respect it. He is the traitor to America, and American institutions, who reckons slavery as one of them, and, as such, screens it from assault. Slavery is a blight, a canker, a poison, in the very heart of our republic; and unless the nation, as such, disengage itself from it, it will most assuredly be our ruin. The patriot, the philanthropist, the Christian, truly enlightened, sees no other alternative. The developments of the present session of our national Congress are making this great truth clearly perceptible even to the dullest apprehension.

C.E. STOWE.

ANDOVER, *May* 30, 1854.

Breakfast In Liverpool—April 11.

THE REV. DR. M'NEILE, who had been requested by the respected host to express to Mrs. Stowe the hearty congratulations of the first meeting of friends she had seen in England, thus addressed her: "Mrs. Stowe: I have been requested by those kind friends under whose hospitable roof we are assembled to give some expression to the sincere and cordial welcome with which, we greet your arrival in this country. I find real difficulty in making this attempt, not from want of matter, nor from want of feeling, but because it is not in the power of any language I can command, to give adequate expression to the affectionate enthusiasm which pervades all ranks of our community, and which is truly characteristic of the humanity and the Christianity of Great Britain. We welcome Mrs. Stowe as the honored instrument of that noble impulse which public opinion and public feeling throughout Christendom have received against the demoralizing and degrading system of human slavery. That system is still, unhappily, identified in the minds of many with the supposed material interests of society, and even with the well being of the slaves themselves; but the plausible arguments and ingenious sophistries by which it has been defended shrink with shame from the facts without exaggeration, the principles without compromise, the exposures without indelicacy, and the irrepressible glow of hearty feeling—O, how true to nature!—which characterize Mrs. Stowe's immortal book. Yet I feel assured that the effect produced by Uncle Tom's Cabin is not mainly or chiefly to be traced to the interest of the narrative, however captivating, nor to the exposures of the slave system, however withering: these would, indeed, be sufficient to produce a good effect; but this book contains more and better than even these; it contains what will never be lost sight of—the genuine application to the several branches of the subject of the sacred word of God. By no part of this wonderful work has my own mind been so permanently impressed as by the thorough legitimacy of the application of Scripture,— no wresting, no mere verbal adaptation, but in every instance the passage cited is made to illustrate something in the narrative, or in the development of character, in strictest accordance with the design of the passage in its original sacred context. We welcome Mrs. Stowe, then, as an honored fellow-laborer in the highest and best of causes; and I am much mistaken if this tone of welcome be not by far the most congenial to her own feelings. We unaffectedly sympathize with much which she must feel, and, as a lady, more peculiarly feel, in passing through that ordeal of gratulation which is sure to attend her steps in every part of our country; and I am persuaded that we cannot manifest our gratitude for her past services in any way more acceptable to herself than by earnest prayer on her behalf that she may be kept in the simplicity of Christ, enjoying in her daily experience the tender consolations of the Divine Spirit, and in the midst of the most flattering commendations saying and feeling, in the instincts of a renewed heart, 'Not unto me, O Lord, not unto me, but unto thy name be the praise, for thy mercy, and for thy truth's sake.'"

PROFESSOR STOWE then rose, and said, "If we are silent, it is not because we do not feel, but because we feel more than we can express. When that book was written, we had no hope except in God. We had no expectation of reward save in the prayers of the poor. The surprising enthusiasm which has been excited by the book all over Christendom is an indication that God has a work to be done in the cause of emancipation. The present aspect of things in the United States is discouraging. Every change in society, every financial revolution, every political and ecclesiastical movement, seems to pass and leave the African race without help. Our only resource is prayer. God surely cannot will that the unhappy condition of this portion of his children should continue forever. There are some indications of a movement in the southern mind. A leading southern paper lately declared editorially that slavery is either right or wrong: if it is wrong, it is to be abandoned: if it is right, it must be defended. The *Southern Press*, a paper established to defend the slavery interest at the seat of government, has proposed that the worst features of the system, such as the separation of families, should be abandoned. But it is evident that with that restriction the system could not exist. For instance, a man wants to buy a cook; but she has a husband and seven children. Now, is he to buy a man and seven children, for whom he has no use, for the sake of having a cook? Nothing on the present occasion has been so grateful to our feelings as the reference made by Dr. M'Neile to the Christian character of the book. Incredible as it may seem to those who are without prejudice, it is nevertheless a fact that this book was condemned by some religious newspapers in the United States as anti-Christian, and its author associated with infidels and disorganizers; and had not it been for the decided expression of the mind of English Christians, and of Christendom itself, on this point, there is reason to fear that the proslavery power of the United States would have succeeded in putting the book under foot. Therefore it is peculiarly gratifying that so full an indorsement has been given the work, in this respect, by eminent Christians of the highest character in Europe; for, however some in the United States may affect to despise what is said by the wise and good of this kingdom and the Christian world, they do feel it, and feel it intensely." In answer to an inquiry by Dr. M'Neile as to the mode in which southern Christians defended the institution, Dr. Stowe remarked that "a great change had taken place in that respect during the last thirty years. Formerly all Christians united in condemning the system; but of late some have begun to defend it on scriptural grounds. The Rev. Mr. Smylie, of Mississippi, wrote a pamphlet in the defensive; and Professor Thornwell, of South Carolina, has published the most candid and able statement of that argument which has been given. Their main reliance is on the system of Mosaic servitude, wholly unlike though it was to the American system of slavery. As to what this American system of slavery is, the best documents for enlightening the minds of British Christians are the commercial newspapers of the slaveholding states. There you see slavery as it is, and certainly without any exaggeration. Read the advertisements for the sale of slaves and for the apprehension of fugitives, the descriptions of the persons of slaves, of dogs for hunting slaves, &c., and you see how the whole matter as viewed by the southern mind. Say what they will about it, practically they generally regard the separation of families no more than the separation of cattle, and the slaves as so much property, and nothing else. Their own papers show that the pictures of the internal slave trade given in Uncle Tom, so far from being overdrawn, fall even below the truth. Go on, then, in forming and expressing your views on this subject. In laboring for the overthrow of American slavery you are pursuing a course of Christian duty as legitimate as in laboring to suppress the suttees of India, the cannibalism of the Fejee Islands, and other barbarities of heathenism, of which human slavery is but a relic. These evils can be finally removed by the benign influence of the love of Christ, and no other power is competent to the work."

Public Meeting In Liverpool—April 13.

THE CHAIRMAN, (A. HODGSON, ESQ.,) in opening the proceedings, thus addressed Mrs. Beecher Stowe: "The modesty of our English ladies, which, like your own, shrinks instinctively from unnecessary publicity, has devolved on me, as one of the trustees of the Liverpool Association, the gratifying office of tendering to you, at then request, a slight testimonial of their gratitude and respect. We had hoped almost to the last moment that Mrs. Cropper would have represented, on this day, the ladies with whom she has cooperated, and among whom she has taken a distinguished lead in the great work which you had the honor and the happiness to originate. But she has felt with you that the path most grateful and most congenial to female exertion, even in its widest and most elevated range, is still a retired and a shady path; and you have taught us that the voice which most effectually kindles enthusiasm in millions is the still small voice which comes forth from the sanctuary of a woman's breast, and from the retirement of a woman's closet—the simple but unequivocal expression of her unfaltering faith, and the evidence of her generous and unshrinking self-devotion. In the same spirit, and as deeply impressed with the retired character of female exertion, the ladies who have so warmly greeted your arrival in this country have still felt it entirely consistent with the most sensitive delicacy to make a public response to your appeal, and to hail with acclamation your thrilling protest against those outrages on our common nature which circumstances have forced on your observation. They engage in no political discussion, they embark in no public controversy; but when an intrepid sister appeals to the instincts of women of every color and of every clime against a system which sanctions the violation of the fondest affections and the disruption of the tenderest ties; which snatches the clinging wife from the agonized husband, and the child from the breast of its fainting mother; which leaves the young and innocent female a helpless and almost inevitable victim of a licentiousness controlled by no law and checked by no public opinion,—it is surely as feminine as it is Christian to sympathize with her in her perilous task, and to rejoice that she has shed such a vivid light on enormities which can exist only while unknown or unbelieved. We acknowledge with regret and shame that that fatal system was introduced into America by Great Britain; but having in our colonies returned from our devious paths, we may without presumption, in the spirit of friendly suggestion, implore our honored transatlantic friends to do the same. The ladies of Great Britain have been admonished by their fair sisters in America, (and I am sure they are bound to take the admonition in good part,) that there are social evils in our own country demanding our special vigilance and care. This is most true; but it is also true that the deepest sympathies and most strenuous efforts are directed, in the first instance, to the evils which exist among ourselves, and that the rays of benevolence which flash across the Atlantic are often but the indication of the intensity of the bright flame which is shedding light and heat on all in its immediate vicinity. I believe this is the case with most of those who have taken a prominent part in this great movement. I am sure it is preeminently the case with respect to many of those by whom you are surrounded; and I hardly know a more miserable fallacy, by which sensible men allow themselves to be deluded, than that which assumes that every emotion of sympathy which is kindled by objects abroad is abstracted from our sympathies at home. All experience points to a directly opposite conclusion; and surely the divine command, 'to go into all the world, and preach the gospel to every creature,' should put to shame and silence the specious but transparent selfishness which would contract the limits of human sympathy, and veil itself under the garb of superior sagacity. But I must not detain you by any further observations. Allow me, in the name of the associated ladies, to present you with this small memorial of great regard, and to tender to you their and my best wishes for your health and happiness while you are sojourning among us, for the blessing of God on your children during your absence, and for your safe return to your native country when your mission shall be accomplished. I have just been requested to state the following particulars: In December last, a few ladies met in this place to consider the best plan of obtaining signatures in Liverpool to an address to the women of America on the subject of negro slavery, in substance coinciding with the one so nobly proposed and carried forward by Lord Shaftesbury. At this meeting it was suggested that it would be a sincere gratification to many if some testimonial could be presented to Mrs. Stowe which would indicate the sense, almost universally entertained, that she had been the instrument in the hands of God of arousing the slumbering sympathies of this country in behalf of the suffering slave. It was felt desirable to render the expression of such a feeling as general as possible; and to effect this it was resolved that a subscription should be set on foot, consisting of contributions of one penny and upwards, with a view to raise a testimonial, to be presented to Mrs. Stowe by the ladies of Liverpool, as an expression of their grateful appreciation of her valuable services in the cause of the negro, and as a token of admiration for the genius and of high esteem for the philanthropy and Christian feeling which animate her great work, Uncle Tom's Cabin. It ought, perhaps, to be added, that some friends, not residents of Liverpool, have united in this tribute. As many of the ladies connected with the effort to obtain signatures to the address may not be aware of the whole number appended, they may be interested in knowing that they amounted in all to twenty-one thousand nine hundred and fifty-three. Of these, twenty thousand nine hundred and thirty-six were obtained by ladies in Liverpool, from their friends either in this neighborhood or at a distance; and one thousand and seventeen were sent to the committee in London from other parts, by those who preferred our form of address. The total number of signatures from all parts of the kingdom to Lord Shaftesbury's address was upwards of five hundred thousand."

PROFESSOR STOWE then said, "On behalf of Mrs. Stowe I will read from her pen the response to your generous offering: 'It is impossible for me to express the feelings of my heart at the kind and generous manner in which I have been received upon English shores. Just when I had begun to realize that a whole wide ocean lay between me and all that is dearest to me, I found most unexpectedly a home and friends waiting to receive me here. I have had not an hour in which to know the heart of a stranger. I have been made to feel at home since the first moment of landing, and wherever I have looked I have seen only the faces of friends. It is with deep feeling that I have found myself on ground that has been consecrated and made holy by the prayers and efforts of those who first commenced the struggle for that sacred cause which has proved so successful in England, and which I have a solemn assurance will yet be successful in my own country. It is a touching thought that here so many have given all that they have, and are, in behalf of oppressed humanity. It is touching to remember that one of the noblest men which England has ever produced now lies stricken under the heavy hand of disease, through a last labor of love in this cause. May God grant us all to feel that nothing is too dear or precious to be given in a work for which such men have lived, and labored, and suffered. No great good is ever wrought out for the human race without the suffering of great hearts. They who would serve their fellow-men are ever reminded that the Captain of their salvation was made perfect through suffering. I gratefully accept the offering confided to my care, and trust it may be so employed that the blessing of many "who are ready to perish" will return upon your heads. Let me ask those—those fathers and mothers in Israel—who have lived and prayed many years for this cause, that as they prayed for their own country in the hour of her struggle, so they will pray now for ours. Love and prayer can hurt no one, can offend no one, and prayer is a real power. If the hearts of all the real Christians of England are poured out in prayer, it will be felt through the heart of the whole American church. Let us all look upward, from our own feebleness and darkness, to Him of whom it is said, "He shall not fail nor be discouraged till he have set judgment in the earth." To him, the only wise God our Saviour, be glory and majesty, dominion and power, both now and ever. Amen.'—These are the words, my friends, which Mrs. Stowe has written, and I cannot forbear to add a few words of my own. It was our intention, as the invitation to visit Great Britain came from Glasgow, to make our first landing there. But it was ordered by Providence that we should land here; and surely there is no place in the kingdom where a landing could be more appropriate, and where the reception could have been more cordial. [Hear, hear!] It was wholly unexpected by us, I can assure you. We know that there were friendly hearts here, for we had received abundant testimonials to that effect from letters which had come to us across the Atlantic—letters wholly unexpected, and which filled our souls with surprise; but we had no thought that there was such a feeling throughout England, and we scarcely know how to conduct ourselves under it, for we are not accustomed to this kind of receptions. In our own country, unhappily, we are very much divided, and the preponderance of feeling expressed is in the other direction, entirely in opposition, and not in favor. [Hear, hear!] We knew that this city had been the scene of some of the greatest, most disinterested, and most powerful efforts in behalf of emancipation. The name of Clarkson was indissolubly associated with this place, for here he came to make his investigations, and here he was in danger of his life, and here he was protected by friends who stood by him through the whole struggle. The names of Cropper, and of Stephen, and of many others in this city, were very familiar to us—[Hear, hear!]—and it was in connection with this city that we received what to our feelings was a most effective testimonial, an unexpected letter from Lord Denman, whom we have always venerated. When I was in England in 1836, there were no two persons whom I more desired to see than the Duke of Wellington and Lord Denman; and soon I sought admission to the House of Lords, where I had the pleasure both of seeing and hearing England's great captain; and I found my way to the Court of Queen's Bench, where I had the pleasure of seeing and hearing England's great judge. But how unexpected was all this to us! When that book was written, in sorrow, and in sadness, and obscurity, and with the heart almost broken in the view of the sufferings which it described, and the still greater sufferings which it dared not describe, there was no expectation of any thing but the prayers of the sufferers and the blessing of God, who has said that the seed which is buried in the earth shall spring up in his own good time; and though it may be long buried, it will still at length come forth and bear fruit. We never could believe that slavery in our land would be a perpetual curse; but we felt, and felt deeply, that there must be a terrible struggle before we could be delivered from it, and that there must be suffering and martyrdom in this cause, as in every other great cause; for a struggle of eighteen years had taught us its strength. And, under God, we rely very much on the Christian public of Great Britain; for every expression of feeling from the wise and good of this land, with whatever petulance it may be met by some, goes to the heart of the American people. [Hear, hear!] You must not judge of the American people by the expressions which have come across the Atlantic in reference to the subject. Nine tenths of the American people, I think, are, in opinion at least, with you on this great subject; [Hear, hear!] but there is a tremendous pressure brought to bear upon all who are in favor of emancipation. The whole political power, the whole money power, almost the whole ecclesiastical power is wielded in defence of slavery, protecting it from all aggression; and it is as much as a man's reputation is worth to utter a syllable boldly and openly on the other side. Let me say to the ladies who have been active in getting up the address on the subject of slavery, that you have been doing a great and glorious work, and a work most appropriate for you to do; for in slavery it is woman that suffers most intensely, and the suffering woman has a claim upon the sympathy of her sisters in other lands. This address will produce a powerful impression throughout the country. There are ladies already of the highest character in the nation pondering how they shall make a suitable response, and what they shall do in reference to it that will be acceptable to the ladies of the United Kingdom, or will be profitable to the slave; and in due season you will see that the hearts of American women are alive to this matter, as well as the hearts of the women of this country. [Hear, hear!] Such was the mighty influence brought to bear upon every thing that threatened slavery, that had it not been for the decided expression on this side of the Atlantic in reference to the work which has exerted, under God, so much influence, there is every reason to fear that it would have been crushed and put under foot, as many other efforts for the overthrow of slavery have been in the United States. But it is impossible; the unanimous voice of Christendom prohibits it; and it shows that God has a work to accomplish, and that he has just commenced it. There are social evils in England. Undoubtedly there are; but the difference between the social evils in England and this great evil of slavery in the United States is just here: In England, the power of the government and the power of Christian sympathy are exerted for the removal of those evils. Look at the committees of inquiry in Parliament, look at the amount of information collected with regard to the suffering poor in their reports, and see how ready the government of Great Britain is to enter into those inquiries, and to remove those evils. Look at the benevolent institutions of the United Kingdom, and see how active all these are in administering relief; and then see the condition of slavery in the United States, where the whole power of the government is used in the contrary direction, where every influence is brought to bear to prevent any mitigation of the evil, and where every voice that is lifted to plead for a mitigation is drowned in vituperation and abuse from those who are determined that the evil shall not be mitigated. This is the difference: England repents and reforms. America refuses to repent and reform. It is said, 'Let each country take care of itself, and let the ladies of England attend to their own business.' Now I have always found that those who labor at home are those who labor abroad; [Hear, hear!] and those who say, 'Let us do the work at home,' are those who do no work of good either at home or abroad. [Hear, hear!] It was just so when the great missionary effort came up in the United States. They said, 'We have a great territory here. Let us send missionaries to our own territories. Why should we send missionaries across the ocean?' But those who sent missionaries across the ocean were those who sent missionaries in the United States; and those who did not send missionaries across the ocean were those who sent missionaries nowhere. [Hear, hear!] They who say, 'Charity begins at home,' are generally those who have no charity; and when I see a lady whose name is signed to this address, I am sure to find a lady who is exercising her benevolence at home. Let me thank you for all the interest you have manifested and for all the kindness which we have received at your hands, which we shall ever remember, both with gratitude to you and to God our Father."

THE REV. C.M. BIRRELL afterwards made a few remarks in proposing a vote of thanks to the ladies who had contributed the testimonial which had been presented to the distinguished writer of Uncle Tom's Cabin. He said it was most delightful to hear of the great good which that remarkable volume had done, and, he humbly believed, by God's special inspiration and guidance, was doing, in the United States of America. It was not confined to the United States of America. The volume was going forth over the whole earth, and great good was resulting, directly and indirectly, by God's providence, from it. He was told a few days ago, by a gentleman fully conversant with the facts, that an edition of Uncle Tom, circulated in Belgium, had created an earnest desire on the part of the people to read the Bible, so frequently quoted in that beautiful work, and that in consequence of it a great run had been made upon the Bible Society's depositories in that kingdom. [Hear, hear!] The priests of the church of Rome, true to their instinct, in endeavoring to maintain the position which they could not otherwise hold, had published another edition, from which, they had entirely excluded all reference to the word of God. [Hear, hear!] He had been also told that at St. Petersburg an edition of Uncle Tom had been translated into the Russian tongue, and that it was being distributed, by command of the emperor, throughout the whole of that vast empire. It was true that the circulation of the work there did not spring from a special desire on the part of the emperor to give liberty to the people of Russia, but because he wished to create a third power in the empire, to act upon the nobles; he wished to cause them to set free their serfs, in order that a third power might be created in the empire to serve as a check upon them. But whatever was the cause, let us thank God, the Author of all gifts, for what is done.

SIR GEORGE STEPHEN seconded the motion of thanks to the ladies, observing that he had peculiar reasons for doing so. He supposed that he was one of the oldest laborers in this cause. Thirty years ago he found that the work of one lady was equal to that of fifty men; and now we had the work of one lady which was equal to that of all the male sex. [Applause.]

Public Meeting In Glasgow—April 15.

THE REV. DR. WARDLAW was introduced by the chairman, and spoke as follows:—

"The members of the Glasgow Ladies' New Antislavery Association and the citizens of Glasgow, now assembled, hail with no ordinary satisfaction, and with becoming gratitude to a kindly protecting Providence, the safe arrival amongst them of Mrs. Harriet Beecher Stowe. They feel obliged by her accepting, with so much promptitude and cordiality, the invitation addressed to her—an invitation intended to express the favor they bore to her, and the honor in which they held her, as the eminently gifted authoress of Uncle Tom's Cabin—a work of humble name, but of high excellence and world-wide celebrity; a work the felicity of whose conception is more than equalled by the admirable tact of its execution, and the Christian benevolence of its design, by its exquisite adaptation to its accomplishment; distinguished by the singular variety and consistent discrimination of its characters; by the purity of its religious and moral principles; by its racy humor, and its touching pathos, and its effectively powerful appeals to the judgment, the conscience, and the heart; a work, indeed, of whose sterling worth the earnest test is to be found in the fact of its having so universally touched and stirred the bosom of our common humanity, in all classes of society, that its humble name has become 'a household word,' from the palace to the cottage, and of the extent of its circulation having been unprecedented in the history of the literature of this or of any other age or country. They would, at the same time, include in their hearty welcome the Rev. C.E. Stowe, Professor of Theological Literature in the Andover Theological Seminary, Massachusetts, whose eminent qualifications, as a classical scholar, a man of general literature, and a theologian, have recently placed him in a highly honorable and responsible position, and who, on the subject of slavery, holds the same principles and breathes the same spirit of freedom with his accomplished partner; and, along with them too, another member of the same singularly talented family with herself. They delight to think of the amount of good to the cause of emancipation and universal liberty which her Cabin has already done, and to anticipate the still larger amount it is yet destined to do, now that the Key to the Cabin has triumphantly shown it to be no fiction; and in whatever further efforts she may be honored of Heaven to make in the same noble cause, they desire, unitedly and heartily, to cheer her on, and bid her 'God speed.' I cannot but feel myself highly honored in having been requested to move this resolution. In doing so, I have the happiness of introducing to a Glasgow audience a lady from the transatlantic continent, the extraordinary production of whose pen, referred to in the resolution, had made her name familiar in our country and through Europe, ere she appeared in person among us. My judgment and my heart alike fully respond to every thing said in the resolution respecting that inimitable work. We are accustomed to make a distinction between works of nature and works of art, but in a sense which, all will readily understand, this is preeminently both. As a work of art, it bears upon it, throughout, the stamp of original and varied genius. And yet, throughout, it equally bears the impress of nature—of human nature—in its worst and its best, and all its intermediate phases. The man who has read that little volume without laughing and crying alternately—without the meltings of pity, the thrillings of horror, and the kindlings of indignation—would supply a far better argument for a distinct race than a negro. [Loud laughter and cheers.] He must have a humanity peculiarly his own. And he who can read it without the breathings of devotion must, if he calls himself a Christian, have a Christianity as unique and questionable as his humanity. [Cheering.] Never did work produce such a sensation. Among us that sensation has happily been all of one kind. It has been the stirring of universal sympathy and unbounded admiration. Not so in the country of its own and of its gifted authoress's birth. There, the ferment has been among the friends as well as the foes of slavery. Among the former all is rage. Among the latter, while there are some—we trust not a few—who take the same high and noble position with the talented authoress, there are too many, we fear, who are frightened by this uncompromising boldness, and who are drawn back rather than drawn forward by it—who 'halt between two opinions,' and are the advocates of medium principles and medium measures. By many among ourselves, the excitement which has been stirred is contemplated with apprehension. They regard it as unfavorable to emancipation, and likely to retard rather than to advance its progress. I must confess myself of a somewhat different mind. That the cause may be obstructed by it for a time, may be true. But it will work well in the long run. Good will ultimately come out of it. Stir is better than stagnancy. Irritation is better than apathy. Whence does it arise? From two sources. The conscience and the honor of the country have both been touched. Conscience winces under the touch. The provocation shows it to be ill at ease. The wound is painful, and it naturally awakens fretfulness and resentment. But by and by the angry excitement will subside, and the salutary conviction will remain and operate. The national honor, too, has been touched. Our friends across the wave boast, and with good reason, of the free principles of their constitution. They glory in their liberty. But they cannot fail to feel the inconsistency of their position, and the exposure of it to the world kindles on the cheek the blush of shame and the reddening fire of displeasure. Now, the blush has aright source. It is the blush of patriotism—it is for their country. But there is anger with the shame; for few things are more galling than to feel that to be wrong which you are unable to justify, and which, yet, you are not prepared to relinquish. [Loud applause.] On the whole, I cannot but regard the agitation which has been produced as an auspicious, rather than a discouraging omen. It was when the waters of the pool were troubled that their healing virtue was imparted. Let us then hope that the troubling of the waters by this ministering angel of mercy may impregnate them with a similar sanative influence, [the reverend doctor here pointed towards Mrs. Stowe, while the audience burst out with enthusiastic acclamations and waving of handkerchiefs,] and thus ultimately contribute to the healing of the ghastly wounds of the chain and the lash, and to the setting of the crushed and bowed down erect in the soundness and dignity of their true manhood. [Loud cheering.] Sorry we are that Mrs. Stowe should appear amongst us in a state of broken health and physical exhaustion. No one who looks at the Cabin and at the Key, and who knows aught of the effect of severe mental labor on the bodily frame, will marvel at this. We fondly trust, and earnestly pray, that her temporary sojourn among us may, by the divine blessing, recruit her strength, and contribute to the prolongation of a life so promising of benefit to suffering humanity, and to the glory of God. [Cheers.] Meanwhile she enjoys the happy consciousness that she is suffering in a good cause. A better there could not be. It is one which involves the well being, corporeal and mental, physical and spiritual, temporal and eternal, of degraded, plundered, oppressed, darkened, brutalized, perishing millions. And, while we delight in furnishing her for a time with a peaceful retreat from 'the wrath of men,' from the resentment of those who, did they but rightly know their own interests, would have smiled upon her, and blessed her. We trust she enjoys, and ever will enjoy, quietness and assurance of an infinitely higher order—the divine Master, whom she serves and seeks to honor; proving to her, in the terms of his own promise, 'a refuge from the storm, and a covert from the tempest.' [Enthusiastic cheering.] It may sound strangely, that, when assembled for the very purpose of denouncing 'property in man,' we should be putting in our claims for a share of property in woman. So, however, it is. We claim Mrs. Stowe as ours—[renewed, cheers]—not ours only, but still ours. She is British and European property as well as American. She is the property of the whole world of literature and the whole world of humanity. [Cheers.] Should our transatlantic friends repudiate the property, they may transfer their share—[laughter and cheers]—most gladly will we accept the transference."

PROFESSOR STOWE, on rising to reply, was greeted with the most enthusiastic applause. He said that he appeared in the name of Mrs. Stowe, and in his own name, for the purpose of cordially thanking the people of Glasgow for the reception that had been given to them. But he could not find words to do it. Was it true that all this affectionate interest was merited? [Cheers.] He could not imagine any book capable of exciting such expressions of attachment; indeed he was inclined to believe it had not been written at all—he "'spected it grew." [Tremendous cheers.] Under the oppression of the fugitive slave law the book had sprung from the soil ready made. He regretted exceedingly that in consequence of the state of Mrs. Stowe's health, and in consequence of the great pressure of engagements on himself, their stay in this country would be necessarily short. But he hoped they would accept of the expression of thanks they offered, and their apology for not being in a condition to meet their kindness as they would desire. When they were about to set out from Andover, a friend of theirs expressed his astonishment that they should enter upon such a journey in the delicate state of Mrs. Stowe's health. The Scotch people, he doubted not, would be kind to them—*they would kill them with kindness*; and he feared it would be so. It was from Glasgow the idea of the invitation they had received had originated; and well might it originate in that city, for when had been the time that Glasgow was not in earnest on the subject of freedom? They had had hard struggles for liberty, and they had been successful, and the people in the United States were now struggling for the same privilege. But they labored under circumstances greatly different from those in Great Britain. Scotland had ever been distinguished for its love of freedom. [Great applause.] The religious denominations in the United States—to a great extent, give few and feeble expressions of disapprobation against the system of slavery. Two denominations had never been silent—the Old Scotch Seceders, or Covenanters, and the disciples of William Penn—not one of their number, in the United States, owns a slave. Not one can own a slave without being ejected from the society.[1] In fact, the general feeling was against slavery; but to avoid trouble, the people hesitate to give publicity to their feelings. Were this done, slavery would soon come to an end. Great sacrifices are sometimes made by slaveholders to get rid of slavery. He went once to preach in the State of Ohio. He found there a little log house. Inside was a delicate woman, feeble and with white hands. She seemed wholly unaccustomed to work. Her husband had the same appearance of delicacy. They were very poor. How had they come into that state? They belonged to a slave State, where they had formerly possessed a little family of slaves. They had felt slavery to be wrong. They set them free, and with the remainder of their little property tried to get their living by farming; but like many similar cases, it had been one of martyrdom. The Professor then proceeded to make some very practical remarks on the character of the fugitive slave law, after which he said that the prosperity of Great Britain in a great measure resulted from the products of slave labor. American cotton was the chief support of the system. We must, both in Britain and America, get free-grown cotton, or slavery will not, at least for a long time to come, be abolished. What he would impress on the minds of Christians was unity in this great work. Let slaveholders be ever so much opposed to each other on other topics, they were unanimous in their endeavors to support slavery. But let the prayers of all Christians and the efforts of all Christians be united; and the system of oppression would speedily be destroyed forever.

Public Meeting In Edinburgh—April 20.

THE LORD PROVOST rose, and stated that a number of letters of apology had been received from parties who had been invited to take part in the meeting, but who had been unable to attend. Among these he might mention Professor Blackie, the Rev. Mr. Gilfillan, of Dundee, Rev. J. Begg, D.D., the Earl of Buchan, Dr. Candlish, and Sir W. Gibson Craig, all of whom expressed their regret that they could not be present. One of them, he observed, was from a gentleman who had long taken an interest in the antislavery cause,—Lord Cockburn,[2]—and his note was so warm, and sympathetic, and hearty on the subject about which they had met, that he could not resist the temptation of reading it. It proceeded, "I regret, that owing to my being obliged to be in Ayrshire, it will not be in my power to join you in the expression of respect and gratitude to Mrs. Stowe; she deserves all the honor that can be done her; she has done more for humanity than was ever accomplished before by a single book of fiction. [Cheers.] It did not require much to raise our British feeling against slavery, but by showing us what substantially are facts, and the necessary tendency of this evil in its most mitigated form, she has greatly strengthened the ground on which this feeling rests. Her work may have no immediate or present influence on the states of her own country that are now unhappily under the curse, and may indeed for a time aggravate its horrors; but it is a prodigious accession to the constantly accumulating mass of views and evidence, which by reason of its force must finally prevail." [Cheers.] The Lord Provost proceeded to say, that they had now assembled chiefly to do honor to their distinguished guest, Mrs. Stowe. [Applause.] They had met, however, also to express their interest in the cause which it had been the great effort of her life to promote—the abolition of slavery. They took advantage of her presence, and the effect which was produced on the public mind of this country, to reiterate their love for the abolition cause, and their detestation of slavery. Before they were aware that Mrs. Stowe was to grace the city of Edinburgh with her presence, a committee had been organized to collect a penny offering—the amount to be contributed in pence, and other small sums, from the masses of this country—to be presented to her as some means of mitigating, through her instrumentality, the horrors of slavery, as they might come under her observation. It was intended at once as a mark of their esteem for her, of their confidence in her, of their conviction that she would do what was right in the cause, and, at the same time, as an evidence of the detestation in which the system of slavery was held in this free country. That penny offering now, he was happy to say, by the spontaneous efforts of the inhabitants of this and other towns, amounted to a considerable sum; to certain gentlemen in Edinburgh forming the committee the whole credit of this organization was due, and he believed one of their number, the Rev. Mr. Ballantyne, would present the offering that evening, and tell them all about it. He would not, therefore, forestall what he would have to say on the subject. They were also to have the pleasure of presenting Mrs. Stowe with an address from the committee in this city, which would be presented by another reverend friend, who would be introduced at the proper time. As there would be a number of speakers to follow during the evening, his own remarks must be exceedingly short; but he could not resist the temptation of saying how happy he felt at being once more in the midst of a great meeting in the city of Edinburgh, for the purpose of expressing their detestation of the system of slavery. They could appeal to their brethren in the United States with clean hands, because they had got rid of the abomination themselves; they could therefore say to them, through their friends who were now present, on their return home, and through the press, which would carry their sentiments even to the slave states—they could say to them that they had washed their own hands of the evil at the largest pecuniary sacrifice that was ever made by any nation for the promotion of any good cause. [Loud applause.] Some parties said that they should not speak harshly of the Americans, because they were full of prejudice with regard to the system which they had seen growing up around them. He said so too with all his heart; he joined in the sentiment that they should not speak harshly, but they might fairly express their opinion of the system with which their American friends were surrounded, and in which he thought all who supported it were guilty participators. [Hear, hear!] They could denounce the wickedness, they could tell them that they thought it was their duty to put an end to it speedily. The cause of the abolition of slavery in our own colonies long hung without any visible progress, notwithstanding the efforts of many distinguished men, who did all they could to mitigate some of its more prominent evils; and yet, so long as they never struck at the root, the progress which they made was almost insensible. They knew how many men had spent their energies, and some of them their lives, in attempting to forward the cause; but how little effect was produced for the first half of the present century! The city of Edinburgh had always, he was glad to say, taken a deep interest in the cause; it was one of the very first to take up the ground of total and entire abolition. [Cheers.] A predecessor of his own in the civic chair was so kind as to preside at a meeting held in Edinburgh twenty-three years ago, in which a very decided step was proposed to be taken in advance, and a resolution was moved by the then Dean of Faculty, to the effect that on the following first of January, 1831, all the children born of slave parents in our colonies were from that date to be declared free. That was thought a great and most important movement by the promoters of the cause. There were, however, parties at that crowded meeting who thought that even this was a mere expedient—that it was a mere pruning of the branches, leaving the whole system intact. One of these was the late Dr. Andrew Thomson—[cheers]—who had the courage to propose that the meeting should at once declare for total and immediate abolition, which proposal was seconded by another excellent citizen, Mr. Dickie. Dr. Thomson replied to some of the arguments which had been put forward, to the effect that the total abolition might possibly occasion bloodshed; and he said that, even if that did follow, it was no fault of his, and that he still stuck to the principle, which he considered right under any circumstances. The chairman, thereupon, threatened to leave the chair on account of the unnecessarily strong language used, and when the sentiments were reiterated by Mr. Dickie, he actually bolted, and left the meeting, which was thrown into great confusion. A few days afterwards, however, another meeting was held—one of the largest and most effective that had been ever held in Edinburgh—at which were present Mr. John Shank More in the chair, the Rev. Dr. Thomson, Rev. Dr Gordon, Dr. Ritchie, Mr. Muirhead, the Rev. Mr. Buchanan of North Leith, Mr. J. Wigham, Jr., Dr. Greville, &c. The Lord Provost proceeded to read extracts from the speeches made at the meeting, showing that the sentiments of the inhabitants of Edinburgh, so far back as 1830, as uttered by some of its most distinguished men,—not violent agitators, but ministers of the gospel, promoters of peace and order, and every good and every benevolent purpose,—were in favor of the immediate and total abolition of slavery in our colonies. He referred especially to the speech of Dr. Andrew Thomson on this occasion, from which he read the following extract: "But if the argument is forced upon me to accomplish this great object, that there must be violence, let it come, for it will soon pass away—let it come and rage its little hour, since it is to be succeeded by lasting freedom, and prosperity, and happiness. Give me the hurricane rather than the pestilence. Give me the hurricane, with its thunders, and its lightnings, and its tempests—give me the hurricane, with its partial and temporary devastations, awful though they be—give me the hurricane, which brings along with it purifying, and healthful, and salutary effects—give me the hurricane rather than the noisome pestilence, whose path is never crossed, whose silence is never disturbed, whose progress is never arrested by one sweeping blast from the heavens—which walks peacefully and sullenly through the length and breadth of the land, breathing poison into every heart, and carrying havoc into every home—enervating all that is strong, defacing all that is beautiful, and casting its blight over the fairest and happiest scenes of human life—and which from day to day, and from year to year, with intolerant and interminable malignity, sends its thousands and tens of thousands of hapless victims into the ever-yawning and never-satisfied grave!"—[Loud and long applause.] The experience which they had had, that all the dangers, all the bloodshed and violence which were threatened, were merely imaginary, and that none of these evils had come upon them although slavery had been totally abolished by us, should, he thought, be an encouragement to their American friends to go home and tell their countrymen that in this great city the views now put forward were advocated long ago—that the persons who now held them said the same years ago of the disturbances and the evils which would arise from pressing the question of immediate and total abolition—that the same kind of arguments and the same predictions of evil were uttered in England—and although she had not the experience, although she had not the opportunity of pointing to the past, and saying the evil had not come in such a case, still, even then, they were willing to face the evil, to stick to the righteous principle, and to say, come what would, justice must be done to the slave, and slavery must be wholly and immediately abolished. [Cheers.] He had said so much on the question of slavery, because he was very sure it would be much more agreeable to their modest and retiring and distinguished guest that one should speak about any other thing than about herself. Uncle Tom's Cabin needed no recommendation from him. [Loud cheers.] It was the most extraordinary book, he thought, that had ever been published; no book had ever got into the same circulation; none had ever produced a tithe of the impression which it had produced within a given time. It was worth all the proslavery press of America put together. The horrors of slavery were not merely described, but they were actually pictured to the eye. They were seen and understood fully; formerly they were mere dim visions, about which there was great difference of opinion; some saw them as in a mist, and others more clearly; but now every body saw and understood slavery. Every body in this great city, if they had a voice in the matter, would be prepared to say that they wished slavery to be utterly extinguished. [Loud cheers.]

PROFESSOR STOWE then rose, and was greeted with loud cheers. He begged to read the following note from Mrs. Stowe, in acknowledgment of the honor:—

"I accept these congratulations and honors, and this offering, which it has pleased Scotland to bestow on me, not for any thing which I have said or done, not as in any sense acknowledging that they are or can be deserved, but with heartfelt, humble gratitude to God, as tokens of mercy to a cause most sacred and most oppressed. In the name of a people despised and rejected of men—in the name of men of sorrows acquainted with grief, from whom the faces of all the great and powerful of the earth have been hid—in the name of oppressed and suffering humanity, I thank you. The offering given is the dearer to me, and the more hopeful, that it is literally the penny offering, given by thousands on thousands, a penny at a time. When, in travelling through your country, aged men and women have met me with such fervent blessings, little children gathered round me with such loving eyes—when honest hands, hard with toil, have been stretched forth with such hearty welcome—when I have seen how really it has come from the depths of the hearts of the common people, and know, as I truly do, what prayers are going up with it from the humblest homes of Scotland, I am encouraged. I believe it is God who inspires this feeling, and I believe God never inspired it in vain. I feel an assurance that the Lord hath looked down from heaven to hear the groaning of the prisoner, and according to the greatness of his power, to loose those that are appointed to die. In the human view, nothing can be more hopeless than this cause; all the wealth, and all the power, and all the worldly influence is against it. But here in Scotland, need we tell the children of the Covenant, that the Lord on high is mightier than all human power? Here, close by the spot where your fathers signed that Covenant, in an hour when Scotland's cause was equally poor and depressed—here, by the spot where holy martyrs sealed it with their blood, it will neither seem extravagance nor enthusiasm to say to the children of such parents, that for the support of this cause, we look, not to the things that are seen, but to the things that are not seen; to that God, who, in the face of all worldly power, gave liberty to Scotland, in answer to your fathers' prayers. Our trust is in Jesus Christ, and in the power of the Holy Ghost, and in the promise that he shall reign till he hath put all things under his feet. There are those faithless ones, who, standing at the grave of a buried humanity, tell us that it is vain to hope for our brother, because he hath lain in the grave three days already. We turn from them to the face of Him who has said, 'Thy brother shall rise again.' There was a time when our great High Priest, our Brother, yet our Lord, lay in the grave three days; and the governors and powers of the earth made it as sure as they could, sealing the stone and setting a watch. But a third day came, and an earthquake, and an angel. So shall it be to the cause of the oppressed; though now small and despised, we are watchers at the sepulchre, like Mary and the trusting women; we can sit through the hours of darkness. We are watching the sky for the golden streaks of dawning, and we believe that the third day will surely come. For Christ our Lord, being raised from the dead, dieth no more; and he has pledged his word that he shall not fail nor be discouraged till he have set judgment on the earth. He shall deliver the poor when He crieth, the needy, and him that hath no helper. The night is far spent—the day is at hand. The universal sighing of humanity in all countries, the whole creation groaning and travailing in pain together—the earnest expectation of the creature waiting for the manifestation of the sons of God—show that the day is not distant when he will break every yoke, and let the oppressed go free. And whatever we are able to do for this sacred cause, let us cast it where the innumerable multitude of heaven cast their crowns, at the feet of the Lamb, saying, 'Worthy is the Lamb that was slain to receive power, and riches, and wisdom, and strength, and honor, and glory, and blessings.'"

The Rev. Professor then continued. "My Lord Provost, Ladies and Gentlemen: This cause, to be successful, must be carried on in a religious spirit, with a deep sense of our dependence on God, and with that love for our fellow-men which the gospel requires. It is because I think I have met this spirit since I reached the shores of Great Britain, in those who have taken an interest in the cause, that I feel encouraged to hope that the expression of your feeling will be effective on the hearts of Christians on the other side of the Atlantic. There are Christians there as sincere, as hearty, and as earnest, as any on the face of the earth. They have looked at this subject, and been troubled; they have hardly known what to do, and their hearts have been discouraged. They have almost turned away their eyes from it, because they have scarcely dared encounter it, the difficulties appeared to them so great. Wrong cannot always receive the support of Christians; wrong must be done away with; and what must be—what God requires to be—that certainly will be. Now, in this age, man is every where beginning to regard the sufferings of his fellow-man as his own. There is an interest felt in man, as man, which was not felt in preceding ages. The facilities of communication are bringing all nations in contact, and whatever wrong exists in any part of the world, is every where felt. There are wrongs and sufferings every where; but those to which we are accustomed, we look upon with most indifference, because being accustomed to them, we do not feel their enormity. You feel the enormity of slavery more than we do, because you are not immediately interested, and regard it at a distance. We regard some of the wrongs that exist in the old world with more sensibility than you can regard them, because we are not accustomed to them, and you are. Therefore, in the spirit of Christian love, it belongs to Christian men to speak to each other with great fidelity. It has been said that you know little or nothing about slavery. O, happy men, that you are ignorant of its enormities. [Hear, hear!] But you do know something about it. You know as much about it as you know of the widow-burning in India, or the cannibalism in the Fejee Islands, or any of those crimes and sorrows of paganism, that induced you to send forth your missionaries. You know it is a great wrong, and a terrible obstacle to the progress of the gospel; and that is enough for you to know to induce you to act. You have as much knowledge as ever induced a Christian community in any part of the world to exert an influence in any other part of the world. Slavery is a relic of paganism, of barbarism; it must be removed by Christianity; and if the light of Christianity shines on it clearly, it certainly will remove it. There are thousands of hearts in the United States that rejoice in your help. Whatever expressions of impatience and petulance you may hear, be assured that these expressions are not the heart of the great body of the people. [Cheers.] A large proportion of that country is free from slavery. There is an area of freedom ten times larger than Great Britain in territory.[3] [Cheers.] But all the power over the slave is in the hands of the slaveholder. You had a power over the slaveholder by your national legislature; our national legislature has no power over the slaveholder. All the legislation that can in that country be brought to bear for the slave, is legislation by the slaveholders themselves. There is where the difficulty lies. It is altogether by persuasion, Christian counsel, Christian sympathy, Christian earnestness, that any good can be effected for the slave. The conscience of the people is against the system—the conscience of the people, even in the slaveholding states; and if we can but get at the conscience without exciting prejudice, it will tend greatly towards the desired effect. But this appeal to the conscience must be unintermittent, constant. Your hands must not be weary, your prayers must not be discontinued; but every day and every hour should we be doing something towards the object. It is sometimes said, Americans who resist slavery are traitors to their country. No; those who would support freedom are the only true friends of their country. Our fathers never intended slavery to be identified with the government of the United States; but in the temptations of commerce the evil was overlooked; and how changed for the worse has become the public sentiment even within the last thirty or forty years! The enormous increase in the consumption of cotton has raised enormously the market value of slaves, and arrayed both avarice and political ambition in defence of slavery. Instruct the conscience, and produce free cotton, and this will be like Cromwell's exhortation to his soldiers, '*Trust in God, and keep your powder dry.*'" [Continued cheers.]

THE REV. DR. R. LEE then said: "I am quite sure that every individual here responds cordially to those sentiments of respect and gratitude towards our honored guest which have been so well expressed by the Lord Provost and the other gentlemen who have addressed us. We think that this lady has not only laid us under a great obligation by giving us one of the most delightful books in the English language, but that she has improved us as men and as Christians, that she has taught us the value of our privileges, and made us more sensible than we were before of the obligation which lies upon us to promote every good work. I have been requested to say a few words on the degradation of American slavery; but I feel, in the presence of the gentleman who last addressed you, and of those who are still to address you, that it would be almost presumption in me to enter on such a subject. It is impossible to speak or to think of the subject of slavery without feeling that there is a double degradation in the matter; for, in the first place, the slave is a man made in the image of God—God's image cut in ebony, as old Thomas Fuller quaintly but beautifully said; and what right have we to reduce him to the image of a brute, and make property of him? We esteem drunkenness as a sin. Why is it a sin? Because it reduces that which was made in the image of God to the image of a brute. We say to the drunkard, 'You are guilty of a sacrilege, because you reduce that which God made in his own image "into the image of an irrational creature."' Slavery does the very same. But there is not only a degradation committed as regards the slave—there is a degradation also committed against himself by him who makes him a slave, and who retains him in the position of a slave; for is it not one of the most commonplace of truths that we cannot do a wrong to a neighbor without doing a greater wrong to ourselves?—that we cannot injure him without also injuring ourselves yet more? I observe there is a certain class of writers in America who are fond of representing the feeling of this country towards America as one of jealousy, if not of hatred.. I think, my lord, that no American ever travelled in this country without being conscious at once that this is a total mistake—that this is a total misapprehension. I venture to say that there is no nation on the face of the earth in which we feel half so much interest, or towards which we feel the tenth part of the affection, which we do towards our brethren in the United States of America. And what is more than that—there is no nation towards which we feel one half so much admiration, and for which we feel half so much respect, as we do for the people of the United States of America. [Cheers.] Why, sir, how can it be otherwise? How is it possible that it should be the reverse? Are they not our bone and our flesh? and their character, whatever it is, is it any thing more than our own, a little exaggerated, perhaps? Their virtues and their vices, their faults and their excellences, are just the virtues and the vices, the faults and the excellences, of that old respectable freeholder, John Bull, from whom they are descended. We are not much surprised that a nation which are slaves themselves should make other men slaves. This cannot very much surprise us: but we are both surprised and we are deeply grieved, that a nation which has conceived so well the idea of freedom—a nation which has preached the doctrines of freedom with such boldness and such fulness—a nation which has so boldly and perfectly realized its idea of freedom in every other respect—should in this only instance have sunk so completely below its own idea, and forgetting the rights of one class of their fellow-creatures, should have deprived them of freedom altogether. I say that our grief and our disapprobation of this in the case of our brethren in America arises very much from this, that in other respects we admire them so much, we are sorry that so noble a nation should allow a blot like this to remain upon its escutcheon. I am not ignorant—nobody can be ignorant—of the great difficulties which encompass the solution of this question in America. It is vain for us to shut our eyes to it. There can be no doubt whatever that great sacrifices will require to be made in order to get rid of this great evil. But the Americans are a most ingenious people; they are full of inventions of all sorts, from the invention of a machine for protecting our feet from the water, to a machine for making ships go by means of heated air; from the one to the other the whole field of discovery is occupied by their inventive genius. There is not an article in common use among us but bears some stamp of America. We rise in the morning, and before we are dressed we have had half a dozen American articles in our hands. And during the day, as we pass through the streets, articles of American invention meet us every where. In short, the ingenuity of the people is proclaimed all over the world. And there can be no doubt that the moment this great, this ingenious people finds that slavery is both an evil and a sin, their ingenuity will be successfully exerted in discovering some invention for preventing its abolition from ruining them altogether. [Cheers.] No doubt their ingenuity will be equal to the occasion; and I may take the liberty of adding, that their ingenuity in that case will find even a richer reward than it has done in those other inventions which have done them so much honor, and been productive of so much profit. I say, that sacrifices must be made; there can be no doubt about that; but I would also observe, that the longer the evil is permitted to continue, the greater and more tremendous will become the sacrifice which will be needed to put an end to it; for all history proves that a nation encumbered, with slavery is surrounded with danger. [Applause.] Has the history of antiquity been written in vain? Does it not teach us that not only domestic and social pollutions are the inevitable results, but does it not teach us also that political insecurity and political revolutions as certainly slumber beneath the institution of slavery as fireworks at the basis of Mount Ætna? [Cheers.] It cannot but be so. Men no more than steam can be compressed without a tremendous revulsion; and let our brethren in America be sure of this, that the longer the day of reckoning is put off by them, the more tremendous at last that reckoning will Be." [Loud, applause.]

In regard to this meeting at Edinburgh, there was a ridiculous story circulated and variously commented on in certain newspapers of the United States, that *the American flag was there exhibited, insulted, torn, and mutilated.* Certain religious papers took the lead in propagating the slander, which, so far as I know or can learn, *had no foundation,* unless it be that, in the arranging of the flag around its staff, the stars might have been more distinctly visible than the stripes. The walls were profusely adorned with drapery, and there were numerous flags disposed in festoons. Truly a wonderful thing to make a story of, and then parade it in the newspapers from Maine to Texas, beginning in Philadelphia!

Public Meeting In Aberdeen—April 21.

Address Of The Citizens.

Mrs H. Beecher Stowe.

Madam: The citizens of Aberdeen have much pleasure in embracing the opportunity now afforded them of expressing at once their esteem for yourself personally, and their interest in the cause of which you have been the distinguished advocate.

While they would, not render a blind homage to mere genius, however exalted, they consider genius such as yours, directed by Christian principle, as that which, for the welfare of humanity, cannot be too highly or too fervently honored.

Without depreciating the labors of the various advocates of slave emancipation who have appeared from time to time on both sides of the Atlantic, they may conscientiously award to you the praise of having brought about the present universal and enthusiastic sentiment in regard to the slavery which exists in America.

The galvanic battery may be arranged and charged, every plate, wire, and fluid being in its appropriate place; but, until some hand shall bring together the extremities of the conducting medium, in vain might we expect to elicit the latent fire.

Every heart may throb with the feeling of benevolence, and every mind respond to the sentiment that man, in regard to man, should be free and equal; but it is the province of genius such as yours to give unity to the universal, and find utterance for the felt.

When society has been prepared for some momentous movement or moral reformation, so that the hidden thoughts of the people want only an interpreter, the thinking community an organ, and suffering humanity a champion, distinguished is the honor belonging to the individual in whom all these requisites are found combined.

To you has been assigned by Providence the important task of educing the latent emotions of humanity, and waking the music that slumbered in the chords of the universal human heart, till it has pealed forth in one deep far rolling and harmonious anthem, of which the heavenly burden is, "Liberty to the captive, and the opening of the prison to them that are bound!"

The production of your accomplished pen, which has already called forth such unqualified eulogy from almost every land where Anglo-Saxon literature finds access, and created so sudden and fervent an excitement on the momentous subject of American slavery, has nowhere been hailed with a more cordial welcome, or produced more salutary effects, than in the city of Aberdeen.

Though long ago imbued, with antislavery principles and interested in the progress of liberty in every part of the world, our community, like many others, required such information, suggestions, and appeals as your valuable work contains in one great department of slavery, in order that their interest might be turned into a specific direction, and their principles reduced, to combined practical effort.

Already they have esteemed it a privilege to engage with some activity in the promotion of the interests of the fugitive slave; and they shall henceforth regard with a deeper interest than ever the movements of their American brethren in this matter, until there exists among them no slavery from which to flee.

While they participate in your abhorrence of slavery in the American states, they trust they need scarcely assure you that they participate also in your love for the American people.

It is in proportion as they love that nation, attached to them by so many ties, that they lament the existence of a system which, so long as it exists, must bring odium upon the national character, as it cannot fail to enfeeble and impair their best social institutions.

They believe it to be a maxim that man cannot hold his fellow-man in slavery without being himself to some extent enslaved. And of this the censorship of the press, together with the expurgatorial indices of various religious societies in the Southern States of America, furnish ample corroboration.

It is hoped that your own nation may speedily be directed to recognize you as its best friend, for having stood forth in the spirit of true patriotism to advocate the claims of a large portion of your countrymen, and to seek the removal of an evil which has done much to neutralize the moral influence of your country's best (and otherwise free) institutions.

Accept, then, from the community of Aberdeen their congratulations on the high literary fame which you have by a single effort so deservedly acquired, and their grateful acknowledgments for your advocacy of a cause in which the best interests of humanity are involved.

Signed in name and by appointment of a public meeting of the citizens of Aberdeen within the County Buildings, this 21st April, 1853, A.D.

GEO. HESSAY,
Provost of Aberdeen.

Public Meeting In Dundee—April 22.

MR. GILFILLAN, who was received with great applause, said he had been intrusted by the Committee of the Ladies' Antislavery Association to present the following address to Mrs. Stowe, which he would read to the meeting:—

"MADAM: We, the ladies of the Dundee Antislavery Association, desire to add our feeble voices to the acclamations of a world, conscious that your fame and character need no testimony from us. We are less anxious to honor you than to prove that our appreciation and respect are no less sincere and no less profound than those of the millions in other places and other lands, whom you have instructed, improved, delighted, and thrilled. We beg permission to lay before you the expressions of a gratitude and an enthusiasm in some measure commensurate with your transcendent literary merit and moral worth. We congratulate you on the success of the *chef-d'oeuvre* of your genius, a success altogether unparalleled, and in all probability never to be paralleled in the history of literature. We congratulate you still more warmly on that nobility and benevolence of nature which made you from childhood the friend of the unhappy slave, and led you to accumulate unconsciously the materials for the immortal tale of Uncle Tom's Cabin. We congratulate you in having in that tale supported with matchless eloquence and pathos the cause of the crushed, the forgotten, the injured, of those who had no help of man at all, and who had even been blasphemously taught by professed ministers of the gospel of mercy that Heaven too was opposed to their liberation, and had blotted them out from the catalogue of man. We recognize, too, with delight, the spirit of enlightened and evangelical piety which breathes through your work, and serves to confute the calumny that none but infidels are interested in the cause of abolition—a calumny which cuts at Christianity with a yet sharper edge than at abolition, but which you have proved to be a foul and malignant falsehood. We congratulate you not only on the richness of the laurels which you have won, but on the dignity, the meekness, and the magnanimity with which these laurels have been worn. We hail in you our most gifted sister in the great cause of liberty—we bid you warmly welcome to our city, and we pray Almighty God, the God of the oppressed, to pour his selectest blessings on your head, and to spare your invaluable life, till yours, and ours, and others' efforts for the cause of abolition are crowned with success, and till the shouts of a universal jubilee shall proclaim that in all quarters of the globe the African is free."

The address was handed to Mrs. Stowe amid great applause. MR. GILFILLAN continued: "In addition to the address which I have now read, I have been requested to add a few remarks; and in making these I cannot but congratulate Dundee on the fact that Mrs. Stowe has visited it, and that she has had a reception worthy of her distinguished merits. [Applause.] It is not Dundee alone that is present here to-night: it is Forfarshire, Fifeshire, and I may also add, Perthshire:—that are here to do honor to themselves in doing honor to our illustrious guest. [Cheers.] There are assembled here representatives of the general feeling that boils in the whole land—not from our streets alone, but from our country valleys—from our glens and our mountains O! I wish that Mrs. Stowe would but spare time to go herself and study that enthusiasm amid its own mountain recesses, amid the uplands and the friths, and the wild solitudes of our own unconquered and unconquerable land. She would see scenery there worthy of that pencil which has painted so powerfully the glories of the Mississippi; ay, and she would find her name known and reverenced in every hamlet, and see copies of Uncle Tom's Cabin in the shepherd's shieling, beside Bunyan's Pilgrim's Progress, the Life of Sir William Wallace, Rob Roy, and the Gaelic Bible. I saw copies of it carried by travellers last autumn among the gloomy grandeurs of Glencoe, and, as Coleridge once said when he saw Thomson's Seasons lying in a Welsh wayside inn, 'That is true fame,' I thought this was fame truer still. [Applause.] It is too late in the day to criticize Uncle Tom's Cabin, or to speculate on its unprecedented history—a history which seems absolutely magical. Why, you are reminded of Aladdin's lamp, and of the palace that was reared by genii in one night. Mrs. Stowe's genius has done a greater wonder than this—it has reared in a marvellously short time a structure which, unlike that Arabian fabric, is a reality, and shall last forever. [Applause.] She must not be allowed, to depreciate herself, and to call her glorious book a mere 'bubble.' Such a bubble there never was before. I wish we had ten thousand such bubbles. [Applause.] If it had been a bubble it would have broken long ago. 'Man,' says Jeremy Taylor, 'is a bubble.' Yea, but he is an immortal one. And such an immortal bubble is Uncle Tom's Cabin; it can only with man expire; and yet a year ago not ten individuals in this vast assembly had ever heard of its author's name. [Applause.] At its artistic merits we may well marvel—to find in a small volume the descriptive power of a Scott, the humor of a Dickens, the keen, observing glance of a Thackeray, the pathos of a Richardson or Mackenzie, combined with qualities of earnestness, simplicity, humanity, and womanhood peculiar to the author herself. But there are three things which, strike me as peculiarly remarkable about Uncle Tom's Cabin: it is the work of an American—of a woman—and of an evangelical Christian. [Cheers.] We have long been accustomed to despise American literature—I mean as compared with our own. I have heard eminent *litterateurs* say, 'Pshaw! the Americans have no national literature.' It was thought that they lived entirely on plunder—the plunder of poor slaves, and of poor British authors. [Loud cheers.] Their own works, when, they came among us, were treated either with contempt or with patronizing wonder—yes, the 'Sketch Book' was a very good book to be an American's. To parody two lines of Pope, we

> Admired such wisdom in a Yankee shape,
>
> And showed an Irving as they show an ape.'

[Loud cheers.] And yet, strange to tell, not only of late have we been almost deluged with editions of new and excellent American writers, but the most popular book of the century has appeared on the west side of the Atlantic. Let us hear no more of the poverty of American brains, or the barrenness of American literature. Had it produced only Uncle Tom's Cabin, it had evaded contempt just as certainly as Don Quixote, had there been no other product of the Spanish mind, would have rendered it forever illustrious. It is the work of a woman, too! None but a woman could have written it. There are in the human mind springs at once delicate and deep, which only the female genius can understand, or the female finger touch. Who but a female could have created the gentle Eva, painted the capricious and selfish Marie St. Clair, or turned loose a Topsy upon the wondering world? [Loud and continued cheering.] And it is to my mind exceedingly delightful, and it must be humiliating to our opponents, to remember that the severest stroke to American slavery has been given by a woman's hand. [Loud cheers.] It was the smooth stone from the brook which, sent from the hand of a youthful David, overthrew Goliath of Gath; but I am less reminded of this than of another incident in Scripture history. When the robber and oppressor of Israel, Abimelech, who had slain his brethren, was rushing against a tower, whither his enemies had fled, we are told that 'a certain woman cast a piece of a millstone upon Abimelech's head, and all to break his skull,' and that he cried hastily to the young man, his armor-bearer, and said unto him, 'Draw thy sword, and slay me, that men say not of me, A woman slew him.' It is a parable of our present position. Mrs. Stowe has thrown a piece of millstone, sharp and strong, at the skull of the giant abomination of her country; he is reeling in his death pangs, and, in the fury of his despair and shame, is crying, but crying in vain, 'Say not, A woman slew me!' [Applause.] But the world shall say, 'A woman slew him,' or, at least, 'gave him the first blow, and drove him to despair and suicide.' [Cheers.] Lastly, it is the work of an evangelical Christian; and the piety of the book has greatly contributed to its power. It has forever wiped away the vile calumny, that all who love their African brother hate their God and Savior. I look, indeed, on Mrs. Stowe's volume, not only as a noble contribution to the cause of emancipation, but to the general cause of Christianity. It is an olive leaf in a dove's mouth, testifying that the waters of scepticism, which have rolled more fearfully far in America than here,— and no wonder, if the Christianity of America in general is a slaveholding, man-stealing, soul-murdering Christianity—that they are abating, and that genuine liberty and evangelical religion are soon to clasp hands, and to smile in unison on the ransomed, regenerated, and truly 'United States.' [Loud and reiterated applause.]"

Address Of The Students Of Glasgow University—April 25.

This address is particularly gratifying on account of its recognition of the use of intoxicating drinks as an evil analogous to slaveholding, and to be eradicated by similar means. The two reforms are in all respects similar movements, to be promoted in the same manner and with the same spirit.

MRS. HARRIET BEECHER STOWE.

MADAM: The Committee of the Glasgow University Abstainers' Society, representing nearly one hundred students, embrace the opportunity which you have so kindly afforded them, of expressing their high esteem for you, and their appreciation of your noble efforts in behalf of the oppressed. They cordially join in the welcome with which you have been so justly received on these shores, and earnestly hope and pray that your visit may be beneficial to your own health, and tend greatly to the furtherance of Christian philanthropy.

The committee have had their previous convictions confirmed, and their hearts deeply affected, by your vivid and faithful delineations of slavery; and they desire to join with thousands on both sides of the Atlantic, who offer fervent thanksgiving to God for having endowed you with those rare gifts, which have qualified you for producing the noblest testimony against slavery, next to the Bible, which the world has ever received.

While giving all the praise to God, from whom cometh every good and perfect gift, they may be excused for mentioning three characteristics of your writings regarding slavery, which awakened their admiration—a sensibility befitting the anguish of suffering millions; the graphic power which presents to view the complex and hideous system, stripped of all its deceitful disguises; and the moral courage that was required to encounter the monster, and drag it forth to the gaze and the execration of mankind.

The committee feel humbled in being called to confess and deplore, as existing among ourselves, another species of slavery, not less ruinous in its tendency, and not less criminal in the sight of God—we mean the slavery by strong drink. We feel too much ashamed of the sad preëminence which these nations have acquired in regard to this vice to take any offence at the reproaches cast upon us from across the Atlantic. Such smiting shall not break our head. We are anxious to profit by it. Yet when it is used as an argument to justify slavery, or to silence our respectful but earnest remonstrances, we take exception to the parallelism on which these arguments are made to rest. We do not justify our slavery. We do not try to defend it from the Scriptures. We do not make laws to uphold it. The unhappy victims of our slavery have all forged and riveted their own fetters. We implore them to forbear; but, alas! in many cases without success. We invite them to be free, and offer our best assistance to undo their bonds. When a fugitive slave knocks at our door, escaping from a cruel master, we try to accost him in the spirit or in the words of a well-known philanthropist, "Come in, brother, and get warm, and get thy breakfast." And when distinguished American philanthropists, who have done so much to undo the heavy burdens in their own land, come over to assist us, we hail their advent with rejoicing, and welcome them as benefactors. We are well aware that a corresponding feeling would be manifested in the United States by a portion, doubtless a large portion, of the population; but certainly not by those who justify or palliate their own oppression by a reference to our lamentable intemperance.

We rejoice, madam, to know that as abstainers we can claim an important place, not only in your sympathies, but in your literary labors. We offer our hearty thanks for the valuable contributions you have already furnished in that momentous cause, and for the efforts of that distinguished family with which you are connected.

We bear our testimony to the mighty impulse imparted to the public mind by the extensive circulation of those memorable sermons which your honored father gave to Europe, as well as to America, more than twenty-five years ago. It will be pleasing to him to know that the force of his arguments is felt in British universities to the present time, and that not only students in augmenting numbers, but learned professors, acknowledge their cogency and yield to their power.

Permit us to add that a movement has already begun, in an influential quarter in England, for the avowed purpose of combining the patriotism and Christianity of these nations in a strenuous agitation for the suppression, by the legislature, of the traffic in alcoholic drinks.

In conclusion, the committee have only further to express their cordial thanks for your kindness in receiving their address, and their desire and prayer that you may be long spared to glorify God, by promoting the highest interests of man; that if it so please him, you may live to see the glorious fruit of your labors here on earth, and that hereafter you may meet the blessed salutation, "Inasmuch as ye have done it unto one of the least of these my brethren, ye have done it unto me."

NORMAN S. KERR, *Secretary*.

STEWART BATES, *President*.

GLASGOW, 25th April, 1853.

Loud Mayor's Dinner At The Mansion House, London—May 2.

MR. JUSTICE TALFOURD,[4] having spoken of the literature of England and America, alluded to two distinguished authors then present. The one was a lady, who had shed a lustre on the literature of America, and whose works were deeply engraven on every English heart. He spoke particularly of the consecration of so much genius to so noble a cause—the cause of humanity; and expressed the confident hope that the great American people would see and remedy the wrongs so vividly depicted. The learned judge, having paid an eloquent tribute to the works of Mr. Charles Dickens, concluded by proposing "Mr. Charles Dickens and the literature of the Anglo-Saxons."

MR. CHARLES DICKENS returned thanks. In referring to Mrs. H.B. Stowe, he observed that, in returning thanks, he could not forget he was in the presence of a stranger who was the authoress of a noble book, with a noble purpose. But he had no right to call her a stranger, for she would find a welcome in every English home.

Stafford House Reception—May 7.

THE DUKE OF SUTHERLAND having introduced Mrs. Stowe to the assembly, the following short address was read and presented to her by the EARL OF SHAFTESBURY:—

"MADAM: I am deputed by the Duchess of Sutherland, and the ladies of the two committees appointed to conduct 'The Address from the Women of England, to the Women of America on the Subject of Slavery,' to express the high gratification they feel in your presence amongst them this day.

"The address, which has received considerably more than half a million of the signatures of the women of Great Britain and Ireland, they have already transmitted to the United States, consigning it to the care of those whom you have nominated as fit and zealous persons to undertake the charge in your absence.

"The earnest desire of these committees, and, indeed, we may say of the whole kingdom, is to cultivate the most friendly and affectionate relations between the two countries; and we cannot but believe that we are fostering such a feeling when we avow our deep admiration of an American lady who, blessed by the possession of vast genius and intellectual powers, enjoys the still higher blessing, that she devotes them to the glory of God and the temporal and eternal interests of the human race."

The following is a copy of the address to which Lord Shaftesbury makes reference:—

> "*The affectionate and Christian Address of many thousands of Women of Great Britain and Ireland to their Sisters, the Women of the United States of America.*
>
> "A common origin, a common faith, and, we sincerely believe, a common cause, urge us at the present moment to address you on the subject of that system of negro slavery which still prevails so extensively, and even under kindly-disposed masters, with such frightful results, in many of the vast regions of the western world.
>
> "We will not dwell on the ordinary topics—on the progress of civilization; on the advance of freedom

every where; on the rights and requirements of the nineteenth century; but we appeal to you very seriously to reflect, and to ask counsel of God, how far such a state of things is in accordance with his holy word, the inalienable rights of immortal souls, and the pure and merciful spirit of the Christian religion.

"We do not shut our eyes to the difficulties, nay, the dangers, that might beset the immediate abolition of that long-established system; we see and admit the necessity of preparation for so great an event; but in speaking of indispensable preliminaries, we cannot be silent on those laws of your country which, in direct contravention of God's own law, instituted in the time of man's innocency, deny, in effect, to the slave the sanctity of marriage, with all its joys, rights, and obligations; which separate, at the will of the master, the wife from the husband, and the children from the parents. Nor can we be silent on that awful system which, either by statute or by custom, interdicts to any race of men, or any portion of the human family, education in the truths of the gospel, and the ordinances of Christianity.

"A remedy applied to these two evils alone would commence the amelioration of their sad condition. We appeal to you, then, as sisters, as wives, and as mothers, to raise your voices to your fellow-citizens, and your prayers to God, for the removal of this affliction from the Christian world. We do not say these things in a spirit of self-complacency, as though our nation were free from the guilt it perceives in others. We acknowledge with grief and shame our heavy share in this great sin. We acknowledge that our forefathers introduced, nay, compelled the adoption of slavery in those mighty colonies. We humbly confess it before Almighty God; and it is because we so deeply feel, and so unfeignedly avow, our own complicity, that we now venture to implore your aid to wipe away our common crime, and our common dishonor."

Congregational Union—May 13.

THE REV. JOHN ANGELL JAMES said, "I will only for one moment revert to the resolution.[5] It does equal honor to the head, and the heart, and the pen of the man who drew it. Beautiful in language, Christian in spirit, noble and generous in design, it is just such a resolution as I shall be glad to see emanate from the Congregational body, and find its way across the Atlantic to America. Sir, we speak most powerfully, when, though we speak firmly, we speak in kindness; and there is nothing in that resolution that can, by possibility, offend the most fastidious taste of any individual present, or any individual in the world, who takes the same views of the evil of slavery, in itself, as we do. [Hear, hear!] I shall not trespass long upon the attention of this audience, for we are all impatient to hear Professor Stowe speak in his own name, and in the name of that distinguished lady whom it is his honor and his happiness to call his wife. [Loud cheers.] His station and his acquirements, his usefulness in America, his connection with our body, his representation of the Pilgrim Fathers who bore the light of Christianity to his own country, all make him welcome here. [Cheers.] But he will not be surprised if it is not on his own account merely that we give him welcome, but also on account of that distinguished woman to whom so marked an allusion has already been made. To her, I am sure, we shall tender no praise, except the praise that comes to her from a higher source than ours; from One who has, by the testimony of her own conscience, echoing the voice from above, said to her, 'Well done, good and faithful servant.' Long, sir, may it be before the completion of the sentence; before the welcome shall be given to her, when she shall hear him say, 'Enter thou into the joy of thy Lord.' [Loud cheers.] But, though we praise her not, or praise with chastened language, we would say, Madam, we do thank you from the bottom of our hearts, [Hear, hear! and immense cheering,] for rising up to vindicate our outraged humanity; for rising up to expound the principles of our still nobler Christianity. For my own part, it is not merely as an exposition of the evils of slavery that makes me hail that wondrous volume to our country and to the world; but it is the living exposition of the principles of the gospel that it contains, and which will expound those principles to many an individual who would not hear them from our lips, nor read them from our pens. I maintain, that Uncle Tom is one of the most beautiful imbodiments of the Christian religion that was ever presented in this world. [Loud cheers.] And it is that which makes me take such delight in it. I rejoice that she killed him. [Laughter and cheers.] He must die under the slave lash—he must die, the martyr of slavery, and receive the crown of martyrdom from both worlds for his testimony to the truth. [Turning to Mrs. Stowe, Mr. James continued:] May the Lord God reward you for what you have done; we cannot, madam—we cannot do it. [Cheers.] We rejoice in the perfect assurance, in the full confidence, that the arrow which is to pierce the system of slavery to the heart has been shot, and shot by a female hand. Right home to the mark it will go. [Cheers.] It is true, the monster may groan and struggle for a long while yet; but die it will; die it must—under the potency of that book. [Loud cheers.] It never can recover. It will be your satisfaction, perhaps, in this world, madam, to see the reward of your labors. Heaven grant that your life may be prolonged, until such time as you see the reward of your labors in the striking off of the last fetter of the last slave that still pollutes the soil of your beloved country. [Cheers.] For beloved it is; and I should do dishonor to your patriotism if I did not say it—beloved it is; and you are prepared to echo the sentiments, by changing the terms, which we often hear in old England, and say,—

'America! with all thy faults I love thee still!'

But still more intense will be my affection, and pure and devoted the ardor of my patriotism, when this greatest of all thine ills, this darkest of the blots upon thine escutcheon, shall be wiped out forever." [Loud applause.]

THE REV. PROFESSOR STOWE rose amid loud, and repeated cheers, and said, "It is extremely painful for me to speak on the subject of American slavery, and especially out of the borders of my own country. [Hear, hear!] I hardly know whether painful or pleasurable emotions predominate, when I look upon the audience to which I speak. I feel a very near affinity to the Congregationalists of England, and especially to the Congregationalists of London. [Cheers.] My ancestors were residents of London; at least, from the time of Edward III.; they lived in Cornhill and Leadenhall Street, and their bones lie buried in the old church of St. Andrew Under-Shaft; and, in the year 1632, on account of their nonconformity, they were obliged to seek refuge in the State of Massachusetts; and I have always felt a love and a veneration for the Congregational churches of England, more than for any other churches in any foreign land. [Cheers.] I can only hope, that my conduct, as a religious man and a minister of Christ, may not bring discredit upon my ancestors, and upon the honorable origin which I claim. [Hear! and cheers.] I wish to say, in the first place, that in the United States the Congregational churches, as a body, are free from slavery. [Cheers.] I do not think that there is a Congregational church in the United States in which a member could openly hold a slave without subjecting himself to discipline.[6] True, I have met with churches very deficient in their duty on this subject, and I am afraid there are members of Congregational churches who hold slaves secretly as security for debt in the Southern States. At the last great Congregational Convention, held in the city of Albany, the churches took a step on the subject of slavery much in advance of any other great ecclesiastical body in the country. I hope it is but the beginning of a series of measures that will eventuate in the separation of this body from all connection with slavery. [Hear, hear!] I am extensively acquainted with the United States; I have lived in different sections of them; I am familiar with people of all classes, and it is my solemn conviction, that nine tenths of the people feel on the subject of slavery as you do; [cheers;] perhaps not so intensely, for familiarity with wrong deadens the conscience; but their convictions are altogether as yours are; and in the slaveholding states, and among slaveholders themselves, conscience is against the system. [Cheers.] There is no legislative control of the subject of slavery, except by slaveholding legislators themselves. Congress has no right to do any thing in the premises. They violated the constitution, as I believe, in passing the Fugitive Slave Act. [Cheers.] I do not believe they had any right to pass it. [Hear, hear!] I stand here not as the representative of any body whatever. I only represent myself, and give you my individual convictions, that have been produced by a long and painful connection with the subject. [Hear, hear!] As to the resolution, I approve it entirely. Its sentiment and its spirit are my own. [Cheers.] At the close of the revolutionary war, which separated the colonies from the mother country, every state of the Union was a slaveholding state; every colony was a slaveholding colony; and now we have seventeen free states. [Cheers.] Slavery has been abolished in one half of the original colonies, and it was declared that there should be neither slavery nor the slave trade in any territory north and west of the Ohio River; so that all that part is entirely free from actual active participation in this curse, laying open a free territory that, I think, must be ten times larger in extent than Great Britain. [Loud cheers.] The State of Massachusetts was the first in which slavery ceased. How did it cease? By an enactment of the legislature? Not at all. They did not feel there was any necessity for such an enactment. The Bill of Rights declared, that all men were born free, and that they had an equal right to the pursuit of happiness and the acquisition of property. In contradiction to that, there were slaves in every part of Massachusetts; and some philanthropic individual advised a slave to bring into court an action for wages against his master during all his time of servitude. The action was brought, and the court decided that the negro was entitled to wages during the whole period. [Cheers.] That put an end to slavery in Massachusetts, and that decision ought to have put an end to slavery in all states of the Union, because the law applied to all. They abolished slavery in all the Northern States—in Maine, New Hampshire, Vermont, Connecticut, and Rhode Island; and it was expected that the whole of the states would follow the example. When I was a child, I never heard a lisp in defence of slavery. [Hear, hear, hear!] Every body condemned it; all looked upon it as a great curse, and all regarded it as a temporary evil, which would soon melt away before the advancing light of truth. [Hear, hear!] But still there was great injustice done to those who had been slaves. Every body regarded the colored race as a degraded race; they were looked upon as inferior; they were not upon terms of social equality. The only thing approaching it was, that the colored children attended the schools with the white children, and took their places on the same forms; but in all other respects they were excluded from the common advantages and privileges of society. In the places of worship they were seated by themselves; and that difference always existed till these discussions came up, and they began to feel mortified at their situation; and hence, wherever they could, they had worship by themselves, and began to build places of worship for themselves; and now you will scarcely find a colored person occupying a seat in our places of worship. This stain still remains, and it is but a type of the feeling that has been generated by slavery. This ought to be known and understood, and this is just one of the out-croppings of that inward feeling that still is doing great injustice to the colored race; but there are symptoms of even that giving way.

"I suppose you all remember Dr. Pennington—[cheers]—a colored minister of great talent and excellence—[Hear, hear!]—though born a slave, and for many years was a fugitive slave. [Hear, hear.] Dr. Pennington is a member of the presbytery of New York; and within the last six months he has been chosen moderator of that presbytery. [Loud cheers.] He has presided in that capacity at the ordination of a minister to one of the most respectable churches of that city. So far so good—we rejoice in it, and we hope that the same sense of justice which has brought about that change, so that a colored man can be moderator of a Presbytery in the city of New York, will go on, till full justice is done to these people, and until the grievous wrongs to which they have been subjected will be entirely done away. [Cheers.] But still, what is the aspect which the great American nation now presents to the Christian world? Most sorry am I to say it; but it is just this—a Christian republic upholding slavery—the only great nation on earth that does uphold it—a great Christian republic, which, so far as the white people are concerned, is the fairest and most prosperous nation on earth—that great Christian republic using all the power of its government to secure and to shield this horrible institution of negro slavery from aggression; and there is no subject on which the government is so sensitive—there is no institution which it manifests such a determination to uphold. [Hear, hear!] And then the most melancholy fact of all is, that the entire Christian church in that republic, with few exceptions, are silent, or are apologists for this great wrong. [Hear, hear!] It makes my heart bleed to think of it; and there are many praying and weeping in secret places over this curse, whose voices are not heard. There is such a pressure on the subject, it is so mixed up with other things, that many sigh over it who know not what to say or what to do in reference to it. And what kind of slavery is it? Is it like the servitude under the Mosaic law, which is brought forward to defend it? Nothing like it. Let me read you a little extract from a correspondent of a New York paper, writing from Paris. I will read it, because it is so graphic, and because I wish to show from what sources you may best ascertain the real nature of American slavery. The commercial newspapers, published by slaveholders, in slaveholding states, will give you a far more graphic idea of what slavery actually is, than you have from Uncle Tom's Cabin; for there the most horrible features are softened. This writer says, 'And now a word on American representatives abroad. I have already made my complaint of the troubles brought on Americans here by that "incendiary" book of Mrs. Stowe's, especially of the difficulty we have in making the French understand our institutions. But there was one partially satisfactory way of answering their questions, by saying that Uncle Tom's Cabin was a romance. And this would have served the purpose pretty well, and spared our blushes for the model republic, if the slaveholders themselves would only withhold their testimony to the truth of what we were willing to let pass as fiction. But they are worse than Mrs. Stowe herself, and their writings are getting to be quoted here quite extensively. The *Moniteur* of to-day, and another widely-circulated journal that lies on my table, both contain extracts from those extremely incendiary periodicals, *The National Intelligencer*, of February 11, and *The N.O. Picayune*, of February 17. The first gives an auctioneer's advertisement of the sale of "a negro boy of eighteen years, a negro girl aged sixteen, three horses, saddles, bridles, wheelbarrows," &c. Then follows an account of the sale, which reads very much like the description, in the dramatic *feuilletons* here, of a famous scene in the *Case de l'Oncle Tom*, as played at the *Ambigu Comique*. The second extract is the advertisement of "our esteemed fellow-citizen, Mr. M.C.G.," who presents his "respects to the inhabitants of O. and the neighbouring parishes," and "informs them that he keeps a fine pack of dogs trained to catch negroes," &c. It is painful to think that there are men in our country who will write, and that there are others found to publish, such tales as these about our peculiar institution. I put it to Mr. G., if he thinks it is patriotic. As a "fellow-citizen," and in his private relations, G. may be an estimable man, for aught I know, a Christian and a scholar, and an ornament to the social circles of O. and the neighboring parishes. But as an author, G. becomes public property, and a fair theme for criticism; and in that capacity, I say G. is publishing the shame of his country. I call him G., without the prefatory Mister, not from any personal disrespect, much as I am grieved at his course as a writer, but because he is now breveted for immortality, and goes down to posterity, like other immortals, without titular prefix.' [Cheers.] Now, here is where you get the true features of slavery. What is the reason that the churches, as a general thing, are silent—that some of them are apologists, and that some, in the extreme Southern States, actually defend slavery, and say it is a good institution, and sanctioned by Scripture? It is simply this—the overwhelming power of the slave system; and whence comes that overwhelming power? It comes from its great influence in the commercial world. [Hear!] Until the time that cotton became so extensively an article of export, there was not a word said in defence of slavery, as far as I know, in the United States. In 1818, the Presbyterian General Assembly passed resolutions unanimously on the subject of slavery, to which this resolution is mildness itself; and not a man could be found to say one word against it. But cotton became a most valuable article of export. In one form and another, it became intimately associated with the commercial affairs of the whole country. The northern manufacturers were intimately connected with this cotton trade, and more than two thirds raised in the United States has been sold in Great Britain; and it is this cotton trade that supports the whole system. That you may rely upon. The sugar and rice, so far as the United States are concerned, are but small interests. The system is supported by this cotton trade, and within two days I have seen an article written with vigor in the *Charleston Mercury*, a southern paper of great influence, saying, that the slaveholders are becoming isolated, by the force of public opinion, from the rest of the world. They are beginning to be regarded as inhuman tyrants, and the slaves the victims of their cruelty; but, says the writer, just so long as you take our cotton, we shall have our slaves. Now, you are as really involved in this matter as we are—[Hear, hear!]—and if you have no other right to speak on the subject, you have a right to speak from being yourselves very active participators in the wrong. You have a great deal of feeling on the subject, honorable and generous feeling, I know—an earnest, philanthropic, Christian feeling; but if you have nothing to do, that feeling will all evaporate, and leave an apathy behind. Now, here is something to be done. It may be a small beginning, but, as you go forward, Providence will develop other plans, and the more you do, the further you will see. I am happy to know that a beginning has been made. There are indications that a way has been so opened in providence that this exigency can be met. Within the last few years, the Chinese have begun to emigrate to the western parts of the United States. They will maintain themselves on small wages; and wherever they come into actual competition with slave labor, it cannot compete with them. Very many of the slaveholders have spoken of this as a very remarkable indication. If slavery had been confined to the original slave states, as it was intended, slavery could not have lived. It was the intention that it should never go beyond those boundaries. Had this been the case, it would increase the number of slaves so much that they would have been valueless as articles of property. I must say this for America, that the slaves increase in the slave states faster than the white people; and it shows that their physical condition is better than was that of the slaves at the West Indies, or in Cuba, where the number actually diminished. We must have more slave territories to make our slaves valuable, and there was the origin of that iniquitous Mexican war, whereby was added the vast territory of Texas; and then it was the intention to make California a slave state; but, I am happy to say, it has been received into the Union as a free state, and God grant it may continue so. [Hear, hear!] What has been the effect of this expansion of slave territory? It has doubled the value of slaves. Since I can remember, a strong slave man would sell for about four hundred or six hundred dollars—that is, about one hundred pounds; but now, during the present season, I have known instances in which a slave man has been sold for two hundred and thirty pounds. There are more slaves raised in Virginia and Maryland than they can use in those states in labor, and, therefore, they sell them at one hundred, two hundred, or three hundred pounds, as the case may be, for cash. All that Mrs. Tyler intimates in that letter about slavery in America, and the impression it is calculated and intended to convey, that they treat their slaves so well, and do not separate their families, and so forth, is all mere humbug. [Laughter and cheers.] It is well known that Virginia has more profit from selling negroes than from any other source. The great sources of profit are tobacco and negroes, and they derive more from the sale of negroes than tobacco. You see the temptation this gives to avarice. Suppose there is a man with no property, except fifteen or twenty negro men, whom he can sell, each one for two hundred pounds, cash; and he has as many negro women, whom he can sell for one hundred and fifty pounds, cash, and the children for one hundred pounds each: here is a temptation to avarice; and it is calculated to silence the voice of conscience; and it is the expansion of the slave territory, and the immense mercantile value of the cotton, that has brought so powerful an influence to bear on the United States in favor of slavery. [Hear, hear.] Now, as to free labor coming into competition with slave labor: You will see, that when the price of slaves is so enormous, it requires an immense outlay to stock a plantation. A good plantation would take two hundred, or three hundred hands. Now, say for every hand employed on this plantation, the man must pay on an average two hundred pounds, which is not exorbitant at the present time. If he has to pay at this rate, what an immense outlay of capital to begin with, and how great the interest on that sum continually accumulating! And then there is the constant exposure to loss. These plantation negroes are very careless of life, and often cholera gets among them, and sweeps off twenty-five or thirty in a few days; and then there is the underground railroad, and, with all the precautions that can be taken, it continues to work. And now you see what an immense risk, and exposure to loss, and a vast outlay of capital, there is in connection with this system.

But, if a man takes a cotton farm, and can employ Chinese laborers, he can get them for one or two shillings a day, and they will do the work as well, if not better than negroes, and there is no outlay or risk. [Hear, hear!]. If good cotton fields can be obtained, as they may in time, here is an opening which will tend to weaken the slave system. If Christians will investigate this subject, and if philanthropists generally will pursue these inquiries in an honest spirit, it is not long before we shall see a movement throughout the civilized world, and the upholders of slavery will feel, where they feel most acutely—in their pockets. Until something of this kind is done, I despair of accomplishing any great amount of good by simple appeals to the conscience and right principle. There are a few who will listen to conscience and a sense of right, but there are unhappily only a few. I suppose, though you have good Christians here, you have many who will put their consciences in their pockets. [Hear, hear!] I have known cases of this kind. There was a young lady in the State of Virginia who was left an orphan, and she had no property except four negro slaves, who were of great commercial value. She felt that slavery was wrong, and she could not hold them. She gave them their freedom—[cheers]—and supported herself by teaching a small school. [Cheers.] Now, notwithstanding all the unfavorable things we see—notwithstanding the dark cloud that hangs over the country, there are hopeful indications that God has not forgotten us, and that he will carry on this work till it is accomplished. [Hear!] But it will be a long while first, I fear; and we must pray, and labor, and persevere; for he that perseveres to the end, and he only, receives the crown. Now, there are very few in the United States who undertake to defend slavery, and say it is right. But the great majority, even of professors of religion, unite to shield it from aggression. 'It is the law of the land,' they say, 'and we must submit to it.' It seems a strange doctrine to come from the lips of the descendants of the Puritans, those who resisted the law of the land because those laws were against their conscience, and finally went over to that new world, in order that they might enjoy the rights of conscience. How would it have been with the primitive church if this doctrine had prevailed? There never would have been any Christian church, for that was against the laws of the land. In regard to the distribution of the Bible, in many states the laws prohibit the teaching of slaves, and the distribution of the Bible is not allowed among them. The American Bible Society does not itself take the responsibility of this. It leaves the whole matter to the local societies in the several states, and it is the local societies that take the responsibility. Well, why should we obey the law of the land in South Carolina on this subject, and disobey the law of the land in Italy? But our missionary societies and Bible societies send Bibles to other parts of the world, and never ask if it is contrary to the law of these lands, and if it is, they push it all the more zealously. They send Bibles to Italy and Spain, and yet the Bible is prohibited by those governments. The American Tract Society and the American Sunday School Union allow none of their issues to utter a syllable against slavery. They expunge even from their European books every passage of this kind, and excuse themselves by the law and the public sentiment. So are the people taught. There has been a great deal said on the subject of influence from abroad; but those who talk in that way interfered with the persecution of the Madiai, and remonstrated with the Tuscan government. We have had large meetings on the subject in New York, and those who refuse the Bible to the slave took part in that meeting, and did not seem to think there was any inconsistency in their conduct.

"The Christian church knows no distinction of nations. In that church there is neither Greek nor Jew, Barbarian, Scythian, bond nor free, but all are one in Christ; and whatever affects one part of the body affects the other, and the whole Christian church every where is bound to help, and encourage, and rebuke, as the case may require. The Christian church is every where bound to its corresponding branch in every other country; and thus you have, not only a right, but it is your duty, to consider the case of the American slave with just the same interest with which you consider the cause of the native Hindoo, when you send out your missionaries there, or with which you consider Madagascar; and to express yourselves in a Christian spirit, and in a Christian way continually, till you see that your admonitions have had a suitable influence. I do not doubt what you say, that you will receive with great pleasure men who come from the United States to promote the cause of temperance, and you may have the opportunity of showing your sincerity before long; and the manner in which you receive them will have a very important bearing on the subject of slavery. [Cheers.] I have not the least doubt you will hail with joy those who will come across the Atlantic to advance and promote still more earnestly those noble institutions, the ragged schools and the ragged churches. [Cheers.] The men who want to do good at home are the men who do good abroad; and the same spirit of Christian liberality that leads you to feel for the American slave will lead you to care for your own poor, and those in adverse circumstances in your own land, I would ask, Is it possible, then, that admonition and reproof given in a Christian spirit, and by a Christian heart, can fail to produce a right influence on a Christian spirit and a Christian heart? I think the thing is utterly impossible; and that if such admonitions as are contained in the resolution, conceived in such a spirit, and so kindly expressed—if they are not received in a Christian spirit, it is because the Christian spirit has unhappily fled. I can answer for myself, at least, and many of my brethren, that it will be so; and, so far from desiring you to withhold your expressions on account of any bad feeling that they might excite, I wish you to reiterate them, and reiterate them in the same spirit in which they are given in this resolution; for I believe that these expressions of impatience and petulance represent the feelings of very few. Who is it that always speaks first? The angry man, and it comes out at once; but the wise man keeps it in till afterwards; and it will not be long before you will find, that whatever you say in a Christian spirit will be responded to on the other side of the water. Now, I believe our churches have neglected their duty on this subject, and are still neglecting it. Many do not seem to know what their duty is. Yet I believe them to be good, conscientious men, and men who will do their duty when they know what it is. Take, for example, the American Board of Foreign Missions. There are not better men, or more conscientious men, on the face of the earth, or men more sincerely desirous of doing their duty; yet, in some things, I believe they are mistaken. I think it would be better to throw over the very few churches connected with the Board which are slaveholding, than to endeavor to sustain them, and to have all this pressure of responsibility still upon them. But yet they are pursuing the course which they conscientiously think to be right. Christian admonition will not be lost upon them.[8] I will say the same of the American Home Missionary Society. They have little to do with slavery, as I have already remarked. Many think they ought not to say any thing upon the subject, because they cannot do so without weakening their influence. But then this question comes: If good men do not speak, who will?—[Hear, hear!]—and, as our Savior said in regard to the children that shouted, Hosannah, 'If these should hold their peace, the stones would immediately cry out.' It is in consequence of their silence that stones have begun to cry out, and they rebuke the silence and apathy of good men; and this is made an argument against religion, which has had effect with unthinking people; so I think it absolutely necessary that men in the church, on that very ground, should speak out their mind on this great subject at whatever risk—[cheers]—and they must take the consequences. In due time God will prosper the right, and in due time the fetters will fall from every slave, and the black man will have the same privileges as the white. [Applause.]"

Royal Highland School Society Dinner, At The Freemason's Tavern, London—May 14.

THE CHAIRMAN, SIR ARCHIBALD ALISON, gave "The health of her Grace the Duchess of Sutherland, and the noble patronesses of the Society," which was received with great applause. It was extremely gratifying, he said, to find a lady, belonging to one of the most ancient and noblest families of the kingdom, displaying so great an interest in their institution. [Cheers.] Not the least of their obligations to her Grace was the opportunity she had given them to offer their respects to a lady, remarkable alike for her genius and her philanthropy, who had come from across the Atlantic, and who, by her philanthropic exertions in the cause of negro emancipation, had enlisted the feelings and called forth the sympathies of thousands and tens of thousands on both sides of the ocean. [Tremendous cheering.] She had shown that the genius, and talents, and energies, which such a cause inspired, had created a species of freemasonry throughout the world; it had set aside nationalities, and bound two nations together which the broad Atlantic could not sever; and created a union of sentiment and purpose which he trusted would continue till the great work of negro emancipation had been finally accomplished. [Cheers.]

PROFESSOR STOWE responded to the allusion which had been made to Mrs. Stowe, and was greeted with hearty applause. He said he had read in his childhood the writings of Sir Walter Scott, and thus became intensely interested in all that pertained to Scotland. [Cheers.] He had read, more recently, his Life of Napoleon, and also Sir Archibald Alison's History of Europe. [Protracted cheers.] But he certainly never expected to be called upon to address such an assembly as that, and under such circumstances. Nothing could exceed the astonishment which was felt by himself and Mrs. Stowe at the cordiality of their reception in every part of Great Britain, from persons of every rank in life. [Cheers.] Every body seemed to have read her book. [Hear, hear! and loud cheers.] Everyone seemed to have been deeply interested, [cheers,] and disposed to return a full-hearted homage to the writer. But all she claimed credit for was truth, and honesty, and earnestness of purpose. He had only to add that he cordially thanked the Royal Highland School Society for the kindness which induced them to invite him and Mrs. Stowe to be present that evening. [Cheers.]

The work in which the society was engaged was one that they both held dear, and in which they felt the deepest interest, inasmuch as that object was to promote the education of youth among those whose poverty rendered them unable to provide the means of education for themselves. [Hear, hear!] In such works as that they had themselves for most of their lives been diligently engaged. [Cheers.]

Antislavery Society, Exeter Hall—May 16.

THE EARL OF SHAFTESBURY, who, on coming forward to open the proceedings, was received with much applause, spoke as follows: "We are assembled here this night to protest, with the utmost intensity, and with all the force which language can command, against the greatest wrong that the wickedness of man ever perpetrated upon his fellow-man—[loud cheers]—a wrong which, great in all ages—great in heathen times—great in all countries—great even under heathen sentiments—is indescribably monstrous in Christian days, and exercised as it is, not unfrequently, over Christian people. [Hear!] It is surely remarkable, and exceedingly disgraceful to a century and a generation so boastful of its progress, and of the institution of so many Bible societies, with so many professions and preachments of Christianity—with so many declarations of the spiritual value of man before God—after so many declarations of this equality of every man in the sight of his fellow-man—that we should be assembled here this evening to protest against the conduct of a mighty and a Protestant people, who, in the spirit of the Romish Babylon, which they had renounced, resort to her most abominable practices—making merchandise of the temples of God, and trafficking in the bodies and souls of men. [Cheers.] We are not here to proclaim and maintain our own immaculate purity. We are not here to stand forward and say, 'I am holier than thou.' We have confessed, and that openly, and freely, and unreservedly, our share, our heavy share, in by-gone days, of vast wickedness; we have, we declare it again, and we had our deep remorse. We sympathize with the preponderating bulk of the American people; we acknowledge and we feel the difficulties which beset them; we rejoice and we believe in their good intentions; but we have no patience—I at least have none—with those professed leaders, be they political or be they clerical, who mislead the people—with those who, blasphemously resting slavery on the Holy Scriptures, desecrate their pulpits by the promulgation of doctrines better suited to the synagogue of Satan—[cheers]—nor with that gentleman who, the greatest officer of the greatest republic in the whole world, in pronouncing an inaugural address to the assembled multitudes, maintains the institution of slavery; and—will you believe it?—invokes the Almighty God to maintain those rights, and thus sanction the violation of his own laws!—[Cries of 'Shame!'] This is, indeed, a dismal prospect for those who tremble at human power; but we have this consolation: Is it not said that, 'When the enemy shall come in like a flood, the Spirit of the Lord shall lift up a standard against him?' [Hear, hear!] He has done so now, and a most wonderful and almost inspired protector has arisen for the suffering of this much injured race. [Loud cheers.] Feeble as her sex, but irresistible as virtue and as truth, she will prove to her adversary, and to ours, that such boasting shall not be for his honor, 'for the Lord will sell Sisera into the hands of a woman.' [Hear, hear! and loud cheers.] Now, I ask you this: Is there one of you who believes that the statements of that marvellous book to which we have alluded present an exaggerated picture?—[Tremendous cries of 'No, no.'] Do they not know, say what they will, that the truth is not fully stated? [Hear, hear!] The reality is worse than the fiction. [Hear, hear!] But, apart from this, there is our solemn declaration that the vileness of the principle is at once exhibited in the mere notion of slavery, and the atrocities of it are the natural and almost inevitable consequences of the profession and exercise of absolute and irresponsible power. [Hear, hear!] But do you doubt the fact? Look to the document. I will quote to you from this book. I have never read any thing more strikingly illustrative or condemnatory of the system we are here to denounce. Here is the judgment pronounced by one of the judges in North Carolina. It is impossible to read this judgment, however terrible the conclusion, without feeling convinced that the man who pronounced it was a man of a great mind, and, in spite of the law he was bound to administer, a man of a great heart. [Hear, hear!] Hear what he says. The case was this: It was a 'case of appeal,' in which the defendant had hired a slave woman for a year. During this time she committed some slight offence, for which the defendant undertook to chastise her. After doing so he shot at her as she was running away. The question then arose, was he justified in using that amount of coercion? and whether the privilege of shooting was not confined to the actual proprietor? The case was argued at some length, and the court, in pronouncing judgment, began by deploring that any judge should ever be called upon to decide such a case, but he had to administer the law, and not to make it. The judge said, 'With whatever reluctance, therefore, the court is bound to express the opinion, that the dominion over a slave in Carolina has not, as it has been argued, any analogy with the authority of a tutor over a pupil, of a master over an apprentice, or of a parent over a child. The court does not recognize these applications. There is no likeness between them. They are in opposition to each other, and there is an impassable gulf between them. The difference is that which exists between freedom and slavery—[Hear, hear!]—and a greater difference cannot be imagined. In the one case, the end in view is the happiness of the youth, born to equal rights with the tutor, whose duty it is to train the young to usefulness by moral and intellectual instruction. If they will not suffice, a moderate chastisement maybe administered. But with slavery it is far otherwise.' Mark these words, for they contain the whole thing. But with slavery it is far otherwise. The end is the profit of the master, and the poor object is one doomed, in his own person, and in his posterity, to live without knowledge, and without capacity to attain any thing which he may call his own. He has only to labor, that another may reap the fruits.' [Hear, hear!] Mark! this is from the sacred bench of justice, pronounced by one of the first intellects in America! 'There is nothing else which can operate to produce the effect; the power of the master must be absolute, to render the submission of the slave perfect. [Hear, hear!] It is inherent in the relation of master and slave;' and then he adds those never-to-be-forgotten words, 'We cannot allow the right of the master to come under discussion in the courts of justice. The slave must be made sensible that there is no appeal from his master, and that his master's power is in no instance usurped; that these rights are conferred by the laws of man, at least, if not by the law of God.' [Loud cries of 'Shame, shame!'] This is the mode in which we are to regard these two classes of beings, both created by the same God, and both redeemed by the same Savior as ourselves, and destined to the same immortality! The judgment, on appeal, was reversed; but, God be praised; there is another appeal, and that appeal we make to the highest of all imaginable courts, where God is the judge, where mercy is the advocate, and where unerring truth will pronounce the decision![Protracted cheering.] There are some who are pleased to tell us that there is an inferiority in the race! That is untrue. [Cheers.] But we are not here to inquire whether our black brethren will become Shakspeares or Herschels. [Hear, hear!] I ask, are they immortal beings? [Great applause.] Do our adversaries, say no? I ask them, then, to show me one word in the handwriting of God which has thus levelled them with the brute beasts. [Hear, hear!] Let us bear in mind those words of our blessed Savior—'Whosoever shall offend one of these little ones who believe in me, it were better that a millstone were hanged about his neck, and that he were cast into the depths of the sea.' [Loud cheers.] Now, then, what is our duty? Is it to stand still? Yes! when we receive the command from the same authority that said to the sun, Stand over Gibeon! [Loud cheers.] Then, and not till then, will we stand still. [Renewed cheers.] Are we to listen to the craven and miserable talk about 'doing more harm than good'? [Hear, hear!] This was an argument which would have checked every noble enterprise which has been undertaken since the world began. It would have strangled Wilberforce, and checked the very Exodus itself from the house of bondage in Egypt. [Hear, hear!] Out on all such craven talk! [Cheers.] Slavery is a mystery, and so is all sin, and we must fight against it; and, by the blessing of God, we will. [Loud cheers.] We must pray to Almighty God, that we and our American brethren—who seem now to be the sole depositories of the Protestant truth, and of civil and religious liberty, may be as one. [Cheers.] We are feeble, if hostile; but, if united, we are the arbiters of the world. [Cheers.] Let us join together for the temporal and spiritual good of our race."

Professor Stowe then came forward, and was received with unbounded demonstrations of applause. When the cheering had subsided, he said "he felt utterly exhausted by the heat and excitement of the meeting, and should therefore be glad to be excused from saying a single word; however, he would utter a few thoughts. The following was the resolution which he had to submit to the meeting: 'That with a view to the correction of public sentiment on this subject in slaveholding communities, it is of the first importance that those who are earnest in condemnation of slavery should observe consistency; and, therefore, that it is their duty to encourage the development of the natural resources of countries where slavery does not exist, and the soil of which is adapted to the growth of products—especially of cotton—now partially or chiefly raised by slave labor; and though the extinction of slavery is less to be expected from a diminished demand for slave produce than from the moral effects of a steadfast abhorrence of slavery itself, and from an unwavering and consistent opposition to it, this meeting would earnestly recommend, that in all cases where it is practicable, a decided preference should be given to the products of free labor, by all who enter their protest against slavery, so that at least they themselves may be clear of any participation in the guilt of the system, and be thus morally strengthened in their condemnation of it.' At the close of the revolutionary war, all the states of America were slaveholding states. In Massachusetts, some benevolent white man caused a slave to try an action for wages in a court of justice. He succeeded, and the consequence was, that slavery fell in Massachusetts. It was then universally acknowledged that slavery was a sin and shame, and ought to be abolished, and it was expected that it would be soon abolished in every state of the Union. Mr. Jefferson, Mr. Madison, and Benjamin Franklin would not allow the word 'slave' to occur in the constitution, and Mr. Edwards, from the pulpit, clearly and broadly denounced slavery. And when he (Professor Stowe) was a boy, in Massachusetts the negro children were admitted to the same schools with the whites. Although there was some prejudice of color then, yet it was not so strong as at present. In 1818, the General Assembly of the Presbyterian church in the United States passed, resolutions against slavery far stronger than those passed at the meeting this evening, and every man, north and south, voted for them. What had caused the change? It was the profitableness of the cotton trade. It was that which had spread the chains of slavery over the Union, and silenced the church upon the subject. He had been asked, what right had Great Britain to interfere? Why, Great Britain took four fifths of the cotton of America, and therefore sustained four fifths of the slavery. That gave them a right to interfere. [Hear, hear!] He admitted that our participation in the guilt was not direct, but without the cotton, trade of Great Britain slavery would have been abolished long ago, for the American manufacturers consumed but one fifth of all the cotton grown in the country. The conscience of the cotton growers was talked of; but had the cotton consumer no conscience? [Cheers.] It seemed to him that the British public had more direct access to the consumer than to the grower of cotton." Professor Stowe then read an extract from a paper published in Charleston, South Carolina, showing the influence of the American cotton trade on the slavery question. "The price of cotton regulated the price of slaves, who were now worth an average of two hundred pounds. A cotton plantation required in some cases two hundred, and in others four hundred slaves. This would give an idea of the capital needed. With free labor there was none of this outlay—there was none of those losses by the cholera, and the 'underground railroad,' to which the slave owners were subjected. [Hear, hear!] The Chinese had come over in large numbers, and could be hired for small wages, on which they managed to live well in their way. If people would encourage free-grown cotton, that would be the strongest appeal they could make to the slaveholder. There were three ways of abolishing slavery. First, by a bloody revolution, which few would approve. [Hear, hear!] Secondly, by persuading slaveholders of the wrong they commit; but this would have little effect so long as they bought their cotton. [Hear, hear!] And the third and most feasible way was, by making slave labor unprofitable, as compared with free labor. [Hear!] When the Chinese first began to emigrate to California, it was predicted that slavery would be 'run out' that way. He hoped it might be so. [Cheers.] The reverend gentleman then reverted to his previous visit to this country, seventeen years ago, and described the rapid strides which had been made in the work of education—especially the education of the poor—in the interval. It was most gratifying to him, and more easily seen by him than it would be by us, with whom the change had been gradual. He had been told in America that the English abolitionists were prompted by jealousy of America, but he had found that to be false. The Christian feeling which had dictated efforts on behalf of ragged schools and factory children, and the welfare of the poor and distressed of every kind, had caused the same Christian hearts to throb for the American slave. It was that Christian philanthropy which received all men as brethren—children of the same father, and therefore he had great hopes of success. [Cheers.]"

My remarks on the cotton business of Britain were made with entire sincerity, and a single-hearted desire to promote the antislavery cause. They are sentiments which I had long entertained, and which I had taken every opportunity to express with the utmost freedom from the time of my first landing in Liverpool, the great cotton mart of England, and where, if any where, they might be supposed capable of giving offence; yet no exception was taken to them, so far as I know, till delivered in Exeter Hall. There they were heard by some with surprise, and by others with extreme displeasure. I was even called *proslavery*, and ranked with Mrs. Julia Tyler, for frankly speaking the truth, under circumstances of great temptation to ignore it.

Still I have the satisfaction of knowing that both my views and my motives were rightly understood and properly appreciated by large-hearted and clear-headed philanthropists, like the Earl of Shaftesbury and Joseph Sturge, and very fairly represented and commented upon by such religious and secular papers as the Christian Times, the British Banner, the London Daily News and Chronicle; and even the *thundering political* Times seemed disposed, in a half-sarcastic way, to admit that I was more than half right.

But it is most satisfactory of all to know that the best of the British abolitionists are now acting, promptly and efficiently, in accordance with those views, and are determined to develop the resources of the British empire for the production of cotton by free labor. The thing is practicable, and not of very difficult accomplishment. It is furthermore absolutely essential to the success of the antislavery cause; for now the great practical leading argument for slavery is, *Without slavery you can have no cotton, and cotton you must and will have.* The latest work that I have read in defence of slavery (Uncle Tom in Paris, Baltimore, 1854) says, (pp. 56-7,) "*Of the cotton which supplies the wants of the civilized world, the south produces 86 per cent.; and without slave labor experience has shown that the cotton plant cannot be cultivated.*"

How the matter is viewed by sagacious and practical minds in Britain, is clear from the following sentences, taken from the National Era:—

"COTTON IS KING.—Charles Dickens, in a late number of his Household Words, after enumerating the striking facts of cotton, says,—

"'Let any social or physical convulsion visit the United States, and England would feel the shock from Land's End to John o'Groat's. The lives of nearly two millions of our countrymen are dependent upon the cotton crops of America; their destiny may be said, without any sort of hyperbole, to hang upon a thread.

"'Should any dire calamity befall the land of cotton, a thousand of our merchant ships would rot idly in dock; ten thousand mills must stop their busy looms, and two million mouths would starve for lack of food to feed them.'

"How many non-slaveholders elsewhere are thus interested in the products of slaves? Is it not worthy the attention of genuine philanthropists to inquire whether cotton cannot be profitably cultivated by free labor?"

Soirée At Willis's Rooms—May 25.

MR. JOSEPH STURGE took the chair, announcing that he did so in the absence of the Earl of Shaftesbury, who was prevented from attending.

It was announced that letters had been received from the Duke of Newcastle and the Earls of Carlisle and Shaftesbury, expressing their sympathy with the object of the meeting, and their regret at being unable to attend.

The Secretary, SAMUEL BOWLEY, ESQ., of Gloucester, then read the address, which was as follows:—

"MADAM: It is with feelings of the deepest interest that the committee of the British and Foreign Antislavery Society, on behalf of themselves and of the society they represent, welcome the gifted authoress of Uncle Tom's Cabin to the shores of Great Britain.

"As humble laborers in the cause of negro emancipation, we hail, with emotions more easily imagined than described, the appearance of that remarkable work, which has awakened a world-wide sympathy on behalf of the suffering negro, and called forth a burst of honest indignation against the atrocious system of slavery, which, we trust, under the divine blessing, will, at no distant period, accomplish its entire abolition. We are not insensible to those extraordinary merits of Uncle Tom's Cabin, as a merely literary production, which have procured for its talented authoress such universal commendation and enthusiastic applause; but we feel it to be our duty to refer rather to the Christian principles and earnest piety which pervade its interesting pages, and to express our warmest desire, we trust we may say heartfelt prayer, that He who bestowed upon you the power and the grace to write such a work may preserve and bless you amid all your honours, and enable you, under a grateful and humble sense of his abundant goodness, to give him all the glory.

"We rejoice to find that the great principles upon which our society is based are so fully and so cordially recognized by yourself and your beloved husband and brother—First, that personal slavery, in all its varied forms, is a direct violation of the blessed, precepts of the gospel, and therefore a sin in the sight of God; and secondly, that every victim of this unjust and sinful system is entitled to immediate and unconditional freedom. For, however we might acquiesce in the course of a nation which, under a sense of its participation in the guilt of slavery, should share the pecuniary loss, if such there were, of its immediate abolition, yet we repudiate the right to demand compensation for human flesh and blood, as (to employ the emphatic words of Lord Brougham) we repudiate and abhor 'the wild and guilty fantasy that man can hold property in man.' And we do not hesitate to express our conviction, strengthened by the experience of emancipation in our own colonies, that on the mere ground of social or political expediency, the immediate termination of slavery would be far less dangerous and far less injurious than, any system of compromise, or any attempt at gradual emancipation.

"Let it be borne in mind, however,—and we record it with peculiar interest on the present occasion,—that it was the pen of a woman that first publicly enunciated the imperative duty of immediate emancipation. Amid vituperation and ridicule, and, far worse, the cold rebuke of Christian friends, Mrs. Elizabeth Heyrick boldly sent forth the thrilling tract which taught the abolitionists of Great Britain this lesson of justice and truth; and we honor her memory for her deeds. Again we are indebted to the pen of a woman for pleading yet more powerfully the cause of justice to the slave; and again we have to admire and honor the Christian heroism which has enabled you, dear madam, to brave the storm of public opinion, and to bear the frowns of the church in your own land, while you boldly sent forth your matchless volume to teach more widely and more attractively the same righteous lesson.

"We desire to feel grateful for the measure of success that has crowned the advocacy of these sound antislavery principles in our own country; but we cannot but feel, that as regards the continuance of slavery in America, we have cause for humiliation and shame in the existence of the melancholy fact that a large proportion of the fruits of the bitter toil and suffering of the slaves in the western world are used to minister to the comfort and the luxury of our own population. When this anomaly of a country's putting down slavery by law on the one hand, and supporting it by its trade and commerce on the other, will be removed, it is not for us to predict; but we are conscious that our position is such as should at least dissipate every sentiment of self-complacency, and make us feel, both nationally and individually, how deep a responsibility still rests upon us to wash our own hands of this iniquity, and to seek by every legitimate means in our power to rid the world of this fearful institution.

"True Christian philanthropy knows no geographical limits, no distinctions of race or color; but wherever it sees its fellow-man the victim of suffering and oppression, it seeks to alleviate his sorrows, or drops a tear of sympathy over the afflictions which it has not the power to remove. We cannot but believe that these enlarged and generous sympathies will be aroused and strengthened in the hearts of thousands and tens of thousands of all classes who have wept over the touching pages of Uncle Tom's Cabin. We have marked the rapid progress of its circulation from circle to circle, and from country to country, with feelings of thrilling interest; for we trust, by the divine blessing upon the softening influence and Christian sentiments it breathes, it will be made the harbinger of a better and brighter day for the happiness and the harmony of the human family. The facilities for international intercourse which we now possess, while they rapidly tend to remove those absurd jealousies which have so long existed between the nations of the earth, are daily increasing the power of public opinion in the world at large, which is so well described by one of our leading statesmen in these forcible words: 'It is quite true, it may be said, what are opinions against armies? Opinions, if they are founded in truth and justice, will in the end prevail against the bayonets of infantry, the fire of artillery, and the charges of cavalry.' Responding most cordially to these sentiments, we rejoice with thanksgiving to God that you, whom we now greet and welcome as our dear and honored friend, have been enabled to exemplify their beauty and their truth; for it is our firm conviction that the united powers of Europe, with all their military array, could not accomplish what you have done, through the medium of public opinion, for the overthrow of American slavery.

"The glittering steel of the warrior, though steeped in the tyrant's blood, would be weak when compared with a woman's pen dipped in the milk of human kindness, and softened by the balm of Christian love. The words that have drawn a tear from the eye of the noble, and moistened the dusky cheek of the hardest sons of toil, shall sink into the heart and weaken the grasp of the slaveholder, and crimson with a blush of shame many an American citizen who has hitherto defended or countenanced by his silence this bitter reproach on the character and constitution of his country.

"To the tender mercies of Him who died to save their immortal souls we commend the downcast slaves for freedom and protection, and, in the heart-cheering belief that you have been raised up as an honored instrument in God's hand to hasten the glorious work of their emancipation, we crave that his blessing, as well as the blessing of him that is ready to perish, may abundantly rest upon you and yours. With sentiments of the highest esteem and respect, dear madam, we affectionately subscribe ourselves your friends and fellow-laborers."

PROFESSOR STOWE was received with prolonged cheering. He said, "Besides the right which I have, owing to the relationship subsisting between us, to answer for the lady whom you have so honored, I may claim a still greater right in my sympathy for her efforts. [Hear!] We are perfectly agreed in every point with regard to the nature of slavery, and the best means of getting rid of it. I have been frequently called on to address public meetings since I have been on these shores, and though under circumstances of great disadvantage, and generally with little time, if any, for preparation, still the very great kindness which has been manifested to Mrs. Stowe and to myself, and to our country, afflicted as it is with this great evil, has enabled me to bear a burden which otherwise I should have found insupportable. But of all the addresses we have received, kind and considerate as they have all been, I doubt whether one has so completely expressed the feelings and sympathies of our own hearts as the one we have just heard. It is precisely the expressions of our own thoughts and feelings on the whole subject of slavery. As this is probably the last time I shall have an opportunity of addressing an audience in England, I wish briefly to give you an outline of our views as to the best means of dealing with that terrible subject of slavery, for in our country it is really terrible in its power and influence. Were it not that Providence seems to be lifting a light in the distance, I should be almost in despair. There is now a system of causes at work which Providence designs should continue to work, until that great curse is removed from the face of the earth. I believe that in dealing with the subject of slavery, and the best means of removing it, the first thing is to show the utter wrongfulness of the whole system. The great moral ground is the chief and primary ground, and the one on which we should always, and under all circumstances, insist. With regard to the work which has created so much excitement, the great excellence of it morally is, that it holds up fully and emphatically the extreme wrongfulness of the system, while at the same time showing an entire Christian and forgiving spirit towards those involved in it; and it is these two characteristics which, in my opinion, have given it its great power. Till I read that book, I had never seen any extensive work that satisfied me on those points. It does show, in the most striking manner, the horrible wrongfulness of the system, and, at the same time, it displays no bitterness, no unfairness, no unkindness, to those involved in it. It is that which gives the work the greater power, for where there is unfairness, those assailed take refuge behind it; while here they have no such refuge. We should always aim, in assailing the system of slavery, to awaken the consciences of those involved in it; for among slaveholders there are all kinds of moral development, as among every other class of people in the world. There are men of tender conscience, as well as men of blunted conscience; men with moral sense, and men with no moral sense whatever; some who have come into the system involuntarily, born in it, and others who have come into it voluntarily. There is a moral nature in every man, more or less developed; and according as it is developed we can, by showing the wrong of a thing, bring one to abhor it. We have the testimony of Christian clergymen in slave holding states, that the greater portion of the Christian people there, and even many slaveholders, believe the system is wrong; and it is only a matter of time, a question of delay, as to when they shall perform their whole duty, and bring it to an end.[2] One would believe that when they saw a thing to be wrong, they would at once do right; but prejudice, habit, interest, education, and a variety of influences check their aspirations to what is right; but let us keep on pressing it upon their consciences, and I believe their consciences will at length respond. Public sentiment is more powerful than force, and it may be excited in many ways. Conversation, the press, the platform, and the pulpit may all be used to awaken the feeling of the people, and bring it to bear on this question. I refer especially to the pulpit; for, if the church and the ministry are silent, who is to speak for the dumb and the oppressed? The thing that has borne on my mind with the most melancholy weight, and caused me most sorrow, is the apparent apathy, the comparative silence, of the church on this subject for the last twenty or five and twenty years in the United States. Previous to that period it did speak, and with words of power; but, unfortunately, it has not followed out those words by acts. The influence of the system has come upon it, and brought it, for a long time, almost to entire silence; but I hope we are beginning to speak again. We hear voices here and there which will excite other voices, and I trust before long they will bring all to speak the same thing on this subject, so that the conscience of the whole nation may be aroused. There is another method of dealing with the subject, which is alluded to in the address, and also in the resolution of the society, at Exeter Hall. It is the third resolution proposed at that meeting, and I will read it, and make some comments as I proceed. It begins, 'That, with a view to the correction of public sentiment on this subject in slaveholding communities, it is of the first importance that those who are earnest in condemnation of slavery should observe consistency, and, therefore, that it is their duty to encourage the development of the natural resources of countries where slavery does not exist, and the soil of which is adapted to the growth of products, especially cotton, now partially or chiefly raised by slave labor.' Now, I concur with this most entirely, and would refer you to countries where cotton can be grown even in your own dominions—in India, Australia, British Guiana, and parts of Africa. But it can be raised by free labor in the United States, and indeed it is already raised there by free labor to a considerable extent; and, provided the plan were more encouraged, it could be raised more abundantly. The resolution goes on to say, 'And though the extinction of slavery is less to be expected from a diminished demand for slave produce than from the moral effects of a steadfast abhorrence of slavery, and from an unwavering and consistent opposition to it,' &c. Now, my own feelings on that subject are not quite so hopeless as here expressed, and it seems to me that you are not aware of the extent to which free labor may come into competition with slave labor. I know several instances, in the most slaveholding states, in which slave labor has been displaced, and free labor substituted in its stead. The weakness of slavery consists in the expense of the slaves, the great capital to be invested in their purchase before any work can be performed, and the constant danger of loss by death or escape. When the Chinese emigrants from the eastern portion of their empire came to the North-western States, their labor was found much cheaper and better than that of slaves. I therefore hope there may be a direct influence from this source, as well as the indirect influence contemplated by the resolution. At all events, it is an encouragement to those who wish the extinction of slavery to keep their eyes open, and assist the process by all the means in their power. The resolution proceeds: 'This meeting would earnestly recommend, in all cases where it is practicable, that a decided preference should be given to the products of free labor by all who enter their protest against slavery, so that at least they themselves may be clear of any participation in the guilt of the system, and be thus morally strengthened in their condemnation of it.' To that there can be no objection; but still the state of society is such that we cannot at once dispense with all the products of slave labor. We may, however, be doing what we can—examining the ways and methods by which this end may be brought about; and, at all events, we need not be deterred from self-denial, nor shrink before minor obstacles. If with foresight we participate in the encouragement of slave labor, we must hold ourselves guilty, in no unimportant sense, of sustaining the system of slavery. I will illustrate my argument by a very simple method. Suppose two ships arrive laden with silks of the same quality, but one a pirate ship, in which the goods have been obtained by robbery, and the other by honest trade. The pirate sells his silks twenty per cent. cheaper than the honest trader: you go to him, and declaim against his dishonesty; but because you can get silks cheaper of him, you buy of him. Would he think you sincere in your denunciations of his plundering his fellow-creatures, or would you exert any influence on him to make him abandon his dishonest practices? I can, however, put another case in which this inconsistency might, perhaps, be unavoidable. Suppose we were in famine or great necessity, and we wished to obtain provisions for our suffering families: suppose, too, there was a certain man with provisions, who, we knew, had come by them dishonestly, but we had no other resource than to purchase of him. In that case we should be justified in purchasing of him, and should not participate in the guilt of the robbery. But still, however great our necessity, we are not justified in refusing to examine the subject, and in discouraging those who are endeavoring to set the thing on the right ground. That is all I wish, and all the resolution contemplates; and, happily, I find that that also is what was implied in the address. I may mention one other method alluded to in the address, and that is prayer to Almighty God. This ought to be, and must be, a religious enterprise. It is impossible for any man to contemplate slavery as it is without feeling intense indignation; and unless he have his heart near to God, and unless he be a man of prayer and devotional spirit, bad passions will arise, and to a very great extent neutralize his efforts to do good. How do you suppose such a religious feeling has been preserved in the book to which the address refers? Because it was written amid prayer from the beginning; and it is only by a constant exercise of the religious spirit that the good it had effected has been accomplished in the way it has. There is one more subject to which I would allude, and that is unity among those who desire to emancipate the slave. I mean a good understanding and unity of feeling among the opponents of slavery. What gives slavery its great strength in the United States? There are only about three hundred thousand slaveholders in the United States out of the whole twenty-five millions of its population, and yet they hold the entire power over the nation. That is owing to their unbroken unity on that one matter, however much, and however fiercely, they may contend among themselves on others. As soon as the subject of slavery comes up, they are of one heart, of one voice, and of one mind, while their opponents unhappily differ, and assail each other when they ought to be assailing the great enemy alone. Why can they not work together, so far as they are agreed, and let those points on which they disagree be waived for the time? In the midst of the battle let them sink their differences, and settle them after the victory is won. I was happy to find at the great meeting of the Peace Society that that course has been adopted. They are not all of one mind on the details of the question, but they are of one mind on the great principle of diffusing peace doctrines among the great nations of Europe. I therefore say, let all the friends of the slave work together until the great work of his emancipation is accomplished, and then they will have time to discuss their differences, though I believe by that time they will all think alike. I thank you sincerely for the kindness you have expressed towards my country, and for the philanthropy you have manifested, and I hope all has been done in such a Christian spirit that every Christian feeling on the other side of the Atlantic will be compelled to respond to it."

Concluding Note.

Since the preceding addresses were delivered, the aspect of things among us has been greatly changed. It is just as was predicted by the sagacious Lord Cockburn, at the meeting in Edinburgh, (see page xxvi.) The spirit of slavery, stimulated to madness by the indignation of the civilized world, in its frenzy bids defiance to God and man, and is determined to make itself respected by enlisting into its service the entire wealth, and power, and political influence of this great nation. Its encroachments are becoming so enormous, and its progress so rapid, that it is now a conflict for the freedom of the citizens rather than for the emancipation of the slaves. The reckless faithlessness and impudent falsehood of our national proslavery legislation, the present season, has scarcely a parallel in history, black as history is with all kinds of perfidy. If the men who mean to be free do not now arise in their strength and shake off the incubus which is strangling and crushing them, they deserve to be slaves, and they will be.

C.E.S.

SUNNY MEMORIES OF FOREIGN LANDS

LETTER I

LIVERPOOL, April 11, 1853.

MY DEAR CHILDREN:—

You wish, first of all, to hear of the voyage. Let me assure you, my dears, in the very commencement of the matter, that going to sea is not at all the thing that we have taken it to be.

You know how often we have longed for a sea voyage, as the fulfilment of all our dreams of poetry and romance, the realization of our highest conceptions of free, joyous existence.

You remember our ship-launching parties in Maine, when we used to ride to the seaside through dark pine forests, lighted up with the gold, scarlet, and orange tints of autumn. What exhilaration there was, as those beautiful inland bays, one by one, unrolled like silver ribbons before us! and how all our sympathies went forth with the grand new ship about to be launched! How graceful and noble a thing she looked, as she sprang from the shore to the blue waters, like a human soul springing from life into immortality! How all our feelings went with her! how we longed to be with her, and a part of her—to go with her to India, China, or any where, so that we might rise and fall on the bosom of that magnificent ocean, and share a part of that glorified existence! That ocean! that blue, sparkling, heaving, mysterious ocean, with all the signs and wonders of heaven emblazoned on its bosom, and another world of mystery hidden beneath its waters! Who would not long to enjoy a freer communion, and rejoice in a prospect of days spent in unreserved fellowship with its grand and noble nature?

Alas! what a contrast between all this poetry and the real prose fact of going to sea! No man, the proverb says, is a hero to his valet de chambre. Certainly, no poet, no hero, no inspired prophet, ever lost so much on near acquaintance as this same mystic, grandiloquent old Ocean. The one step from the sublime to the ridiculous is never taken with such alacrity as in a sea voyage.

In the first place, it is a melancholy fact, but not the less true, that ship life is not at all fragrant; in short, particularly on a steamer, there is a most mournful combination of grease, steam, onions, and dinners in general, either past, present, or to come, which, floating invisibly in the atmosphere, strongly predisposes to that disgust of existence, which, in half an hour after sailing, begins to come upon you; that disgust, that strange, mysterious, ineffable sensation which steals slowly and inexplicably upon you; which makes every heaving billow, every white-capped wave, the ship, the people, the sight, taste, sound, and smell of every thing a matter of inexpressible loathing! Man cannot utter it.

It is really amusing to watch the gradual progress of this epidemic; to see people stepping on board in the highest possible feather, alert, airy, nimble, parading the deck, chatty and conversable, on the best possible terms with themselves and mankind generally; the treacherous ship, meanwhile, undulating and heaving in the most graceful rises and pauses imaginable, like some voluptuous waltzer; and then to see one after another yielding to the mysterious spell!

Your poet launches forth, "full of sentiment sublime as billows," discoursing magnificently on the color of the waves and the glory of the clouds; but gradually he grows white about the mouth, gives sidelong looks towards the stairway; at last, with one desperate plunge, he sets, to rise no more!

Here sits a stout gentleman, who looks as resolute as an oak log. "These things are much the effect of imagination," he tells you; "a little self-control and resolution," &c. Ah me! it is delightful, when these people, who are always talking about resolution, get caught on shipboard. As the backwoodsman said to the Mississippi River, about the steamboat, they "get their match." Our stout gentleman sits a quarter of an hour, upright as a palm tree, his back squared against the rails, pretending to be reading a paper; but a dismal look of disgust is settling down about his lips; the old sea and his will are evidently having a pitched battle. Ah, ha! there he goes for the stairway; says he has left a book in the cabin, but shoots by with a most suspicious velocity. You may fancy his finale.

Then, of course, there are young ladies,—charming creatures,—who, in about ten minutes, are going to die, and are sure they shall die, and don't care if they do; whom anxious papas, or brothers, or lovers consign with all speed to those dismal lower regions, where the brisk chambermaid, who has been expecting them, seems to think their agonies and groans a regular part of the play.

I had come on board thinking, in my simplicity, of a fortnight to be spent something like the fortnight on a trip to New Orleans, on one of our floating river palaces; that we should sit in our state rooms, read, sew, sketch, and chat; and accordingly I laid in a magnificent provision in the way of literature and divers matters of fancy work, with which to while away the time. Some last, airy touches, in the way of making up bows, disposing ribbons, and binding collarets, had been left to these long, leisure hours, as matters of amusement.

Let me warn you, if you ever go to sea, you may as well omit all such preparations. Don't leave so much as the unlocking of a trunk to be done after sailing. In the few precious minutes when the ship stands still, before she weighs her anchor, set your house, that is to say, your state room, as much in order as if you were going to be hanged; place every thing in the most convenient position to be seized without trouble at a moment's notice; for be sure that in half an hour after sailing an infinite desperation will seize you, in which the grasshopper will be a burden. If any thing is in your trunk, it might almost as well be in the sea, for any practical probability of your getting to it.

Moreover, let your toilet be eminently simple, for you will find the time coming when to button a cuff or arrange a ruff will be a matter of absolute despair. You lie disconsolate in your berth, only desiring to be let alone to die; and then, if you are told, as you always are, that "you mustn't give way," that "you must rouse yourself" and come on deck, you will appreciate the value of simple attire. With every thing in your berth dizzily swinging backwards and forwards, your bonnet, your cloak, your tippet, your gloves, all present so many discouraging impossibilities; knotted strings cannot be untied, and modes of fastening which seemed curious and convenient, when you had nothing else to do but fasten them, now look disgustingly impracticable. Nevertheless, your fate for the whole voyage depends upon your rousing yourself to get upon deck at first; to give up, then, is to be condemned to the Avernus, the Hades of the lower regions, for the rest of the voyage.

Ah, *those* lower regions!—the saloons—every couch and corner filled with prostrate, despairing forms, with pale cheeks, long, willowy hair and sunken eyes, groaning, sighing, and apostrophizing the Fates, and solemnly vowing between every lurch of the ship, that "you'll never catch them going to sea again, that's what you won't;" and then the bulletins from all the state rooms—"Mrs. A. is sick, and Miss B. sicker, and Miss C. almost dead, and Mrs. E., F., and G. declare that they shall give up." This threat of "giving up" is a standing resort of ladies in distressed circumstances; it is always very impressively pronounced, as if the result of earnest purpose; but how it is to be carried out practically, how ladies *do* give up, and what general impression is made on creation when they do, has never yet appeared. Certainly the sea seems to care very little about the threat, for he goes on lurching all hands about just as freely afterwards as before.

There are always some three or four in a hundred who escape all these evils. They are not sick, and they seem to be having a good time generally, and always meet you with "What a charming run we are having! Isn't it delightful?" and so on. If you have a turn for being disinterested, you can console your miseries by a view of their joyousness. Three or four of our ladies were of this happy order, and it was really refreshing to see them.

For my part, I was less fortunate. I could not and would not give up and become one of the ghosts below, and so I managed, by keeping on deck and trying to act as if nothing was the matter, to lead a very uncertain and precarious existence, though with a most awful undertone of emotion, which seemed to make quite another thing of creation.

I wonder that people who wanted to break the souls of heroes and martyrs never thought of sending them to sea and keeping them a little seasick. The dungeons of Olmutz, the leads of Venice, in short, all the naughty, wicked places that tyrants ever invented for bringing down the spirits of heroes, are nothing to the berth of a ship. Get Lafayette, Kossuth, or the noblest of woman, born, prostrate in a swinging, dizzy berth of one of these sea coops, called state rooms, and I'll warrant almost any compromise might be got out of them.

Where in the world the soul goes to under such influences nobody knows; one would really think the sea tipped it all out of a man, just as it does the water out of his wash basin. The soul seems to be like one of the genii enclosed in a vase, in the Arabian Nights; now, it rises like a pillar of cloud, and floats over land and sea, buoyant, many-hued, and glorious; again, it goes down, down, subsiding into its copper vase, and the cover is clapped on, and there you are. A sea voyage is the best device for getting the soul back into its vase that I know of.

But at night!—the beauties of a night on shipboard!—down in your berth, with the sea hissing and fizzing, gurgling and booming, within an inch of your ear; and then the steward conies along at twelve o'clock and puts out your light, and there you are! Jonah in the whale was not darker or more dismal. There, in profound ignorance and blindness, you lie, and feel yourself rolled upwards, and downwards, and sidewise, and all ways, like a cork in a tub of water; much such a sensation as one might suppose it to be, were one headed up in a barrel and thrown into the sea.

Occasionally a wave comes with a thump against your ear, as if a great hammer were knocking on your barrel, to see that all within was safe and sound. Then you begin to think of krakens, and sharks, and porpoises, and sea serpents, and all the monstrous, slimy, cold, hobgoblin brood, who, perhaps, are your next door neighbors; and the old blue-haired Ocean whispers through the planks, "Here you are; I've got you. Your grand ship is my plaything. I can do what I like with it."

Then you hear every kind of odd noise in the ship—creaking, straining, crunching, scraping, pounding, whistling, blowing off steam, each of which to your unpractised ear is significant of some impending catastrophe; you lie wide awake, listening with all your might, as if your watching did any good, till at last sleep overcomes you, and the morning light convinces you that nothing very particular has been the matter, and that all these frightful noises are only the necessary attendants of what is called a good run.

Our voyage out was called "a good run." It was voted, unanimously, to be "an extraordinarily good passage," "a pleasant voyage;" yet the ship rocked the whole time from side to side with a steady, dizzy, continuous motion, like a great cradle. I had a new sympathy for babies, poor little things, who are rocked hours at a time without so much as a "by your leave" in the case. No wonder there are so many stupid people in the world.

There is no place where killing time is so much of a systematic and avowed object as in one of these short runs. In a six months' voyage people give up to their situation, and make arrangements to live a regular life; but the ten days that now divide England and America are not long enough for any thing. The great question is how to get them off; they are set up, like tenpins, to be bowled at; and happy he whose ball prospers. People with strong heads, who can stand the incessant swing of the boat, may read or write. Then there is one's berth, a never-failing resort, where one may analyze at one's leisure the life and emotions of an oyster in the mud. Walking the deck is a means of getting off some half hours more. If a ship heaves in sight, or a porpoise tumbles up, or, better still, a whale spouts, it makes an immense sensation.

Our favorite resort is by the old red smoke pipe of the steamer, which rises warm and luminous as a sort of tower of defence. The wind must blow an uncommon variety of ways at once when you cannot find a sheltered side, as well as a place to warm your feet. In fact, the old smoke pipe is the domestic hearth of the ship; there, with the double convenience of warmth and fresh air, you can sit by the railing, and, looking down, command the prospect of the cook's offices, the cow house, pantries, &c.

Our cook has specially interested me—a tall, slender, melancholy man, with a watery-blue eye, a patient, dejected visage, like an individual weary of the storms and commotions of life, and thoroughly impressed with the vanity of human wishes. I sit there hour after hour watching him, and it is evident that he performs all his duties in this frame of sad composure. Now I see him resignedly stuffing a turkey, anon compounding a sauce, or mournfully making little ripples in the crust of a tart; but all is done under an evident sense that it is of no use trying.

Many complaints have been made of our coffee since we have been on board, which, to say the truth, has been as unsettled as most of the social questions of our day, and, perhaps, for that reason quite as generally unpalatable; but since I have seen our cook, I am quite persuaded that the coffee, like other works of great artists, has borrowed the hues of its maker's mind. I think I hear him soliloquize over it—"To what purpose is coffee?—of what avail tea?—thick or clear?—all is passing away—a little egg, or fish skin, more or less, what are they?" and so we get melancholy coffee and tea, owing to our philosophic cook.

After dinner I watch him as he washes dishes: he hangs up a whole row of tin; the ship gives a lurch, and knocks them all down. He looks as if it was just what he expected. "Such is life!" he says, as he pursues a frisky tin pan in one direction, and arrests the gambols of the ladle in another; while the wicked sea, meanwhile, with another lurch, is upsetting all his dishwater. I can see how these daily trials, this performing of most delicate and complicated gastronomic operations in the midst of such unsteady, unsettled circumstances, have gradually given this poor soul a despair of living, and brought him into this state of philosophic melancholy. Just as Xantippe made a sage of Socrates, this whisky, frisky, stormy ship life has made a sage of our cook. Meanwhile, not to do him injustice, let it be recorded, that in all dishes which require grave conviction and steady perseverance, rather than hope and inspiration, he is eminently successful. Our table excels in viands of a reflective and solemn character; mighty rounds of beef, vast saddles of mutton, and the whole tribe of meats in general, come on in a superior style. English plum pudding, a weighty and serious performance, is exhibited in first-rate order. The jellies want lightness,—but that is to be expected.

I admire the thorough order and system with which every thing is done on these ships. One day, when the servants came round, as they do at a certain time after dinner, and screwed up the shelf of decanters and bottles out of our reach, a German gentleman remarked, "Ah, that's always the way on English ships; every thing done at such a time, without saying 'by your leave,' If it had been on an American ship now, he would have said, 'Gentlemen, are you ready to have this shelf raised?'"

No doubt this remark is true and extends to a good many other things; but in a ship in the middle of the ocean, when the least confusion or irregularity in certain cases might be destruction to all on board, it does inspire confidence to see that there is even in the minutest things a strong and steady system, that goes on without saying "by your leave." Even the rigidness with which lights are all extinguished at twelve o'clock, though it is very hard in some cases, still gives you confidence in the watchfulness and care with which all on board is conducted.

On Sunday there was a service. We went into the cabin, and saw prayer books arranged at regular intervals, and soon a procession of the sailors neatly dressed filed in and took their places, together with such passengers as felt disposed, and the order of morning prayer was read. The sailors all looked serious and attentive. I could not but think that this feature of the management of her majesty's ships was a good one, and worthy of imitation. To be sure, one can say it is only a form. Granted; but is not a serious, respectful *form* of religion better than nothing? Besides, I am not willing to think that these intelligent-looking sailors could listen to all those devout sentiments expressed in the prayers, and the holy truths embodied in the passages of Scripture, and not gain something from it. It is bad to have only *the form* of religion, but not so bad as to have neither the form nor the fact.

When the ship has been out about eight days, an evident bettering of spirits and condition obtains among the passengers. Many of the sick ones take heart, and appear again among the walks and ways of men; the ladies assemble in little knots, and talk of getting on shore. The more knowing ones, who have travelled before, embrace this opportunity to show their knowledge of life by telling the new hands all sorts of hobgoblin stories about the custom house officers and the difficulties of getting landed in England. It is a curious fact, that old travellers generally seem to take this particular delight in striking consternation into younger ones.

"You'll have all your daguerreotypes taken away," says one lady, who, in right of having crossed the ocean nine times, is entitled to speak *ex cathedra* on the subject.

"All our daguerreotypes!" shriek four or five at once. "Pray tell, what for?"

"They *will* do it," says the knowing lady, with an awful nod; "unless you hide them, and all your books, they'll burn up—"

"Burn our books!" exclaim the circle. "O, dreadful! What do they do that for?"

"They're very particular always to burn up all your books. I knew a lady who had a dozen burned," says the wise one.

"Dear me! will they take our *dresses?*" says a young lady, with increasing alarm.

"No, but they'll pull every thing out, and tumble them well over, I can tell you."

"How horrid!"

An old lady, who has been very sick all the way, is revived by this appalling intelligence.

"I hope they won't tumble over my *caps!*" she exclaims.

"Yes, they will have every thing out on deck," says the lady, delighted with the increasing sensation. "I tell you you don't know these custom house officers."

"It's too bad!" "It's dreadful!" "How horrid!" exclaim all.

"I shall put my best things in my pocket," exclaims one. "They don't search our pockets, do they?"

"Well, no, not here; but I tell you they'll search your *pockets* at Antwerp and Brussels," says the lady.

Somebody catches the sound, and flies off into the state rooms with the intelligence that "the custom house officers are so dreadful—they rip open your trunks, pull out all your things, burn your books, take away your daguerreotypes, and even search your pockets;" and a row of groans is heard ascending from the row of state rooms, as all begin to revolve what they have in their trunks, and what they are to do in this emergency.

"Pray tell me," said I to a gentlemanly man, who had crossed four or five times, "is there really so much annoyance at the custom house?"

"Annoyance, ma'am? No, not the slightest."

"But do they really turn out the contents of the trunks, and take away people's daguerreotypes, and burn their books?"

"Nothing of the kind, ma'am. I apprehend no difficulty. I never had any. There are a few articles on which duty is charged. I have a case of cigars, for instance; I shall show them to the custom house officer, and pay the duty. If a person seems disposed to be fair, there is no difficulty. The examination of ladies' trunks is merely nominal; nothing is deranged."

So it proved. We arrived on Sunday morning; the custom house officers, very gentlemanly men, came on board; our luggage was all set out, and passed through a rapid examination, which in many cases amounted only to opening the trunk and shutting it, and all was over. The whole ceremony did not occupy two hours.

So ends this letter. You shall hear further how we landed at some future time.

LETTER II

Dear Father:—

It was on Sunday morning that we first came in sight of land. The day was one of a thousand—clear, calm, and bright. It is one of those strange, throbbing feelings, that come only once in a while in life; this waking up to find an ocean crossed and long-lost land restored again in another hemisphere; something like what we should suppose might be the thrill of awakening from life to immortality, and all the wonders of the world unknown. That low, green line of land in the horizon is Ireland; and we, with water smooth as a lake and sails furled, are running within a mile of the shore. Every body on deck, full of spirits and expectation, busy as can be looking through spyglasses, and exclaiming at every object on shore,—

"Look! there's Skibareen, where the worst of the famine was," says one.

"Look! that's a ruined Martello tower," says another.

We new voyagers, who had never seen any ruin more imposing than that of a cow house, and, of course, were ravenous for old towers, were now quite wide awake, but were disappointed to learn that these were only custom house rendezvous. Here is the county of Cork. Some one calls out,—

"There is O'Connell's house;" and a warm dispute ensues whether a large mansion, with a stone chapel by it, answers to that name. At all events the region looks desolate enough, and they say the natives of it are almost savages. A passenger remarks, that "O'Connell never really did any thing for the Irish, but lived on his capacity for exciting their enthusiasm." Thereupon another expresses great contempt for the Irish who could be so taken in. Nevertheless, the capability of a disinterested enthusiasm is, on the whole, a nobler property of a human being than a shrewd self-interest. I like the Irish all the better for it.

Now we pass Kinsale lighthouse; there is the spot where the Albion was wrecked. It is a bare, frowning cliff, with walls of rock rising perpendicularly out of the sea. Now, to be sure, the sea smiles and sparkles around the base of it, as gently as if it never could storm; yet under other skies, and with a fierce south-east wind, how the waves would pour in here! Woe then to the distressed and rudderless vessel that drifts towards those fatal rocks! This gives the outmost and boldest view of the point.

View East of Kinsale.

The Albion struck just round the left of the point, where the rock rises perpendicularly out of the sea. I well remember, when a child, of the newspapers being filled with the dreadful story of the wreck of the ship Albion—how for hours, rudderless and helpless, they saw themselves driving with inevitable certainty against these pitiless rocks; and how, in the last struggle, one human being after another was dashed against them in helpless agony.

What an infinite deal of misery results from man's helplessness and ignorance and nature's inflexibility in this one matter of crossing the ocean! What agonies of prayer there were during all the long hours that this ship was driving straight on to these fatal rocks, all to no purpose! It struck and crushed just the same. Surely, without the revelation of God in Jesus, who could believe in the divine goodness? I do not wonder the old Greeks so often spoke of their gods as cruel, and believed the universe was governed by a remorseless and inexorable fate. Who would come to any other conclusion, except from the pages of the Bible?

But we have sailed far past Kinsale point. Now blue and shadowy loom up the distant form of the Youghal Mountains, (pronounced *Yoole.*) The surface of the water is alive with fishing boats, spreading their white wings and skimming about like so many moth millers.

About nine o'clock we were crossing the sand bar, which lies at the mouth of the Mersey River, running up towards Liverpool. Our signal pennants are fluttering at the mast head, pilot full of energy on one wheel house, and a man casting the lead on the other.

"By the mark, five," says the man. The pilot, with all his energy, is telegraphing to the steersman. This is a very close and complicated piece of navigation, I should think, this running up the Mersey, for every moment we are passing some kind of a signal token, which warns off from some shoal. Here is a bell buoy, where the waves keep the bell always tolling; here, a buoyant lighthouse; and "See there, those shoals, how pokerish they look!" says one of the passengers, pointing to the foam on our starboard bow. All is bustle, animation, exultation. Now float out the American stars and stripes on our bow.

Before us lies the great city of Liverpool. No old Cathedral, no castles, a real New Yorkish place.

"There, that's the fort," cries one. Bang, bang, go the two guns from our forward gangway.

"I wonder if they will fire from the fort," says another.

"How green that grass looks!" says a third; "and what pretty cottages!"

"All modern, though," says somebody, in tones of disappointment. Now we are passing the Victoria Dock. Bang, bang, again. We are in a forest of ships of all nations; their masts bristling like the tall pines in Maine; their many colored flags streaming like the forest leaves in autumn.

"Hark," says one; "there's, a chime of bells from the city; how sweet! I had quite forgotten it was Sunday."

Here we cast anchor, and the small steam tender conies puffing alongside. Now for the custom house officers. State rooms, holds, and cabins must all give up their trunks; a general muster among the baggage, and passenger after passenger comes forward as their names are called, much as follows: "Snooks." "Here, sir." "Any thing contraband here, Mr. Snooks? Any cigars, tobacco, &c.?" "Nothing, sir."

A little unlocking, a little fumbling. "Shut up; all right; ticket here." And a little man pastes on each article a slip of paper, with the royal arms of England and the magical letters V.R., to remind all men that they have come into a country where a lady reigns, and of course must behave themselves as prettily as they can.

We were inquiring of some friends for the most convenient hotel, when we found the son of Mr. Cropper, of Dingle Bank, waiting in the cabin, to take us with him to their hospitable abode. In a few moments after the baggage had been examined, we all bade adieu to the old ship, and went on board the little steam tender, which carries passengers up to the city.

This Mersey River would be a very beautiful one, if it were not so dingy and muddy. As we are sailing up in the tender towards Liverpool, I deplore the circumstance feelingly. "What does make this river so muddy?"

"O," says a bystander, "don't you know that

'The quality of mercy is not strained'?"

And now we are fairly alongside the shore, and we are soon going to set our foot on the land of Old England.

Say what we will, an American, particularly a New Englander, can never approach the old country without a kind of thrill and pulsation of kindred. Its history for two centuries was our history. Its literature, laws, and language are our literature, laws, and language. Spenser, Shakspeare, Bacon, Milton, were a glorious inheritance, which we share in common. Our very life-blood is English life-blood. It is Anglo-Saxon vigor that is spreading our country from Atlantic to Pacific, and leading on a new era in the world's development. America is a tall, sightly young shoot, that has grown from the old royal oak of England; divided from its parent root, it has shot up in new, rich soil, and under genial, brilliant skies, and therefore takes on a new type of growth and foliage, but the sap in it is the same.

I had an early opportunity of making acquaintance with my English brethren; for, much to my astonishment, I found quite a crowd on the wharf, and we walked up to our carriage through a long lane of people, bowing, and looking very glad to see us. When I came to get into the hack it was surrounded by more faces than I could count. They stood very quietly, and looked very kindly, though evidently very much determined to look. Something prevented the hack from moving on; so the interview was prolonged for some time. I therefore took occasion to remark the very fair, pure complexions, the clear eyes, and the general air of health and vigor, which seem to characterize our brethren and sisters of the island. There seemed to be no occasion to ask them, how they did, as they were evidently quite well. Indeed, this air of health is one of the most striking things when one lands in England.

They were not burly, red-faced, and stout, as I had sometimes conceived of the English people, but just full enough to suggest the idea of vigor and health. The presence of so many healthy, rosy people looking at me, all reduced as I was, first by land and then by sea sickness, made me feel myself more withered and forlorn than ever. But there was an earnestness and a depth of kind feeling in some of the faces, which I shall long remember. It seemed as if I had not only touched the English shore, but felt the English heart.

Our carriage at last drove on, taking us through Liverpool, and a mile or two out, and at length wound its way along the gravel paths of a beautiful little retreat, on the banks of the Mersey, called the "Dingle." It opened to my eyes like a paradise, all wearied as I was with the tossing of the sea. I have since become familiar with these beautiful little spots, which are so common in England; but now all was entirely new to me.

We rode by shining clumps of the Portugal laurel, a beautiful evergreen, much resembling our mountain rhododendron; then there was the prickly, polished, dark-green holly, which I had never seen before, but which is, certainly, one of the most perfect of shrubs. The turf was of that soft, dazzling green, and had that peculiar velvet-like smoothness, which seem characteristic of England. We stopped at last before the door of a cottage, whose porch was overgrown with ivy. From that moment I ceased to feel myself a stranger in England. I cannot tell you how delightful to me, dizzy and weary as I was, was the first sight of the chamber of reception which had been prepared for us. No item of cozy comfort that one could desire was omitted. The sofa and easy chair wheeled up before a cheerful coal fire, a bright little teakettle steaming in front of the grate, a table with a beautiful vase of flowers, books, and writing apparatus, and kind friends with words full of affectionate cheer,—all these made me feel at home in a moment.

The hospitality of England has become famous in the world, and, I think, with reason. I doubt not there is just as much hospitable feeling in other countries; but in England the matter of coziness and home comfort has been so studied, and matured, and reduced to system, that they really have it in their power to effect more, towards making their guests comfortable, than perhaps any other people.

After a short season allotted to changing our ship garments and for rest, we found ourselves seated at the dinner table. While dining, the sister-in-law of our friends came in from the next door, to exchange a word or two of welcome, and invite us to breakfast with them the following morning.

Between all the excitements of landing, and meeting so many new faces, and the remains of the dizzy motion of the ship, which still haunted me, I found it impossible to close my eyes to sleep that first night till the dim gray of dawn. I got up as soon as it was light, and looked out of the window; and as my eyes fell on the luxuriant, ivy-covered porch, the clumps of shining, dark-green holly bushes, I said to myself, "Ah, really, this is England!"

I never saw any plant that struck me as more beautiful than this holly. It is a dense shrub growing from six to eight feet high, with a thickly varnished leaf of green. The outline of the leaf is something like this. I do not believe it can ever come to a state of perfect development under the fierce alternations of heat and cold which obtain in our New England climate, though it grows in the Southern States. It is one of the symbolical shrubs of England, probably because its bright green in winter makes it so splendid a Christmas decoration. A little bird sat twittering on one of the sprays. He had a bright red breast, and seemed evidently to consider himself of good blood and family, with the best reason, as I afterwards learned, since he was no other than the identical robin redbreast renowned in song and story; undoubtedly a lineal descendant of that very cock robin whose death and burial form so vivid a portion of our childish literature.

I must tell you, then, as one of the first remarks on matters and things here in England, that "robin redbreast" is not at all the fellow we in America take him to be. The character who flourishes under that name among us is quite a different bird; he is twice as large, and has altogether a different air, and as he sits up with military erectness on a rail fence or stump, shows not even a family likeness to his diminutive English namesake. Well, of course, robin over here will claim to have the real family estate and title, since he lives in a country where such matters are understood and looked into. Our robin is probably some fourth cousin, who, like others, has struck out a new course for himself in America, and thrives upon it.

We hurried to dress, remembering our engagements to breakfast this morning with a brother of our host, whose cottage stands on the same ground, within a few steps of our own. I had not the slightest idea of what the English mean by a breakfast, and therefore went in all innocence, supposing that I should see nobody but the family circle of my acquaintances. Quite to my astonishment, I found a party of between thirty and forty people. Ladies sitting with their bonnets on, as in a morning call. It was impossible, however, to feel more than a momentary embarrassment in the friendly warmth and cordiality of the circle by whom we were surrounded.

The English are called cold and stiff in their manners; I had always heard they were so, but I certainly saw nothing of it here. A circle of family relatives could not have received us with more warmth and kindness. The remark which I made mentally, as my eye passed around the circle, was— Why, these people are just like home; they look like us, and the tone of sentiment and feeling is precisely such as I have been accustomed to; I mean with the exception of the antislavery question.

That question has, from the very first, been, in England, a deeply religious movement. It was conceived and carried on by men of devotional habits, in the same spirit in which the work of foreign missions was undertaken in our own country; by just such earnest, self-denying, devout men as Samuel J. Mills and Jeremiah Evarts.

It was encountered by the same contempt and opposition, in the outset, from men of merely worldly habits and principles; and to this day it retains that hold on the devotional mind of the English nation that the foreign mission cause does in America.

Liverpool was at first to the antislavery cause nearly what New York has been with us. Its commercial interests were largely implicated in the slave trade, and the virulence of opposition towards the first movers of the antislavery reform in Liverpool was about as great as it is now against abolitionists in Charleston.

When Clarkson first came here to prosecute his inquiries into the subject, a mob collected around him, and endeavored to throw him off the dock into the water; he was rescued by a gentleman, some of whose descendants I met on this occasion.

The father of our host, Mr. Cropper, was one of the first and most efficient supporters of the cause in Liverpool; and the whole circle was composed of those who had taken a deep interest in that struggle. The wife of our host was the daughter of the celebrated Lord Chief Justice Denman, a man who, for many years, stood unrivalled, at the head of the legal mind in England, and who, with a generous ardor seldom equalled, devoted all his energies to this sacred cause.

When the publication of Uncle Tom's Cabin turned the attention of the British public to the existing horrors of slavery in America, some palliations of the system appeared in English papers. Lord Denman, though then in delicate health and advanced years, wrote a series of letters upon the subject—an exertion which entirely prostrated his before feeble health. In one of the addresses made at table, a very feeling allusion was made to Lord Denman's labors, and also to those of the honored father of the two Messrs. Cropper.

As breakfast parties are things which we do not have in America, perhaps mother would like to know just how they are managed. The hour is generally somewhere between nine and twelve, and the whole idea and spirit of the thing is that of an informal and social gathering. Ladies keep their bonnets on, and are not dressed in full toilet. On this occasion we sat and chatted together socially till the whole party was assembled in the drawing room, and then breakfast was announced. Each gentleman had a lady assigned him, and we walked into the dining room, where stood the tables tastefully adorned with flowers, and spread with an abundant cold collation, while tea and coffee were passed round by servants. In each plate was a card, containing the name of the person for whom it was designed. I took my place by the side of the Rev. Dr. McNiel, one of the most celebrated clergymen of the established church in Liverpool.

The conversation was flowing, free, and friendly. The old reminiscences of the antislavery conflict in England were touchingly recalled, and the warmest sympathy was expressed for those in America who are carrying on the same cause.

In one thing I was most agreeably disappointed. I had been told that the Christians of England were intolerant and unreasonable in their opinions on this subject; that they could not be made to understand the peculiar difficulties which beset it in America, and that they therefore made no distinction and no allowance in their censures. All this I found, so far as this circle were concerned, to be strikingly untrue. They appeared to be peculiarly affectionate in their feelings as regarded our country; to have the highest appreciation of, and the deepest sympathy with, our religious community, and to be extremely desirous to assist us in our difficulties. I also found them remarkably well informed upon the subject. They keep their eyes upon our papers, our public documents and speeches in Congress, and are as well advised in regard to the progress of the moral conflict as our Foreign Missionary Society is with the state of affairs in Hindostan and Burmah.

Several present spoke of the part which England originally had in planting slavery in America, as placing English Christians under a solemn responsibility to bring every possible moral influence to bear for its extinction. Nevertheless, they seem to be the farthest possible from an unkind or denunciatory spirit, even towards those most deeply implicated. The remarks made by Dr. McNiel to me were a fair sample of the spirit and attitude of all present.

"I have been trying, Mrs. S.," he said, "to bring my mind into the attitude of those Christians at the south who defend the institution of slavery. There are *real* Christians there who do this—are there not?"

I replied, that undoubtedly there were some most amiable and Christian people who defend slavery on principle, just as there had been some to defend every form of despotism.

"Do give me some idea of the views they take; it is something to me so inconceivable. I am utterly at a loss how it can be made in any way plausible."

I then stated that the most plausible view, and that which seemed to have the most force with good men, was one which represented the institution of slavery as a sort of wardship or guardian relation, by which an inferior race were brought under the watch and care of a superior race to be instructed in Christianity.

He then inquired if there was any system of religious instruction actually pursued.

In reply to this, I gave him some sketch of the operations for the religious instruction of the negroes, which had been carried on by the Presbyterian and other denominations. I remarked that many good people who do not take very extended views, fixing their attention chiefly on the efforts which they are making for the religious instruction of slaves, are blind to the sin and injustice of allowing their legal position to remain what it is.

"But how do they shut their eyes to the various cruelties of the system,— the separation of families—the domestic slave trade?"

I replied, "In part, by not inquiring into them. The best kind of people are, in general, those who *know* least of the cruelties of the system; they never witness them. As in the city of London or Liverpool there may be an amount of crime and suffering which many residents may live years without seeing or knowing, so it is in the slave states."

Every person present appeared to be in that softened and charitable frame of mind which disposed them to make every allowance for the situation of Christians so peculiarly tempted, while, at the same time, there was the most earnest concern, in view of the dishonor brought upon Christianity by the defence of such a system.

One other thing I noticed, which was an agreeable disappointment to me. I had been told that there was no social intercourse between the established church and dissenters. In this party, however, were people of many different denominations. Our host belongs to the established church; his brother, with whom we are visiting, is a Baptist, and their father was a Friend; and there appeared to be the utmost social cordiality. Whether I shall find this uniformly the case will appear in time.

After the breakfast party was over, I found at the door an array of children of the poor, belonging to a school kept under the superintendence of Mrs. E. Cropper, and called, as is customary here, a ragged school. The children, however, were any thing but ragged, being tidily dressed, remarkably clean, with glowing cheeks and bright eyes. I must say, so far as I have seen them, English children have a much healthier appearance than those of America. By the side of their bright bloom ours look pale and faded.

Another school of the same kind is kept in this neighborhood, under the auspices of Sir George Stephen, a conspicuous advocate of the antislavery cause.

I thought the fair patroness of this school seemed not a little delighted with the appearance of her protégés, as they sung, with great enthusiasm, Jane Taylor's hymn, commencing,

> "I thank the goodness and the grace
>
> That on my birth have smiled,
>
> And made me in these Christian days
>
> A happy English child."

All the little rogues were quite familiar with Topsy and Eva, and *au fait* in the fortunes of Uncle Tom; so that, being introduced as the maternal relative of these characters, I seemed to find favor in their eyes. And when one of the speakers congratulated them that they were born in a land where no child could be bought or sold, they responded with enthusiastic cheers—cheers which made me feel rather sad; but still I could not quarrel with English people for taking all the pride and all the comfort which this inspiriting truth can convey.

They had a hard enough struggle in rooting up the old weed of slavery, to justify them in rejoicing in their freedom. Well, the day will come in America, as I trust, when as much can be said for us.

After the children were gone came a succession of calls; some from very aged people, the veterans of the old antislavery cause. I was astonished and overwhelmed by the fervor of feeling some of them manifested; there seemed to be something almost prophetic in the enthusiasm with which they expressed their hope of our final success in America. This excitement, though very pleasant, was wearisome, and I was glad of an opportunity after dinner to rest myself, by rambling uninterrupted, with my friends, through the beautiful grounds of the Dingle.

Two nice little boys were my squires on this occasion, one of whom, a sturdy little fellow, on being asked his name, gave it to me in full as Joseph Babington Macaulay, and I learned that his mother, by a former marriage, had been the wife of Macaulay's brother. Uncle Tom Macaulay, I found, was a favorite character with the young people. Master Harry conducted me through the walks to the conservatories, all brilliant with azaleas and all sorts of flowers, and then through a long walk on the banks of the Mersey.

Here the wild flowers attracted my attention, as being so different from those of our own country. Their daisy is not our flower, with its wide, plaited ruff and yellow centre. The English daisy is

"The wee modest crimson-tipped flower,"

which Burns celebrates. It is what we raise in greenhouses, and call the mountain daisy. Its effect, growing profusely about fields and grass plats, is very beautiful.

We read much, among the poets, of the primrose,

"Earliest daughter of the Spring."

This flower is one, also, which we cultivate in gardens to some extent. The outline of it is as follows: The hue a delicate straw color; it grows in tufts in shady places, and has a pure, serious look, which reminds one of the line of Shakspeare—

"Pale primroses, which die unmarried."

It has also the faintest and most ethereal perfume,—a perfume that seems to come and go in the air like music; and you perceive it at a little distance from a tuft of them, when you would not if you gathered and smelled them. On the whole, the primrose is a poet's and a painter's flower. An artist's eye would notice an exquisite harmony between the yellow-green hue of its leaves and the tint of its blossoms. I do not wonder that it has been so great a favorite among the poets. It is just such a flower as Mozart and Raphael would have loved.

Then there is the bluebell, a bulb, which also grows in deep shades. It is a little purple bell, with a narrow green leaf, like a ribbon. We often read in English stories, of the gorse and furze; these are two names for the same plant, a low bush, with strong, prickly leaves, growing much like a juniper. The contrast of its very brilliant yellow, pea-shaped blossoms, with the dark green of its leaves, is very beautiful. It grows here in hedges and on commons, and is thought rather a plebeian affair. I think it would make quite an addition to our garden shrubbery. Possibly it might make as much sensation with us as our mullein does in foreign greenhouses.

After rambling a while, we came to a beautiful summer house, placed in a retired spot, so as to command a view of the Mersey River. I think they told me that it was Lord Denman's favorite seat. There we sat down, and in common with the young gentlemen and ladies of the family, had quite a pleasant talk together. Among other things we talked about the question which is now agitating the public mind a good deal,—Whether it is expedient to open the Crystal Palace to the people on Sunday. They said that this course was much urged by some philanthropists, on the ground that it was the only day when the working classes could find any leisure to visit it, and that it seemed hard to shut them out entirely from all the opportunities and advantages which they might thus derive; that to exclude the laborer from recreation on the Sabbath, was the same as saying that he should never have any recreation. I asked, why the philanthropists could not urge employers to give their workmen a part of Saturday for this purpose; as it seemed to me unchristian to drive trade so that the laboring man had no time but Sunday for intellectual and social recreation. We rather came to the conclusion that this was the right course; whether the people of England will, is quite another matter.

The grounds of the Dingle embrace three cottages; those of the two Messrs. Cropper, and that of a son, who is married to a daughter of Dr. Arnold. I rather think this way of relatives living together is more common here in England than it is in America; and there is more idea of home permanence connected with the family dwelling-place than with us, where the country is so wide, and causes of change and removal so frequent. A man builds a house in England with the expectation of living in it and leaving it to his children; while we shed our houses in America as easily as a snail does his shell. We live a while in Boston, and then a while in New York, and then, perhaps, turn up at Cincinnati. Scarcely any body with us is living where they expect to live and die. The man that dies in the house he was born in is a wonder. There is something pleasant in the permanence and repose of the English family estate, which we, in America, know very little of. All which is apropos to our having finished our walk, and got back to the ivy-covered porch again.

The next day at breakfast, it was arranged that we should take a drive out to Speke Hall, an old mansion, which is considered a fine specimen of ancient house architecture. So the carriage was at the door. It was a cool, breezy, April morning, but there was an abundance of wrappers and carriage blankets provided to keep us comfortable. I must say, by the by, that English housekeepers are bountiful in their provision for carriage comfort. Every household has a store of warm, loose over garments, which are offered, if needed, to the guests; and each carriage is provided with one or two blankets, manufactured and sold expressly for this use, to envelope one's feet and limbs; besides all which, should the weather be cold, comes out a long stone reservoir, made flat on both sides, and filled with hot water, for foot stools. This is an improvement on the primitive simplicity of hot bricks, and even on the tin foot stove, which has nourished in New England.

Being thus provided with all things necessary for comfort, we rattled merrily away, and I, remembering that I was in England, kept my eyes wide open to see what I could see. The hedges of the fields were just budding, and the green showed itself on them, like a thin gauze veil. These hedges are not all so well kept and trimmed as I expected to find them. Some, it is true, are cut very carefully; these are generally hedges to ornamental grounds; but many of those which separate the fields straggle and sprawl, and have some high bushes and some low ones, and, in short, are no more like a hedge than many rows of bushes that we have at home. But such as they are, they are the only dividing lines of the fields, and it is certainly a more picturesque mode of division than our stone or worm fences. Outside of every hedge, towards the street, there is generally a ditch, and at the bottom of the hedge is the favorite nestling-place for all sorts of wild flowers. I remember reading in stories about children trying to crawl through a gap in the hedge to get at flowers, and tumbling into a ditch on the other side, and I now saw exactly how they could do it.

As we drive we pass by many beautiful establishments, about of the quality of our handsomest country houses, but whose grounds are kept with a precision and exactness rarely to be seen among us. We cannot get the gardeners who are qualified to do it; and if we could, the painstaking, slow way of proceeding, and the habit of creeping thoroughness, which are necessary to accomplish such results, die out in America. Nevertheless, such grounds are exceedingly beautiful to look upon, and I was much obliged to the owners of these places for keeping their gates hospitably open, as seems to be the custom here.

After a drive of seven or eight miles, we alighted in front of Speke Hall. This house is a specimen of the old fortified houses of England, and was once fitted up with a moat and drawbridge, all in approved feudal style. It was built somewhere about the year 1500. The sometime moat was now full of smooth, green grass, and the drawbridge no longer remains.

This was the first really old thing that we had seen since our arrival in England. We came up first to a low, arched, stone door, and knocked with a great old-fashioned knocker; this brought no answer but a treble and bass duet from a couple of dogs inside; so we opened the door, and saw a square court, paved with round stones, and a dark, solitary yew tree in the centre. Here in England, I think, they have vegetable creations made on purpose to go with old, dusky buildings; and this yew tree is one of them. It has altogether a most goblin-like, bewitched air, with its dusky black leaves and ragged branches, throwing themselves straight out with odd twists and angular lines, and might put one in mind of an old raven with some of his feathers pulled out, or a black cat with her hair stroked the wrong way, or any other strange, uncanny thing. Besides this they live almost forever; for when they have grown so old that any respectable tree ought to be thinking of dying, they only take another twist, and so live on another hundred years. I saw some in England seven hundred years old, and they had grown queerer every century. It is a species of evergreen, and its leaf resembles our hemlock, only it is longer. This sprig gives you some idea of its general form. It is always planted about churches and graveyards; a kind of dismal emblem of immortality. This sepulchral old tree and the bass and treble dogs were the only occupants of the court. One of these, a great surly mastiff, barked out of his kennel on one side, and the other, a little wiry terrier, out of his on the opposite side, and both strained on their chains, as if they would enjoy making even more decided demonstrations if they could.

There was an aged, mossy fountain for holy water by the side of the wall, in which some weeds were growing. A door in the house was soon opened by a decent-looking serving woman, to whom we communicated our desire to see the hall.

We were shown into a large dining hall with a stone floor, wainscoted with carved oak, almost as black as ebony. There were some pious sentences and moral reflections inscribed in old English text, carved over the doors, and like a cornice round the ceiling, which was also of carved oak. Their general drift was, to say that life is short, and to call for watchfulness and prayer. The fireplace of the hall yawned like a great cavern, and nothing else, one would think, than a cart load of western sycamores could have supplied an appropriate fire. A great two-handed sword of some ancestor hung over the fireplace. On taking it down it reached to C———'s shoulder, who, you know, is six feet high.

We went into a sort of sitting room, and looked out through a window, latticed with little diamond panes, upon a garden wildly beautiful. The lattice was all wreathed round with jessamines. The furniture of this room was modern, and it seemed the more unique from its contrast with the old architecture.

We went up stairs to see the chambers, and passed through a long, narrow, black oak corridor, whose slippery boards had the authentic ghostly squeak to them. There was a chamber, hung with old, faded tapestry of Scripture subjects. In this chamber there was behind the tapestry a door, which, being opened, displayed a staircase, that led delightfully off to nobody knows where. The furniture was black oak, carved, in the most elaborate manner, with cherubs' heads and other good and solemn subjects, calculated to produce a ghostly state of mind. And, to crown all, we heard that there was a haunted chamber, which was not to be opened, where a white lady appeared and walked at all approved hours.

Now, only think what a foundation for a story is here. If our Hawthorne could conjure up such a thing as the Seven Gables in one of our prosaic country towns, what would he have done if he had lived here? Now he is obliged to get his ghostly images by looking through smoked glass at our square, cold realities; but one such old place as this is a standing romance. Perhaps it may add to the effect to say, that the owner of the house is a bachelor, who lives there very retired, and employs himself much in reading.

The housekeeper, who showed us about, indulged us with a view of the kitchen, whose snowy, sanded floor and resplendent polished copper and tin, were sights for a housekeeper to take away in her heart of hearts. The good woman produced her copy of Uncle Tom, and begged the favor of my autograph, which I gave, thinking it quite a happy thing to be able to do a favor at so cheap a rate.

After going over the house we wandered through the grounds, which are laid out with the same picturesque mixture of the past and present. There was a fine grove, under whose shadows we walked, picking primroses, and otherwise enacting the poetic, till it was time to go. As we passed out, we were again saluted with a *feu de joie* by the two fidelities at the door, which we took in very good part, since it is always respectable to be thorough in whatever you are set to do.

Coming home we met with an accident to the carriage which obliged us to get out and walk some distance. I was glad enough of it, because it gave me a better opportunity for seeing the country. We stopped at a cottage to get some rope, and a young woman came out with that beautiful, clear complexion which I so much admire here in England; literally her cheeks were like damask roses.

I told Isa I wanted to see as much of the interior of the cottages as I could; and so, as we were walking onward toward home, we managed to call once or twice, on the excuse of asking the way and distance. The exterior was very neat, being built of brick or stone, and each had attached to it a little flower garden. Isa said that the cottagers often offered them a slice of bread or tumbler of milk.

They have a way here of building the cottages two or three in a block together, which struck me as different from our New England manner, where, in the country, every house stands detached.

In the evening I went into Liverpool, to attend a party of friends of the antislavery cause. In the course of the evening, Mr. Stowe was requested to make some remarks. Among other things he spoke upon the support the free part of the world give to slavery, by the purchase of the produce of slave labor; and, in particular, on the great quantity of slave-grown cotton purchased by England; suggesting it as a subject for inquiry, whether this cannot be avoided.

One or two gentlemen, who are largely concerned in the manufacture and importation of cotton, spoke to him on the subject afterwards, and said it was a thing which ought to be very seriously considered. It is probable that the cotton trade of Great Britain is the great essential item which supports slavery, and such considerations ought not, therefore, to be without their results.

When I was going away, the lady of the house said that the servants were anxious to see me; so I came into the dressing room to give them, an opportunity.

While at Mr. C.'s, also, I had once or twice been called out to see servants, who had come in to visit those of the family. All of them had read Uncle Tom's Cabin, and were full of sympathy. Generally speaking, the servants seem to me quite a superior class to what are employed in that capacity with us. They look very intelligent, are dressed with great neatness, and though their manners are very much more deferential than those of servants in our country, it appears to be a difference arising quite as much from self-respect and a sense of propriety as from servility. Every body's manners are more deferential in England than in America.

The next day was appointed to leave Liverpool. It had been arranged that, before leaving, we should meet the ladies of the Negroes' Friend Society, an association formed at the time of the original antislavery agitation in England. We went in the carriage with our friends Mr. and Mrs. E. Cropper. On the way they were conversing upon the labors of Mrs. Chisholm, the celebrated female philanthropist, whose efforts for the benefit of emigrants are awakening a very general interest among all classes in England. They said there had been hesitation on the part of some good people, in regard to coöperating with her, because she is a Roman Catholic.

It was agreed among us, that the great humanities of the present day are a proper ground on which all sects can unite, and that if any feared the extension of wrong sentiments, they had only to supply emigrant ships more abundantly with the Bible. Mr. C. said that this is a movement exciting very extensive interest, and that they hoped Mrs. Chisholm would visit Liverpool before long.

The meeting was a very interesting one. The style of feeling expressed in all the remarks was tempered by a deep and earnest remembrance of the share which England originally had in planting the evil of slavery in the civilized world, and her consequent obligation, as a Christian nation, now not to cease her efforts until the evil is extirpated, not merely from her own soil, but from all lands.

The feeling towards America was respectful and friendly, and the utmost sympathy was expressed with her in the difficulties with which she is environed by this evil. The tone of the meeting was deeply earnest and religious. They presented us with a sum to be appropriated for the benefit of the slave, in any way we might think proper.

A great number of friends accompanied us to the cars, and a beautiful bouquet of flowers was sent, with a very affecting message from, a sick gentleman, who, from the retirement of his chamber, felt a desire to testify his sympathy.

Now, if all this enthusiasm for freedom and humanity, in the person of the American slave, is to be set down as good for nothing in England, because there are evils there in society which require redress, what then shall we say of ourselves? Have we not been enthusiastic for freedom in the person of the Greek, the Hungarian, and the Pole, while protecting a much worse despotism than any from which they suffer? Do we not consider it our duty to print and distribute the Bible in all foreign lands, when there are three millions of people among whom we dare not distribute it at home, and whom it is a penal offence even to teach to read it? Do we not send remonstrances to Tuscany, about the Madiai, when women are imprisoned in Virginia for teaching slaves to read? Is all this hypocritical, insincere, and impertinent in us? Are we never to send another missionary, or make another appeal for foreign lands, till we have abolished slavery at home? For my part, I think that imperfect and inconsistent outbursts of generosity and feeling are a great deal better than none. No nation, no individual is wholly consistent and Christian; but let us not in ourselves or in other nations repudiate the truest and most beautiful developments of humanity, because we have not yet attained perfection.

All experience has proved that the sublime spirit of foreign missions always is suggestive of home philanthropies, and that those whose heart has been enlarged by the love of all mankind are always those who are most efficient in their own particular sphere.

LETTER III

Glasgow, April 16, 1853.

Dear Aunt E.:—

You shall have my earliest Scotch letter; for I am sure nobody can sympathize in the emotions of the first approach to Scotland as you can. A country dear to us by the memory of the dead and of the living; a country whose history and literature, interesting enough of itself, has become to us still more so, because the reading and learning of it formed part of our communion for many a social hour, with friends long parted from earth.

The views of Scotland, which lay on my mother's table, even while I was a little child, and in poring over which I spent so many happy, dreamy hours,—the Scotch ballads, which were the delight of our evening fireside, and which seemed almost to melt the soul out of me, before I was old enough to understand their words,—the songs of Burns, which had been a household treasure among us,—the enchantments of Scott,—all these dimly returned upon me. It was the result of them all which I felt in nerve and brain.

And, by the by, that puts me in mind of one thing; and that is, how much of our pleasure in literature results from its reflection on us from, other minds. As we advance in life, the literature which has charmed us in the circle of our friends becomes endeared to us from the reflected remembrance of them, of their individualities, their opinions, and their sympathies, so that our memory of it is a many-colored cord, drawn from many minds.

So in coming near to Scotland, I seemed to feel not only my own individuality, but all that my friends would have felt, had they been with me. For sometimes we seem to be encompassed, as by a cloud, with a sense of the sympathy of the absent and the dead.

We left Liverpool with hearts a little tremulous and excited by the vibration of an atmosphere of universal sympathy and kindness. We found ourselves, at length, shut from the warm adieus of our friends, in a snug compartment of the railroad car. The English cars are models of comfort and good keeping. There are six seats in a compartment, luxuriously cushioned and nicely carpeted, and six was exactly the number of our party. Nevertheless, so obstinate is custom that we averred at first that we preferred our American cars, deficient as they are in many points of neatness and luxury, because they are so much more social.

"Dear me," said Mr. S., "six Yankees shut up in a car together! Not one Englishman to tell us any thing about the country! Just like the six old ladies that made their living by taking tea at each other's houses."

But that is the way here in England: every arrangement in travelling is designed to maintain that privacy and reserve which is the dearest and most sacred part of an Englishman's nature. Things are so arranged here that, if a man pleases, he can travel all through England with his family, and keep the circle an unbroken unit, having just as little communication with any thing outside of it as in his own house.

From one of these sheltered apartments in a railroad car, he can pass to preëngaged parlors and chambers in the hotel, with his own separate table, and all his domestic manners and peculiarities unbroken. In fact, it is a little compact home travelling about.

Now, all this is very charming to people who know already as much about a country as they want to know; but it follows from it that a stranger might travel all through England, from one end to the other and not be on conversing terms with a person in it. He may be at the same hotel, in the same train with people able to give him all imaginable information, yet never touch them at any practicable point of communion. This is more especially the case if his party, as ours was, is just large enough to fill the whole apartment.

As to the comforts of the cars, it is to be said, that for the same price you can get far more comfortable riding in America. Their first class cars are beyond all praise, but also beyond all price; their second class are comfortless, cushionless, and uninviting. Agreeably with our theory of democratic equality, we have a general car, not so complete as the one, nor so bare as the other, where all ride together; and if the traveller in thus riding sees things that occasionally annoy him, when he remembers that the whole population, from the highest to the lowest, are accommodated here together, he will certainly see hopeful indications in the general comfort, order, and respectability which prevail; all which we talked over most patriotically together, while we were lamenting that there was not a seventh to our party, to instruct us in the localities.

Every thing upon the railroad proceeds with systematic accuracy. There is no chance for the most careless person to commit a blunder, or make a mistake. At the proper time the conductor marches every body into their places and locks them in, gives the word, "All right," and away we go. Somebody has remarked, very characteristically, that the starting word of the English is "all right," and that of the Americans "go ahead."

Away we go through Lancashire, wide awake, looking out on all sides for any signs of antiquity. In being thus whirled through English scenery, I became conscious of a new understanding of the spirit and phraseology of English poetry. There are many phrases and expressions with which we have been familiar from childhood, and which, we suppose, in a kind of indefinite way, we understand, which, after all, when we come on English ground, start into a new significance: take, for instance, these lines from L'Allegro:—

> "Sometimes walking, not unseen,
>
> By hedge-row elms on hillocks green.
>
> * * * *
>
> Straight mine eye hath caught new pleasures,
>
> While the landscape round it measures;
>
> Russet lawns and fallows gray,
>
> Where the nibbling flocks do stray;
>
> Mountains, on whose barren breast
>
> The laboring clouds do often rest;
>
> Meadows trim with daisies pied,
>
> Shallow brooks and livers wide:
>
> Towers and battlements it sees
>
> Bosom'd high in tufted trees."

Now, these hedge-row elms. I had never even asked myself what they were till I saw them; but you know, as I said in a former letter, the hedges are not all of them carefully cut; in fact many of them are only irregular rows of bushes, where, although the hawthorn is the staple element, yet firs, and brambles, and many other interlopers put in their claim, and they all grow up together in a kind of straggling unity; and in the hedges trees are often set out, particularly elms, and have a very pleasing effect.

Then, too, the trees have more of that rounding outline which is expressed by the word "bosomed." But here we are, right under the walls of Lancaster, and Mr. S. wakes me up by quoting, "Old John o' Gaunt, time-honored Lancaster."

"Time-honored," said I; "it looks as fresh as if it had been built yesterday: you do not mean to say that is the real old castle?"

"To be sure, it is the very old castle built in the reign of Edward III., by John of Gaunt."

It stands on the summit of a hill, seated regally like a queen upon a throne, and every part of it looks as fresh, and sharp, and clear, as if it were the work of modern times. It is used now for a county jail. We have but a moment to stop or admire the merciless steam car drives on. We have a little talk about the feudal times, and the old past days; when again the cry goes up,—

"O, there's something! What's that?"

"O, that is Carlisle."

"Carlisle!" said I; "what, the Carlisle of Scott's ballad?"

"What ballad?"

"Why, don't you remember, in the Lay of the Last Minstrel, the song of Albert Graeme, which has something about Carlisle's wall in every verse?

'It was an English, laydie bright

When sun shines fair on Carlisle wall,

And she would marry a Scottish knight,

For love will still be lord of all.'

I used to read this when I was a child, and wonder what 'Carlisle wall' was."

Carlisle is one of the most ancient cities in England, dating quite back to the time of the Romans. Wonderful! How these Romans left their mark every where!

Carlisle has also its ancient castle, the lofty, massive tower of which forms a striking feature of the town.

This castle was built by William Rufus. David, King of Scots, and Robert Bruce both tried their hands upon it, in the good old times, when England and Scotland were a mutual robbery association. Then the castle of the town was its great feature; castles were every thing in those days. Now the castle has gone to decay, and stands only for a curiosity, and the cotton factory has come up in its place. This place is famous for cottons and ginghams, and moreover for a celebrated biscuit bakery. So goes the world,—the lively vigorous shoots of the present springing out of the old, mouldering trunk of the past.

Mr. S. was in an ecstasy about an old church, a splendid Gothic, in which Paley preached. He was archdeacon of Carlisle. We stopped here for a little while to take dinner. In a large, handsome room tables were set out, and we sat down to a regular meal.

One sees nothing of a town from a railroad station, since it seems to be an invariable rule, not only here, but all over Europe, to locate them so that you can see nothing from them.

By the by, I forgot to say, among the historical recollections of this place, that it was the first stopping-place of Queen Mary, after her fatal flight into England. The rooms which she occupied are still shown in the castle, and there are interesting letters and documents extant from lords whom Elizabeth sent here to visit her, in which they record her beauty, her heroic sentiments, and even her dress; so strong was the fascination in which she held all who approached her. Carlisle is the scene of the denouement of Guy Mannering, and it is from this town that Lord Carlisle gets his title.

And now keep up a bright lookout for ruins and old houses. Mr. S., whose eyes are always in every place, allowed none of us to slumber, but looking out, first on his own side and then on ours, called our attention to every visible thing. If he had been appointed on a mission of inquiry he could not have been more zealous and faithful, and I began to think that our desire for an English cicerone was quite superfluous.

And now we pass Gretna Green, famous in story—that momentous place which marks the commencement of Scotland. It is a little straggling village, and there is a roadside inn, which has been the scene of innumerable Gretna Green marriages.

Owing to the fact that the Scottish law of marriage is far more liberal in its construction than the English, this place has been the refuge of distressed lovers from time immemorial; and although the practice of escaping here is universally condemned as very naughty and improper, yet, like every other impropriety, it is kept in countenance by very respectable people. Two lord chancellors have had the amiable weakness to fall into this snare, and one lord chancellor's son; so says the guide book, which is our Koran for the time being. It says, moreover, that it would be easy to add a lengthened list of *distingués* married at Gretna Green; but these lord chancellors (Erskine and Eldon) are quoted as being the most melancholy monuments. What shall meaner mortals do, when law itself, in all her majesty, wig, gown, and all, goes by the board?

Well, we are in Scotland at last, and now our pulse rises as the sun declines in the west. We catch glimpses of the Solway Frith, and talk about Redgauntlet.

One says, "Do you remember the scene on the sea shore, with which it opens, describing the rising of the tide?"

And says another, "Don't you remember those lines in the Young Lochinvar song?—

'Love swells like the Solway, but ebbs like its tide.'"

I wonder how many authors it will take to enchant our country from Maine to New Orleans, as every foot of ground is enchanted here in Scotland.

The sun went down, and night drew on; still we were in Scotland. Scotch ballads, Scotch tunes, and Scotch literature were in the ascendant. We sang "Auld Lang Syne," "Scots wha ha'," and "Bonnie Doon," and then, changing the key, sang Dundee, Elgin, and Martyrs.

"Take care," said Mr. S.; "don't get too much excited."

"Ah," said I, "this is a thing that comes only once in a lifetime; do let us have the comfort of it. We shall never come into Scotland for the *first time* again."

"Ah," said another, "how I wish Walter Scott was alive!"

While we were thus at the fusion point of enthusiasm, the cars stopped at Lockerby, where the real Old Mortality is buried. All was dim and dark outside, but we soon became conscious that there was quite a number collected, peering into the window, and, with a strange kind of thrill, I heard my name inquired for in the Scottish accent. I went to the window; there were men, women, and children there, and hand after hand was presented, with the words, "Ye're welcome to Scotland!"

Then they inquired for, and shook hands with, all the party, having in some mysterious manner got the knowledge of who they were, even down to little G———, whom they took to be my son. Was it not pleasant, when I had a heart so warm for this old country? I shall never forget the thrill of those words, "Ye're welcome to Scotland," nor the "Gude night."

After that we found similar welcomes in many succeeding stopping-places; and though I did wave a towel out of the window, instead of a pocket handkerchief, and commit other awkwardnesses, from not knowing how to play my part, yet I fancied, after all, that Scotland and we were coming on well together. Who the good souls were that were thus watching for us through the night, I am sure I do not know; but that they were of the "one blood," which unites all the families of the earth, I felt.

As we came towards Glasgow, we saw, upon a high hill, what we supposed to be a castle on fire—great volumes of smoke rolling up, and fire looking out of arched windows.

"Dear me, what a conflagration!" we all exclaimed. We had not gone very far before we saw another, and then, on the opposite side of the car, another still.

"Why, it seems to me the country is all on fire."

"I should think," said Mr. S., "if it was in old times, that there had been a raid from the Highlands, and set all the houses on fire."

"Or they might be beacons," suggested C.

To this some one answered out of the Lay of the Last Minstrel,—

> "Sweet Teviot, by thy silver tide
>
> The glaring bale-fires blaze no more."

As we drew near to Glasgow these illuminations increased, till the whole air was red with the glare of them.

"What can they be?"

"Dear me," said Mr. S., in a tone of sudden recollection, "it's the iron works! Don't you know Glasgow is celebrated for its iron works?"

So, after all, in these peaceful fires of the iron works, we got an idea how the country might have looked in the old picturesque times, when the Highlanders came down and set the Lowlands on fire; such scenes as are commemorated in the words of Roderick Dhu's song:—

> "Proudly our pibroch, has thrilled in Glen Fruin,
>
> And Banmachar's groans to our slogan replied;
>
> Glen Luss and Ross Dhu, they are smoking in ruins,
>
> And the best of Loch Lomond lies dead on her side."

To be sure the fires of iron founderies are much less picturesque than the old beacons, and the clink of hammers than the clash of claymores; but the most devout worshipper of the middle ages would hardly wish to change them.

Dimly, by the flickering light of these furnaces, we see the approach to the old city of Glasgow. There, we are arrived! Friends are waiting in the station house. Earnest, eager, friendly faces, ever so many. Warm greetings, kindly words. A crowd parting in the middle, through which we were conducted into a carriage, and loud cheers of welcome, sent a throb, as the voice of living Scotland.

I looked out of the carriage, as we drove on, and saw, by the light of a lantern, Argyle Street. It was past twelve o'clock when I found myself in a warm, cozy parlor, with friends, whom I have ever since been glad to remember. In a little time we were all safely housed in our hospitable apartments, and sleep fell on me for the first time in Scotland.

LETTER IV

Dear Aunt E.:—

The next morning I awoke worn and weary, and scarce could the charms of the social Scotch breakfast restore me. I say Scotch, for we had many viands peculiarly national. The smoking porridge, or parritch, of oatmeal, which is the great staple dish throughout Scotland. Then there was the bannock, a thin, wafer-like cake of the same material. My friend laughingly said when he passed it, "You are in the 'land o' cakes,' remember." There was also some herring, as nice a Scottish fish as ever wore scales, besides dainties innumerable which were not national.

Our friend and host was Mr. Baillie Paton. I believe that it is to his suggestion in a public meeting, that we owe the invitation which brought us to Scotland.

By the by, I should say that "baillie" seems to correspond to what we call a member of the city council. Mr. Paton told us, that they had expected us earlier, and that the day before quite a party of friends met at his house to see us, among whom was good old Dr. Wardlaw.

After breakfast the calling began. First, a friend of the family, with three beautiful children, the youngest of whom was the bearer of a handsomely bound album, containing a pressed collection of the sea mosses of the Scottish coast, very vivid and beautiful.

If the bloom of English children appeared to me wonderful, I seemed to find the same thing intensified, if possible, in Scotland. The children are brilliant as pomegranate blossoms, and their vivid beauty called forth unceasing admiration. Nor is it merely the children of the rich, or of the higher classes, that are thus gifted. I have seen many a group of ragged urchins in the streets and closes with all the high coloring of Rubens, and all his fulness of outline. Why is it that we admire ragged children on canvas so much more than the same in nature?

All this day is a confused dream to me of a dizzy and overwhelming kind. So many letters that it took C—— from nine in the morning till two in the afternoon to read and answer them in the shortest manner; letters from all classes of people, high and low, rich and poor, in all shades and styles of composition, poetry and prose; some mere outbursts of feeling; some invitations; some advice and suggestions; some requests and inquiries; some presenting books, or flowers, or fruit.

Then came, in their turn, deputations from Paisley, Greenock, Dundee, Aberdeen, Edinburgh, and Belfast in Ireland; calls of friendship, invitations of all descriptions to go every where, and to see every thing, and to stay in so many places. One kind, venerable minister, with his lovely daughter, offered me a retreat in his quiet manse on the beautiful shores of the Clyde.

For all these kindnesses, what could I give in return? There was scarce time for even a grateful thought on each. People have often said to me that it must have been an exceeding bore. For my part, I could not think of regarding it so. It only oppressed me with an unutterable sadness.

To me there is always something interesting and beautiful about a universal popular excitement of a generous character, let the object of it be what it may. The great desiring heart of man, surging with one strong, sympathetic swell, even though it be to break on the beach of life and fall backwards, leaving the sands as barren as before, has yet a meaning and a power in its restlessness, with which I must deeply sympathize. Nor do I sympathize any the less, when the individual, who calls forth such an outburst, can be seen by the eye of sober sense to be altogether inadequate and disproportioned to it.

I do not regard it as any thing against our American nation, that we are capable, to a very great extent, of these sudden personal enthusiasms, because I think that, with an individual or a community, the capability of being exalted into a temporary enthusiasm of self-forgetfulness, so far from being a fault, has in it a quality of something divine.

Of course, about all such things there is a great deal which a cool critic could make ridiculous, but I hold to my opinion of them nevertheless.

In the afternoon I rode out with the lord provost to see the cathedral. The lord provost answers to the lord mayor in England. His title and office in both countries continue only a year, except in cases of reëlection.

As I saw the way to the cathedral blocked up by a throng of people, who had come out to see me, I could not help saying, "What went ye out for to see? a reed shaken with the wind?" In fact, I was so worn out, that I could hardly walk through the building.

It is in this cathedral that part of the scene of Rob Roy is laid. This was my first experience in cathedrals. It was a new thing to me altogether, and as I walked along under the old buttresses and battlements without, and looked into the bewildering labyrinths of architecture within, I saw that, with silence and solitude to help the impression, the old building might become a strong part of one's inner life. A grave yard crowded with flat stones lies all around it. A deep ravine separates it from another cemetery on an opposite eminence, rustling with dark pines. A little brook murmurs with its slender voice between.

On this opposite eminence the statue of John Knox, grim and strong, stands with its arm uplifted, as if shaking his fist at the old cathedral which in life he vainly endeavored to battle down.

Knox was very different from Luther, in that he had no conservative element in him, but warred equally against accessories and essentials.

At the time when the churches of Scotland were being pulled down in a general iconoclastic crusade, the tradesmen of Glasgow stood for the defence of their cathedral, and forced the reformers to content themselves with having the idolatrous images of saints pulled down from their niches and thrown into the brook, while, as Andrew Fairservice hath it, "The auld kirk stood as crouse as a cat when the fleas are caimed aff her, and a' body was alike pleased."

We went all through the cathedral, which is fitted up as a Protestant place of worship, and has a simple and massive grandeur about it. In fact, to quote again from our friend Andrew, we could truly say, "Ah, it's a brave kirk, nane o' yere whig-malceries, and curliewurlies, and opensteek hems about it—a' solid, weel-jointed mason wark, that will stand as lang as the warld, keep hands and gun-powther aff it."

I was disappointed in one thing: the painted glass, if there has ever been any, is almost all gone, and the glare of light through the immense windows is altogether too great, revealing many defects and rudenesses in the architecture, which would have quite another appearance in the colored rays through painted windows—an emblem, perhaps, of the cold, definite, intellectual rationalism, which has taken the place of the many-colored, gorgeous mysticism of former times.

After having been over the church, we requested, out of respect to Baillie Nicol Jarvie's memory, to be driven through the Saut Market. I, however, was so thoroughly tired that I cannot remember any thing about it.

I will say, by the way, that I have found out since, that nothing is so utterly hazardous to a person's strength as looking at cathedrals. The strain upon the head and eyes in looking up through these immense arches, and then the sepulchral chill which abides from generation to generation in them, their great extent, and the variety which tempts you to fatigue which you are not at all aware of, have overcome, as I was told, many before me.

Mr. S. and C——, however, made amends, by their great activity and zeal, for all that I could not do, and I was pleased to understand from them, that part of the old Tolbooth, where Rob Roy and the baillie had their rencontre, was standing safe and sound, with stuff enough in it for half a dozen more stories, if any body could be found to write them. And Mr. S. insisted upon it, that I should not omit to notify you of this circumstance.

Well, in consequence of all this, the next morning I was so ill as to need a physician, unable to see any one that called, or to hear any of the letters. I passed most of the day in bed, but in the evening I had to get up, as I had engaged to drink tea with two thousand people. Our kind friends Dr. and Mrs. Wardlaw came after us, and Mr. S. and I went in the carriage with them.

Dr. Wardlaw is a venerable-looking old man; we both thought we saw a striking resemblance in him to our friend Dr. Woods, of Andover. He is still quite active in body and mind, and officiates to his congregation with great acceptance. I fear, however, that he is in ill health, for I noticed, as we were passing along to church, that he frequently laid his hand upon his heart, and seemed in pain. He said he hoped he should be able to get through the evening, but that when he was not well, excitement was apt to bring on a spasm about the heart; but with it all he seemed so cheerful, lively, and benignant, that I could not but feel my affections drawn towards him. Mrs. Wardlaw is a gentle, motherly woman, and it was a great comfort to have her with me on such an occasion.

Our carriage stopped at last at the place. I have a dim remembrance of a way being made for us through a great crowd all round the house, and of going with Mrs. Wardlaw up into a dressing room, where I met and shook hands with many friendly people. Then we passed into a gallery, where a seat was reserved for our party, directly in front of the audience. Our friend Baillie Paton presided. Mrs. Wardlaw and I sat together, and around us many friends, chiefly ministers of the different churches, the ladies and gentlemen of the Glasgow Antislavery Society, and others.

I told you it was a tea party; but the arrangements were altogether different from any I had ever seen. There were narrow tables stretched up and down the whole extent of the great hall, and every person had an appointed seat. These tables were set out with cups and saucers, cakes, biscuit, &c., and when the proper time came, attendants passed along serving tea. The arrangements were so accurate and methodical that the whole multitude actually took tea together, without the least apparent inconvenience or disturbance.

There was a gentle, subdued murmur of conversation all over the house, the sociable clinking of teacups and teaspoons, while the entertainment was going on. It seemed to me such an odd idea, I could not help wondering what sort of a teapot that must be, in which all this tea for two thousand people was made. Truly, as Hadji Baba says, I think they must have had the "father of all teakettles" to boil it in. I could not help wondering if old mother Scotland had put two thousand teaspoonfuls of tea for the company, and one for the teapot, as is our good Yankee custom.

We had quite a sociable time up in our gallery. Our tea table stretched quite across the gallery, and we drank tea "in sight of all the people." By *we*, I mean a great number of ministers and their wives, and ladies of the Antislavery Society, besides our party, and the friends whom I have mentioned before. All seemed to be enjoying themselves.

After tea they sang a few verses of the seventy-second psalm in the old Scotch version.

> "The people's poor ones he shall judge,
>
> The needy's children save;
>
> And those shall he in pieces break,
>
> Who them oppressed have.
>
> For he the needy shall preserve,
>
> When he to him doth call;
>
> The poor, also, and him that hath
>
> No help of man at all.
>
> Both from deceit and violence
>
> Their soul he shall set free;
>
> And in his sight right precious
>
> And dear their blood shall be.

> Now blessed be the Lord, our God,
>
> The God of Israel,
>
> For he alone doth wondrous works,
>
> In glory that excel.
>
> And blessed be his glorious name
>
> To all eternity;
>
> The whole earth let his glory fill:
>
> Amen; so let it be."

When I heard the united sound of all the voices, giving force to these simple and pathetic words, I thought I could see something of the reason why that rude old translation still holds its place in Scotland.

The addresses were, many of them, very beautiful; the more so for the earnest and religious feeling which they manifested. That of Dr. Wardlaw, in particular, was full of comfort and encouragement, and breathed a most candid and catholic spirit. Could our friends in America see with what earnest warmth the religious heart of Scotland beats towards them, they would be willing to suffer a word of admonition from those to whom love gives a right to speak. As Christians, all have a common interest in what honors or dishonors Christianity, and an ocean between us does not make us less one church.

Most of the speeches you will see recorded in the papers. In the course of the evening there was a second service of grapes, oranges, and other fruits, served round in the same quiet manner as the tea. On account of the feeble state of my health, they kindly excused me before the exercises of the evening were over.

The next morning, at ten o'clock, we rode with a party of friends to see some of the *notabilia*. First, to Bothwell Castle, of old the residence of the Black Douglas. The name had for me the quality of enchantment. I cannot understand nor explain the nature of that sad yearning and longing with which one visits the mouldering remains of a state of society which one's reason wholly disapproves, and which one's calm sense of right would think it the greatest misfortune to have recalled; yet when the carriage turned under the shadow of beautiful ancient oaks, and Mr. S. said, "There, we are in the grounds of the old Black Douglas family!" I felt every nerve shiver. I remembered the dim melodies of the Lady of the Lake. Bothwell's lord was the lord of this castle, whose beautiful ruins here adorn the banks of the Clyde.

Whatever else we have or may have in America, we shall never have the wild, poetic beauty of these ruins. The present noble possessors are fully aware of their worth as objects of taste, and, therefore, with the greatest care are they preserved. Winding walks are cut through the grounds with much ingenuity, and seats or arbors are placed at every desirable and picturesque point of view.

To the thorough-paced tourist, who wants to *do* the proprieties in the shortest possible time, this arrangement is undoubtedly particularly satisfactory; but to the idealist, who would like to roam, and dream, and feel, and to come unexpectedly on the choicest points of view, it is rather a damper to have all his raptures prearranged and foreordained for him, set down in the guide book and proclaimed by the guide, even though it should be done with the most artistic accuracy.

Nevertheless, when we came to the arbor which commanded the finest view of the old castle, and saw its gray, ivy-clad walls, standing forth on a beautiful point, round which swept the brown, dimpling waves of the Clyde, the indescribable sweetness, sadness, wildness of the whole scene would make its voice heard in our hearts. "Thy servants take pleasure in her dust, and favor the stones thereof," said an old Hebrew poet, who must have felt the inexpressibly sad beauty of a ruin. All the splendid phantasmagoria of chivalry and feudalism, knights, ladies, banners, glittering arms, sweep before us; the cry of the battle, the noise of the captains, and the shouting; and then in contrast this deep stillness, that green, clinging ivy, the gentle, rippling river, those weeping birches, dipping in its soft waters—all these, in their quiet loveliness, speak of something more imperishable than brute force.

The ivy on the walls now displays a trunk in some places as large as a man's body. In the days of old Archibald the Grim, I suppose that ivy was a little, weak twig, which, if he ever noticed, he must have thought the feeblest and slightest of all things; yet Archibald has gone back to dust, and the ivy is still growing on. Such force is there in gentle things.

I have often been dissatisfied with the admiration, which a poetic education has woven into my nature, for chivalry and feudalism; but, on a closer examination, I am convinced that there is a real and proper foundation for it, and that, rightly understood, this poetic admiration is not inconsistent with the spirit of Christ.

For, let us consider what it is we admire in these Douglases, for instance, who, as represented by Scott, are perhaps as good exponents of the idea as any. Was it their hardness, their cruelty, their hastiness to take offence, their fondness for blood and murder? All these, by and of themselves, are simply disgusting. What, then, do we admire? Their courage, their fortitude, their scorn of lying and dissimulation, their high sense of personal honor, which led them to feel themselves the protectors of the weak, and to disdain to take advantage of unequal odds against an enemy. If we read the book of Isaiah, we shall see that some of the most striking representations of God appeal to the very same principles of our nature.

The fact is, there can be no reliable character which has not its basis in these strong qualities. The beautiful must ever rest in the arms of the sublime. The gentle needs the strong to sustain it, as much as the rock flowers need rocks to grow on, or yonder ivy the rugged wall which it embraces. When we are admiring these things, therefore, we are only admiring some sparkles and glimmers of that which is divine, and so coming nearer to Him in whom all fulness dwells.

After admiring at a distance, we strolled through the ruins themselves. Do you remember, in the Lady of the Lake, where the exiled Douglas, recalling to his daughter the images of his former splendor, says,—

> "When Blantyre hymned, her holiest lays,
>
> And Bothwell's walls flung back the praise"?

These lines came forcibly to my mind, when I saw the mouldering ruins of Blantyre priory rising exactly opposite to the castle, on the other side of the Clyde.

The banks of the River Clyde, where we walked, were thick set with Portuguese laurel, which I have before mentioned as similar to our rhododendron. I here noticed a fact with regard to the ivy which had often puzzled me; and that is, the different shapes of its leaves in the different stages of its growth. The young ivy has this leaf; but when it has become more than a century old every trace and indentation melts away, and it assumes this form, which I found afterwards to be the invariable shape of all the oldest ivy, in all the ruins of Europe which I explored.

This ivy, like the spider, takes hold with her hands in kings' palaces, as every twig is furnished with innumerable little clinging fingers, by which it draws itself close, as it were, to the very heart of the old rough stone.

Its clinging and beautiful tenacity has given rise to an abundance of conceits about fidelity, friendship, and woman's love, which have become commonplace simply from their appropriateness. It might, also, symbolize that higher love, unconquerable and unconquered, which has embraced this ruined world from age to age, silently spreading its green over the rents and fissures of our fallen nature, giving "beauty for ashes, and garments of praise for the spirit of heaviness."

There is a modern mansion, where the present proprietor of the estate lives. It was with an emotion partaking of the sorrowful, that we heard that the Douglas line, as such, was extinct, and that the estate had passed to distant connections. I was told that the present Lord Douglas is a peaceful clergyman, quite a different character from old Archibald the Grim.

The present residence is a plain mansion, standing on a beautiful lawn, near the old castle. The head gardener of the estate and many of the servants came out to meet us, with faces full of interest. The gardener walked about to show us the localities, and had a great deal of the quiet intelligence and self-respect which, I think, is characteristic of the laboring classes here. I noticed that on the green sweep of the lawn, he had set out here and there a good many daisies, as embellishments to the grass, and these in many places were defended by sticks bent over them, and that, in one place, a bank overhanging the stream was radiant with yellow daffodils, which appeared to have come up and blossomed there accidentally. I know not whether these were planted there, or came up of themselves.

We next went to the famous Bothwell bridge, which Scott has immortalized in Old Mortality. We walked up and down, trying to recall the scenes of the battle, as there described, and were rather mortified, after we had all our associations comfortably located upon it, to be told that it was not the same bridge—it had been newly built, widened, and otherwise made more comfortable and convenient.

Of course, this was evidently for the benefit of society, but it was certainly one of those cases where the poetical suffers for the practical. I comforted myself in my despondency, by looking over at the old stone piers underneath, which were indisputably the same. We drove now through beautiful grounds, and alighted at an elegant mansion, which in former days belonged to Lockhart, the son-in-law of Scott. It was in this house that Old Mortality was written.

As I was weary, the party left me here, while they went on to see the Duke of Hamilton's grounds. Our kind hostess showed me into a small study, where she said Old Mortality was written. The window commanded a beautiful view of many of the localities described. Scott was as particular to consult for accuracy in his local descriptions as if he had been writing a guide book.

He was in the habit of noting down in his memorandum book even names and characteristics of the wild flowers and grasses that grew about a place. When a friend once remarked to him, that he should have supposed his imagination could have supplied such trifles, he made an answer that is worth remembering by every artist—that no imagination could long support its freshness, that was not nourished by a constant and minute observation of nature.

Craignethan Castle, which is the original of Tillietudlem, we were informed, was not far from thence. It is stated in Lockhart's Life of Scott, that the ruins of this castle excited in Scott such delight and enthusiasm, that its owner urged him to accept for his lifetime the use of a small habitable house, enclosed within the circuit of the walls.

After the return of the party from Hamilton Park, we sat down to an elegant lunch, where my eye was attracted more than any thing else, by the splendor of the hothouse flowers which adorned the table. So far as I have observed, the culture of flowers, both in England and Scotland, is more universally an object of attention than with us. Every family in easy circumstances seems, as a matter of course, to have their greenhouse, and the flowers are brought to a degree of perfection which I have never seen at home.

I may as well say here, that we were told by a gentleman, whose name I do not now remember, that this whole district had been celebrated for its orchards; he added, however, that since the introduction of the American apple into the market, its superior excellence had made many of these orchards almost entirely worthless. It is a curious fact, showing how the new world is working on the old.

After taking leave of our hospitable friends, we took to our carriages again. As we were driving slowly through the beautiful grounds, admiring, as we never failed to do, their perfect cultivation, a party of servants appeared in sight, waving their hats and handkerchiefs, and cheering us as we passed. These kindly expressions from them were as pleasant as any we received.

In the evening we had engaged to attend another *soirée*, gotten up by the working classes, to give admission to many who were not in circumstances to purchase tickets for the other. This was to me, if any thing, a more interesting *réunion*, because this was just the class whom I wished to meet. The arrangements of the entertainment were like those of the evening before.

As I sat in the front gallery and looked over the audience with an intense interest, I thought they appeared on the whole very much like what I might have seen at home in a similar gathering. Men, women, and children were dressed in a style which showed both self-respect and good taste, and the speeches were far above mediocrity. One pale young man, a watchmaker, as I was told afterwards, delivered an address, which, though doubtless it had the promising fault of too much elaboration and ornament, yet I thought had passages which would do honor to any literary periodical whatever.

There were other orators less highly finished, who yet spoke "right on," in a strong, forcible, and really eloquent way, giving the grain of the wood without the varnish. They contended very seriously and sensibly, that although the working men of England and Scotland had many things to complain of, and many things to be reformed, yet their condition was world-wide different from that of the slave.

One cannot read the history of the working classes in England, for the last fifty years, without feeling sensibly the difference between oppressions under a free government and slavery. So long as the working class of England produces orators and writers, such as it undoubtedly has produced; so long as it has in it that spirit of independence and resistance of wrong, which has shown itself more and more during the agitations of the last fifty years; and so as long as the law allows them to meet and debate, to form associations and committees, to send up remonstrances and petitions to government,—one can see that their case is essentially different from that of plantation slaves.

I must say, I was struck this night with the resemblance between the Scotchman and the New Englander. One sees the distinctive nationality of a country more in the middle and laboring classes than in the higher, and accordingly at this meeting there was more nationality, I thought, than at the other.

The highest class of mind in all countries loses nationality, and becomes universal; it is a great pity, too, because nationality is picturesque always. One of the greatest miracles to my mind about Kossuth was, that with so universal an education, and such an extensive range of language and thought, he was yet so distinctively a Magyar.

One thing has surprised and rather disappointed us. Our enthusiasm for Walter Scott does not apparently meet a response in the popular breast. Allusions to Bannockburn and Drumclog bring down the house, but enthusiasm for Scott was met with comparative silence. We discussed this matter among ourselves, and rather wondered at it.

The fact is, Scott belonged to a past, and not to the coming age. He beautified and adorned that which is waxing old and passing away. He loved and worshipped in his very soul institutions which the majority of the common people have felt as a restraint and a burden. One might naturally get a very different idea of a feudal castle by starving to death in the dungeon of it, than by writing sonnets on it at a picturesque distance. Now, we in America are so far removed from feudalism,—it has been a thing so much of mere song and story with us, and our sympathies are so unchecked by any experience of inconvenience or injustice in its consequences,—that we are at full liberty to appreciate the picturesque of it, and sometimes, when we stand overlooking our own beautiful scenery, to wish that we could see,

"On yon bold brow, a lordly tower;

In that soft vale, a lady's bower;

In yonder meadow, far away,

The turrets of a cloister gray;"

when those who know by experience all the accompaniments of these ornaments, would have quite another impression.

Nevertheless, since there are two worlds in man, the real and the ideal, and both have indisputably a right to be, since God made the faculties of both, we must feel that it is a benefaction to mankind, that Scott was thus raised up as the link, in the ideal world, between the present and the past. It is a loss to universal humanity to have the imprint of any phase of human life and experience entirely blotted out. Scott's fictions are like this beautiful ivy, with which all the ruins here are overgrown,—they not only adorn, but, in many cases, they actually hold together, and prevent the crumbling mass from falling into ruins.

To-morrow we are going to have a sail on the Clyde.

LETTER V

April 17.

My Dear Sister:—

To-day a large party of us started on a small steamer, to go down the Clyde. It has been a very, very exciting day to us. It is so stimulating to be where every name is a poem. For instance, we start at the Broomielaw. This Broomielaw is a kind of wharf, or landing. Perhaps in old times it was a haugh overgrown with broom, from whence it gets its name; this is only my conjecture, however.

We have a small steamer quite crowded with people, our excursion party being very numerous. In a few minutes after starting, somebody says,—

"O, here's where the Kelvin enters." This starts up,—

"Let us haste to Kelvin Grove."

Then soon we are coming to Dumbarton Castle, and all the tears we shed over Miss Porter's William Wallace seem to rise up like a many-colored mist about it. The highest peak of the rock is still called Wallace's Seat, and a part of the castle, Wallace's Tower; and in one of its apartments a huge two-handed sword of the hero is still shown. I suppose, in fact, Miss Porter's sentimental hero is about as much like the real William Wallace as Daniel Boone is like Sir Charles Grandison. Many a young lady, who has cried herself sick over Wallace in the novel, would have been in perfect horror if she could have seen the real man. Still Dumbarton Castle is not a whit the less picturesque for that.

Now comes the Leven,—that identical Leven Water known in song,—and on the right is Leven Grove.

"There," said somebody to me, "is the old mansion of the Earls of Glencairn." Quick as thought, flashed through my mind that most eloquent of Burns's poems, the Lament for James, Earl of Glencairn.

"The bridegroom may forget the bride

Was made his wedded wife yestreen;

The monarch may forget the crown

That on his head an hour hath been;

> The mother may forget the child
>
> That smiles sae sweetly on her knee;
>
> But I'll remember thee, Glencairn,
>
> And a' that thou hast done for me."

This mansion is now the seat of Graham of Gartmor.

Now we are shown the remains of old Cardross Castle, where it was said Robert Bruce breathed his last. And now we come near the beautiful grounds of Roseneath, a green, velvet-like peninsula, stretching out into the widening waters.

"Peninsula!" said C——. "Why, Walter Scott said it was an island."

Certainly, he did declare most explicitly in the person of Mr. Archibald, the Duke of Argyle's serving man, to Miss Dollie Dutton, when she insisted on going to it by land, that Roseneath was an island. It shows that the most accurate may be caught tripping sometimes.

Of course, our heads were full of David Deans, Jeanie, and Effie, but we saw nothing of them. The Duke of Argyle's Italian mansion is the most conspicuous object.

Hereupon there was considerable discussion on the present Duke of Argyle among the company, from which we gathered that he stood high in favor with the popular mind. One said that there had been an old prophecy, probably uttered somewhere up in the Highlands, where such things are indigenous, that a very good duke of Argyle was to arise having red hair, and that the present duke had verified the prediction by uniting both requisites. They say that he is quite a young man, with a small, slight figure, but with a great deal of energy and acuteness of mind, and with the generous and noble traits which have distinguished his house in former times. He was a pupil of Dr. Arnold, a member of the National Scotch Kirk, and generally understood to be a serious and religious man. He is one of the noblemen who have been willing to come forward and make use of his education and talent in the way of popular lectures at lyceums and athenæums; as have also the Duke of Newcastle, the Earl of Carlisle, and some others. So the world goes on. I must think, with all deference to poetry, that it is much better to deliver a lyceum lecture than to head a clan in battle; though I suppose, a century and a half ago, had the thing been predicted to McCallummore's old harper, he would have been greatly at a loss to comprehend the nature of the transaction.

Somewhere about here, I was presented, by his own request, to a broad-shouldered Scotch farmer, who stood some six feet two, and who paid me the compliment to say, that he had read my book, and that he would walk six miles to see me any day. Such a flattering evidence of discriminating taste, of course, disposed my heart towards him; but when I went up and put my hand into his great prairie of a palm, I was as a grasshopper in my own eyes. I inquired who he was, and was told he was one of the Duke of Argyle's farmers. I thought to myself, if all the duke's farmers were of this pattern, that he might be able to speak to the enemy in the gates to some purpose.

Roseneath occupies the ground between the Gare Loch and Loch Long. The Gare Loch is the name given to a bay formed by the River Clyde, here stretching itself out like a lake. Here we landed and went on shore, passing along the sides of the loch, in the little village of Row.

As we were walking along a carriage came up after us, in which were two ladies. A bunch of primroses, thrown from this carriage, fell at my feet. I picked it up, and then the carriage stopped, and the ladies requested to know if I was Mrs. Stowe. On answering in the affirmative, they urged me so earnestly to come under their roof and take some refreshment, that I began to remember, what I had partly lost sight of, that I was very tired; so, while the rest of the party walked on to get a distant view of Ben Lomond, Mr. S. and I suffered ourselves to be taken into the carriage of our unknown friends, and carried up to a charming little Italian villa, which stood, surrounded by flower gardens and pleasure grounds, at the head of the loch. We were ushered into a most comfortable parlor, where a long window, made of one clear unbroken sheet of plate glass, gave a perfect view of the loch with all its woody shores, with Roseneath Castle in the distance. My good hostesses literally overwhelmed me with kindness; but as there was nothing I really needed so much as a little quiet rest, they took me to a cozy bedroom, of which they gave me the freedom, for the present. Does not every traveller know what a luxury it is to shut one's eyes sometimes? The chamber, which is called "Peace," is now, as it was in Christian's days, one of the best things that Charity or Piety could offer to the pilgrim. Here I got a little brush from the wings of dewy-feathered sleep.

After a while our party came back, and we had to be moving. My kind friends expressed so much joy at having met me, that it was really almost embarrassing. They told me that they, being confined to the house by ill health, and one of them by lameness, had had no hope of ever seeing me, and that this meeting seemed a wonderful gift of Providence. They bade me take courage and hope, for they felt assured that the Lord would yet entirely make an end of slavery through the world.

It was concluded, after we left here, that, instead of returning by the boat, we should take carriage and ride home along the banks of the river. In our carriage were Mr. S. and myself, Dr. Robson and Lady Anderson. About this time I commenced my first essay towards giving titles, and made, as you may suppose, rather an odd piece of work of it, generally saying "Mrs." first, and "Lady" afterwards, and then begging pardon. Lady Anderson laughed, and said she would give me a general absolution. She is a truly genial, hearty Scotch woman, and seemed to enter happily into the spirit of the hour.

As we rode on we found that the news of our coming had spread through the village. People came and stood in their doors, beckoning, bowing, smiling, and waving their handkerchiefs, and the carriage was several times stopped by persons who came to offer flowers. I remember, in particular, a group of young girls brought to the carriage two of the most beautiful children I ever saw, whose little hands literally deluged us with flowers.

At the village of Helensburgh we stopped a little while to call upon Mrs. Bell, the wife of Mr. Bell, the inventor of the steamboat. His invention in this country was about the same time of that of Fulton in America. Mrs. Bell came to the carriage to speak to us. She is a venerable woman, far advanced in years. They had prepared a lunch for us, and quite a number of people had come together to meet us, but our friends said that there was not time for us to stop.

We rode through several villages after this, and met quite warm welcome. What pleased me was, that it was not mainly from the literary, nor the rich, nor the great, but the plain, common people. The butcher came out of his stall, and the baker from his shop, the miller, dusty with his flour, the blooming, comely, young mother, with her baby in her arms, all smiling and bowing with that hearty, intelligent, friendly look, as if they knew we should be glad to see them.

Once, while we stopped to change horses, I, for the sake of seeing something more of the country, walked on. It seems the honest landlord and his wife were greatly disappointed at this; however, they got into the carriage and rode on to see me, and I shook hands with them with a right good will.

We saw several of the clergymen, who came out to meet us, and I remember stopping, just to be introduced to a most delightful family who came out, one by one, gray-headed father and mother, with comely brothers and fair sisters, looking all so kindly and home-like, that I would have been glad to use the welcome that they gave me to their dwelling.

This day has been a strange phenomenon to me. In the first place, I have seen in all these villages how universally the people read. I have seen how capable they are of a generous excitement and enthusiasm, and how much may be done by a work of fiction, so written as to enlist those sympathies which are common to all classes. Certainly, a great deal may be effected in this way, if God gives to any one the power, as I hope he will to many. The power of fictitious writing, for good as well as evil, is a thing which ought most seriously to be reflected on. No one can fail to see that in our day it is becoming a very great agency.

We came home quite tired, as you may well suppose. You will not be surprised that the next day I found myself more disposed to keep my bed than to go out. I regretted it, because, being Sunday, I would like to have heard some of the preachers of Glasgow. I was, however, glad of one quiet day to recall my thoughts, for I had been whirling so rapidly from scene to scene, that I needed time to consider where I was; especially as we were to go to Edinburgh on the morrow.

Towards sunset Mr. S. and I strolled out entirely alone to breathe a little fresh air. We walked along the banks of the Kelvin, quite down to its junction with the Clyde. The Kelvin Grove of the ballad is all cut away, and the Kelvin flows soberly between stone walls, with a footpath on each side, like a stream that has learned to behave itself.

"There," said Mr. S., as we stood on the banks of the Clyde, now lying flushed and tranquil in the light of the setting sun, "over there is Ayrshire."

"Ayrshire!" I said; "what, where Burns lived?"

"Yes, there is his cottage, far down to the south, and out of sight, of course; and there are the bonny banks of Ayr."

It seemed as if the evening air brought a kind of sigh with it. Poor Burns! how inseparably he has woven himself with the warp and woof of every Scottish association!

We saw a great many children of the poor out playing—rosy, fine little urchins, worth, any one of them, a dozen bleached, hothouse flowers. We stopped to hear them talk, and it was amusing to hear the Scotch of Walter Scott and Burns shouted out with such a right good will. We were as much struck by it as an honest Yankee was in Paris by the proficiency of the children in speaking French.

The next day we bade farewell to Glasgow, overwhelmed with kindness to the last, and only oppressed by the thought, how little that was satisfactory we were able to give in return.

Again in the railroad car on our way to Edinburgh. A pleasant two hours' trip is this from Glasgow to Edinburgh. When the cars stopped at Linlithgow station, the name started us as out of a dream.

There, sure enough, before our eyes, on a gentle eminence stood the mouldering ruins of which Scott has sung:—

> "Of all the palaces so fair,
>
> Built for the royal dwelling,
>
> In Scotland, far beyond compare
>
> Linlithgow is excelling;
>
> And in its park in genial June,
>
> How sweet the merry linnet's tune,
>
> How blithe the blackbird's lay!
>
> The wild buck's bells from thorny brake.
>
> The coot dives merry on the lake,—
>
> The saddest heart might pleasure take,
>
> To see a scene so gay."

Here was born that woman whose beauty and whose name are set in the strong, rough Scotch heart, as a diamond in granite. Poor Mary! When her father, who lay on his death bed at that time in Falkland, was told of her birth, he answered, "Is it so? Then God's will be done! It [the kingdom] came with a lass, and it will go with a lass!" With these words he turned his face to the wall, and died of a broken heart. Certainly, some people appear to be born under an evil destiny.

Here, too, in Linlithgow church, tradition says that James IV. was warned, by a strange apparition, against that expedition to England which cost him his life. Scott has worked this incident up into a beautiful description, in the fourth canto of Marmion.

The castle has a very sad and romantic appearance, standing there all alone as it does, looking down into the quiet lake. It is said that the internal architectural decorations are exceedingly rich and beautiful, and a resemblance has been traced between its style of ornament and that of Heidelberg Castle, which has been accounted for by the fact that the Princess Elizabeth, who was the sovereign lady of Heidelberg, spent many of the earlier years of her life in this place.

Not far from here we caught a glimpse of the ruins of Niddrie Castle, where Mary spent the first night after her escape from Lochleven.

The Avon here at Linlithgow is spanned by a viaduct, which is a fine work of art. It has twenty-five arches, which are from seventy to eighty feet high and fifty wide.

As the cars neared Edinburgh we all exclaimed at its beauty, so worthily commemorated by Scott:—

> "Such dusky grandeur clothes the height,
>
> Where the huge castle holds its state,
>
> And all the steeps slope down,
>
> Whose ridgy back heaves to the sky,
>
> Piled deep and massy, close and high,
>
> Mine own romantic town!"

Edinburgh has had an effect on the literary history of the world for the last fifty years, that cannot be forgotten by any one approaching her. The air seemed to be full of spirits of those who, no longer living, have woven a part of the thread of our existence. I do not know that the shortness of human life ever so oppressed me as it did on coming near to the city.

At the station house the cars stopped amid a crowd of people, who had assembled to meet us. The lord provost met us at the door of the car, and presented us to the magistracy of the city, and the committees of the Edinburgh antislavery societies. The drab dresses and pure white bonnets of many Friends were conspicuous among the dense moving crowd, as white doves seen against a dark cloud. Mr. S. and myself, and our future hostess, Mrs. Wigham, entered the carriage with the lord provost, and away we drove, the crowd following with their shouts and cheers. I was inexpressibly touched and affected by this. While we were passing the monument of Scott, I felt an oppressive melancholy. What a moment life seems in the presence of the noble dead! What a momentary thing is art, in all its beauty! Where are all those great souls that have created such an atmosphere of light about Edinburgh? and how little a space was given them to live and to enjoy!

We drove all over Edinburgh, up to the castle, to the university, to Holyrood, to the hospitals, and through many of the principal streets, amid shouts, and smiles, and greetings. Some boys amused me very much by their pertinacious attempts to keep up with the carriage.

"Heck," says one of them, "that's *her*, see the *courls*."

The various engravers, who have amused themselves by diversifying my face for the public, having all, with great unanimity, agreed in giving prominence to this point, I suppose the urchins thought they were on safe ground there. I certainly think I answered one good purpose that day, and that is, of giving the much oppressed and calumniated class, called boys, an opportunity to develop all the noise that was in them—a thing for which I think they must bless me in their remembrances.

At last the carriage drove into a deep gravelled yard, and we alighted at a porch covered with green ivy, and found ourselves once more at home.

LETTER VI.

My Dear Sister:—

You may spare your anxieties about me, for I do assure you, that if I were an old Sevres China jar, I could not have more careful handling than I do. Every body is considerate; a great deal to say, when there appears to be so much excitement. Every body seems to understand how good for nothing I am; and yet, with all this consideration, I have been obliged to keep my room and bed for a good part of the time. One agreeable feature of the matter is, it gave me an opportunity to make the acquaintance of the celebrated homoeopathic physician, Dr. Henderson, in whose experiments and experience I had taken some interest while in America.

Of the multitudes who have called, I have seen scarcely any.

Mrs. W., with whom I am staying, is a most thoughtful nurse. They are Friends, and nothing can be more a pattern of rational home enjoyment, without ostentation and without parade, than a Quaker family.

Though they reject every thing in arrangement which savors of ostentation and worldly show, yet their homes are exquisite in point of comfort. They make great use of flowers and natural specimens in adorning their apartments, and also indulge to a chaste and moderate extent in engravings and works of art. So far as I have observed, they are all "tee-totalers;" giving, in this respect, the whole benefit of their example to the temperance cause.

To-morrow evening is to be the great tea party here. How in the world I am ever to live through it, I don't know.

The amount of letters we found waiting for us here in Edinburgh was, if possible, more appalling than in Glasgow. Among those from persons whom you would be interested in hearing of, I may mention, a very kind and beautiful one from the Duchess of Sutherland, and one also from the Earl of Carlisle, both desiring to make appointments for meeting us as soon as we come to London. Also a very kind and interesting note from the Rev. Mr. Kingsley and lady. I look forward with a great deal of interest to passing a little time with them in their rectory. Letters also from Mr. Binney and Mr. Sherman, two of the leading Congregational clergymen of London. The latter officiates at Surrey Chapel, which was established by Rowland Hill. Both contain invitations to us to visit them in London.

As to all engagements, I am in a state of happy acquiescence, having resigned myself, as a very tame lion, into the hands of my keepers.

Whenever the time comes for me to do any thing, I try to behave as well as I can, which, as Dr. Young says, is all that an angel could do in the same circumstances.

As to these letters, many of them are mere outbursts of feeling; yet they are interesting as showing the state of the public mind. Many of them are on kindred topics of moral reform, in which they seem to have an intuitive sense that we should be interested. I am not, of course, able to answer them all, but C—— does, and it takes a good part of every day. One was from a shoemaker's wife in one of the islands, with a copy of very fair verses. Many have come accompanying little keepsakes and gifts. It seems to me rather touching and sad, that people should want to give me things, when I am not able to give an interview, or even a note, in return. C—— wrote from six to twelve o'clock, steadily, answering letters.

April 26. Last night came off the *soirée*. The hall was handsomely decorated with flags in front. We went with the lord provost in his carriage. The getting in to the hall is quite an affair, I assure you, the doorway is blocked up by such a dense crowd; yet there is something very touching about these crowds. They open very gently and quietly, and they do not look at you with a rude stare, but with faces full of feeling and intelligence. I have seen some looks that were really beautiful; they go to my heart. The common people appear as if they knew that our hearts were with them. How else should it be, as Christians of America?—a country which, but for one fault, all the world has reason to love.

We went up, as before, into a dressing room, where I was presented to many gentlemen and ladies. When we go in, the cheering, clapping, and stamping at first strikes one with a strange sensation; but then every body looks so heartily pleased and delighted, and there is such an all-pervading atmosphere of geniality and sympathy, as makes one in a few moments feel quite at home. After all I consider that these cheers and applauses, are Scotland's voice to America, a recognition of the brotherhood of the countries.

We were arranged at this meeting much as in Glasgow. The lord provost presided; and in the gallery with us were distinguished men from the magistracy, the university, and the ministry, with their wives, besides the members of the antislavery societies. The lord provost, I am told, has been particularly efficient in all benevolent operations, especially those for the education of the poorer classes. He is also a zealous supporter of the temperance cause.

Among the speakers, I was especially interested in Dr. Guthrie, who seems to be also a particular favorite of the public. He is a tall, thin man, with a kind of quaintness in his mode of expressing himself, which sometimes gives an air of drollery to his speaking. He is a minister of the Free Church, and has more particularly distinguished himself by his exertions in behalf of the poorer classes.

One passage in his speech I will quote, for I was quite amused with it. It was in allusion to the retorts which had been made in Mrs. Tyler's letter to the ladies of England, on the defects in the old country.

"I do not deny," he said, "that there are defects in our country. What I say of them is this—that they are incidental very much to an old country like our own. Dr. Simpson knows very well, and so does every medical man, that when a man gets old he gets very infirm, his blood vessels get ossified, and so on; but I shall not enter into that part of the subject. What is true of an old country is true of old men, and old women, too. I am very much disposed to say of this young nation of America, that their teasing us with our defects might just get the answer which a worthy member of the church of Scotland gave to his son, who was so dissatisfied with the defects in the church, that he was determined to go over to a younger communion. 'Ah, Sandy, Sandy, man, when your lum reeks as lang as ours, it will, may be, need sweeping too.'[10] Now, I do not deny that we need sweeping; every body knows that I have been singing out about sweeping for the last five years. Let me tell my good friends in Edinburgh, and in the country, that the sooner you sweep the better; for the chimney may catch fire, and reduce your noble fabric to ashes.

"They told us in that letter about the poor needlewomen, that had to work sixteen hours a day. "Tis true, and pity 'tis 'tis true.' But does the law compel them to work sixteen hours a day? I would like to ask the writer of the letter. Are they bound down to their garrets and cellars for sixteen hours a day? May they not go where they like, and ask better wages and better work? Can the slave do that? Do they tell us of our ragged children? I know something about ragged children. But are our ragged children condemned to the street? If I, or the lord provost, or any other benevolent man, should take one of them from the street and bring it to the school, dare the policeman—miscalled officer of justice—put his foot across the door to drag it out again to the street? Nobody means to defend our defects; does any man attempt to defend them? Were not these noble ladies and excellent women, titled and untitled, among the very first to seek to redress them?"

I wish I could give you the strong, broad Scotch accent.

The national penny offering, consisting of a thousand golden sovereigns on a magnificent silver salver, stood conspicuously in view of the audience. It has been an unsolicited offering, given in the smallest sums, often from the extreme poverty of the giver. The committee who collected it in Edinburgh and Glasgow bore witness to the willingness with which the very poorest contributed the offering of their sympathy. In one cottage they found a blind woman, and said, "Here, at least, is one who will feel no interest, as she cannot have read the book."

"Indeed," said the old lady, "if I cannot read, my son has read it to me, and I've got my penny saved to give."

It is to my mind extremely touching to see how the poor, in their poverty, can be moved to a generosity surpassing that of the rich. Nor do I mourn that they took it from their slender store, because I know that a penny given from a kindly impulse is a greater comfort and blessing to the poorest giver than even a penny received.

As in the case of the other meeting, we came out long before the speeches were ended. Well, of course, I did not sleep any all night. The next day I felt quite miserable. Mrs. W. went with Mr. S. and myself for a quiet drive in her carriage.

It was a beautiful, sunny day that we drove out to Craigmiller Castle, formerly one of the royal residences. It was here that Mary retreated after the murder of Rizzio, and where, the chronicler says, she was often heard in those days wishing that she were in her grave. It seems so strange to see it standing there all alone, in the midst of grassy fields, so silent, and cold, and solitary. I got out of the carriage and walked about it. The short, green grass was gemmed with daisies, and sheep were peacefully feeding and resting, where was once all the life and bustle of a court.

We had no one to open the inside of the castle for us, where there are still some tolerably preserved rooms, but we strolled listlessly about, looking through the old arches, and peeping through slits and loopholes into the interior.

The last verse of Queen Mary's lamentation seemed to be sighing in the air:—

> "O, soon for me shall simmer's suns
>
> Nae mair light up the morn;
>
> Nae mair for me the autumn wind
>
> Wave o'er the yellow corn.
>
> But in the narrow house of death
>
> Let winter round me rave,
>
> And the next flowers that deck the spring

Bloom on my peaceful grave."

Only yesterday, it seemed, since that poor heart was yearning and struggling, caught in the toils of this sorrowful life. How many times she looked on this landscape through sad eyes! I suppose just such little daisies grew here in the grass then, and perhaps she stooped and picked them, wishing, just as I do, that the pink did not grow on the under side of them, where it does not show. Do you know that this little daisy is the *gowan* of Scotch poetry? So I was told by a "charming young Jessie" in Glasgow, one day when I was riding out there.

The view from Craigmiller is beautiful—Auld Reekie, Arthur's Seat, Salisbury Crags, and far down the Frith of Forth, where we can just dimly see the Bass Hock, celebrated as a prison, where the Covenanters were immured.

It was this fortress that Habakkuk Mucklewrath speaks of in his ravings, when he says, "Am not I Habakkuk Mucklewrath, whose name is changed to Magor-Missabib, because I am made a terror unto myself, and unto all that are around me? I heard it: when did I hear it? Was it not in the tower of the Bass, that overhangeth the wide, wild sea? and it howled in the winds, and it roared in the billows, and it screamed, and it whistled, and it clanged, with the screams, and the clang, and the whistle of the sea birds, as they floated, and flew, and dropped, and dived, on the bosom of the waters."

These Salisbury Crags, which overlook Edinburgh, have a very peculiar outline; they resemble an immense elephant crouching down. We passed Mushats Cairn, where Jeanie Deans met Robertson; and saw Liberton, where Reuben Butler was a schoolmaster. Nobody doubts, I hope, the historical accuracy of these points.

Thursday, 21st. We took cars for Aberdeen. The appropriation of old historical names to railroad stations often reminds me of Hood's whimsical lines on a possible railroad in the Holy Land. Think of having Bannockburn shouted by the station master, as the train runs whistling up to a small station house. Nothing to be seen there but broad, silent meadows, through which the burn wimples its way. Here was the very Marathon of Scotland. I suppose we know more about it from the "Scots wha ha' wi' Wallace bled," than we do from history; yet the real scene, as narrated by the historian, has a moral grandeur in it.

The chronicler tells us, that when on this occasion the Scots formed their line of battle, and a venerable abbot passed along, holding up the cross before them, the whole army fell upon their knees.

"These Scots will not fight," said Edward, who was reconnoitring at a distance. "See! they are all on their knees now to beg for mercy."

"They kneel," said a lord who stood by, "but it is to God alone; trust me, those men will win or die."

The bold lyric of Burns is but an inspired kind of version of the real address which Bruce is said to have made to his followers; and whoever reads it will see that its power lies not in appeal to brute force, but to the highest elements of our nature, the love of justice, the sense of honor, and to disinterestedness, self-sacrifice, courage unto death.

These things will live and form high and imperishable elements of our nature, when mankind have learned to develop them in other spheres than that of physical force. Burns's lyric, therefore, has in it an element which may rouse the heart to noble endurance and devotion, even when the world shall learn war no more.

We passed through the town of Stirling, whose castle, magnificently seated on a rocky throne, looks right worthy to have been the seat of Scotland's court, as it was for many years. It brought to our minds all the last scenes of the Lady of the Lake, which are laid here with a minuteness of local description and allusion characteristic of Scott.

According to our guide book, one might find there the visible counterpart of every thing which he has woven into his beautiful fiction—"the Lady's Rock, which rang to the applause of the multitude;" "the Franciscan steeple, which pealed the merry festival;" "the sad and fatal mound," apostrophized by Douglas,—

> "That oft has heard the death-axe sound
>
> As on the noblest of the land,

>   Fell the stern headsman's bloody hand;"—

the room in the castle, where "a Douglas by his sovereign bled;" and not far off the ruins of Cambuskenneth Abbey. One could not but think of the old days Scott has described.

> "The castle gates were open flung,
> The quivering drawbridge rocked and rung,
> And echoed loud the flinty street
> Beneath the coursers' clattering feet,
> As slowly down the steep descent
> Fair Scotland's king and nobles went,
> While all along the crowded way
> Was jubilee and loud huzza."

The place has been long deserted as a palace; but it is one of the four fortresses, which, by the articles of union between Scotland and England, are always to be kept in repair.

We passed by the town of Perth, the scene of the "Fair Maid's" adventures. We had received an invitation to visit it, but for want of time were obliged to defer it till our return to Scotland.

Somewhere along here Mr. S. was quite excited by our proximity to Scone, the old crowning-place of the Scottish kings; however, the old castle is entirely demolished, and superseded by a modern mansion, the seat of the Earl of Mansfield.

Still farther on, surrounded by dark and solemn woods, stands Glamis Castle, the scene of the tragedy in Macbeth. We could see but a glimpse of it from the road, but the very sound of the name was enough to stimulate our imagination. It is still an inhabited dwelling, though much to the regret of antiquarians and lovers of the picturesque, the characteristic outworks and defences of the feudal ages, which surrounded it, have been levelled, and velvet lawns and gravel walks carried to the very door. Scott, who passed a night there in 1793, while it was yet in its pristine condition, comments on the change mournfully, as undoubtedly a true lover of the past would. Albeit the grass plats and the gravel walks, to the eye of sense, are undoubtedly much more agreeable and convenient. Scott says in his Demonology, that he never came any where near to being overcome with a superstitious feeling, except twice in his life, and one was on the night when he slept in Glamis Castle. The poetical and the practical elements in Scott's mind ran together, side by side, without mixing, as evidently as the waters of the Alleghany and Monongahela at Pittsburg. Scarcely ever a man had so much relish for the supernatural, and so little faith in it. One must confess, however, that the most sceptical might have been overcome at Glamis Castle, for its appearance, by all accounts, is weird and strange, and ghostly enough to start the dullest imagination.

On this occasion Scott says, "After a very hospitable reception from the late Peter Proctor, seneschal of the castle, I was conducted to my apartment in a distant part of the building. I must own, that when I heard door after door shut, after my conductor had retired, I began to consider myself as too far from the living, and somewhat too near the dead. We had passed through what is called 'the King's Room,' a vaulted apartment, garnished with stags' antlers and similar trophies of the chase, and said by tradition to be the spot of Malcolm's murder, and I had an idea of the vicinity of the castle chapel. In spite of the truth of history, the whole night scene in Macbeth's castle rushed at once upon my mind, and struck my imagination more forcibly than even when I have seen its terrors represented by the late John Kemble and his inimitable sister. In a word, I experienced sensations which, though not remarkable either for timidity or superstition, did not fail to affect me to the point of being disagreeable, while they were mingled at the same time with a strange and indescribable kind of pleasure."

Externally, the building is quaint and singular enough; tall and gaunt, crested with innumerable little pepper box turrets and conical towers, like an old French chateau.

Besides the tragedy of Macbeth, another story of still more melancholy interest is connected with it, which a pen like that of Hawthorne, might work up with gloomy power.

In 1537 the young and beautiful Lady Glamis of this place was actually tried and executed for witchcraft. Only think, now! what capabilities in this old castle, with its gloomy pine shades, quaint architecture, and weird associations, with this bit of historic verity to start upon.

Walter Scott says, there is in the castle a secret chamber; the entrance to which, by the law of the family, can be known only to three persons at once—the lord of the castle, his heir apparent, and any third person whom they might choose to take into their confidence. See, now, the materials which the past gives to the novelist or poet in these old countries. These ancient castles are standing romances, made to the author's hands. The castle started a talk upon Shakspeare, and how much of the tragedy he made up, and how much he found ready to his hand in tradition and history. It seems the story is all told in Holingshed's Chronicles; but his fertile mind has added some of the most thrilling touches, such as the sleep walking of Lady Macbeth. It always seemed to me that this tragedy had more of the melancholy majesty and power of the Greek than any thing modern. The striking difference is, that while fate was the radical element of those, free will is not less distinctly the basis of this. Strangely enough, while it commences with a supernatural oracle, there is not a trace of fatalism in it; but through all, a clear, distinct recognition of moral responsibility, of the power to resist evil, and the guilt of yielding to it. The theology of Shakspeare is as remarkable as his poetry. A strong and clear sense of man's moral responsibility and free agency, and of certain future retribution, runs through all his plays.

I enjoyed this ride to Aberdeen more than any thing we had seen yet, the country is so wild and singular. In the afternoon we came in sight of the German Ocean. The free, bracing air from the sea, and the thought that it actually *was* the German Ocean, and that over the other side was Norway, within a day's sail of us, gave it a strange, romantic charm.

"Suppose we just run over to Norway," said one of us; and then came the idea, what we should do if we got over there, seeing none of us understood Norse.

The whole coast along here is wild and rock-bound; occasionally long points jut into the sea; the blue waves sparkle and dash against them in little jets of foam, and the sea birds dive and scream around them.

On one of these points, near the town of Stonehaven, are still seen the ruins of Dunottar Castle, bare and desolate, surrounded on all sides by the restless, moaning waves; a place justly held accursed as the scene of cruelties to the Covenanters, so appalling and brutal as to make the blood boil in the recital, even in this late day.

During the reigns of Charles and James, sovereigns whom Macaulay justly designates as Belial and Moloch, this castle was the state prison for confining this noble people. In the reign of James, one hundred and sixty-seven prisoners, men, women, and children, for refusing the oath of supremacy, were arrested at their firesides: herded together like cattle; driven at the point of the bayonet, amid the gibes, jeers, and scoffs of soldiers, up to this dreary place, and thrust promiscuously into a dark vault in this castle; almost smothered in filth and mire; a prey to pestilent disease, and to every malignity which brutality could inflict, they died here unpitied. A few escaping down the rocks were recaptured, and subjected to shocking tortures.

A moss-grown gravestone, in the parish churchyard of Dunottar, shows the last resting-place of these sufferers.

Walter Scott, who visited this place, says, "The peasantry continue to attach to the tombs of these victims an honor which they do not render to more splendid mausoleums; and when they point them out to their sons, and narrate the fate of the sufferers, usually conclude by exhorting them to be ready, should the times call for it, to resist to the death in the cause of civil and religious liberty, like their brave forefathers."

It is also related by Gilfillan, that a minister from this vicinity, having once lost his way in travelling through a distant part of Scotland, vainly solicited the services of a guide for some time, all being engaged in peat-cutting; at last one of the farmers, some of whose ancestors had been included among the sufferers, discovering that he came from this vicinity, had seen the gravestones, and could repeat the inscriptions, was willing to give up half a day's work to guide him on his way.

It is well that such spots should be venerated as sacred shrines among the descendants of the Covenanters, to whom Scotland owes what she is, and all she may become.

It was here that Scott first became acquainted with Robert Paterson, the original of Old Mortality.

Leaving Stonehaven we passed, on a rising ground a little to our left, the house of the celebrated Barclay of Ury. It remains very much in its ancient condition, surrounded by a low stone wall, like the old fortified houses of Scotland.

Barclay of Ury was an old and distinguished soldier, who had fought under Gustavus Adolphus in Germany, and one of the earliest converts to the principles of the Friends in Scotland. As a Quaker, he became an object of hatred and abuse at the hands of the magistracy and populace; but he endured all these insults and injuries with the greatest patience and nobleness of soul.

"I find more satisfaction," he said, "as well as honor, in being thus insulted for my religious principles, than when, a few years ago, it was usual for the magistrates, as I passed the city of Aberdeen, to meet me on the road and conduct me to public entertainment in their hall, and then escort me out again, to gain my favor."

Whittier has celebrated this incident in his beautiful ballad, called "Barclay of Ury." The son of this Barclay was the author of that Apology which bears his name, and is still a standard work among the Friends. The estate is still possessed by his descendants.

A little farther along towards Aberdeen, Mr. S. seemed to amuse himself very much with the idea, that we were coming near to Dugald Dalgetty's estate of Drumthwacket, an historical remembrance which I take to be somewhat apocryphal.

It was towards the close of the afternoon that we found ourselves crossing the Dee, in view of Aberdeen. My spirits were wonderfully elated: the grand sea scenery and fine bracing air; the noble, distant view of the city, rising with its harbor and shipping, all filled me with delight. Besides which the Dee had been enchanted for me from my childhood, by a wild old ballad which I used to hear sung to a Scottish tune, equally wild and pathetic. I repeated it to C——, and will now to you.

> "The moon had climbed the highest hill
>
> That rises o'er the banks of Dee,
>
> And from her farthest summit poured
>
> Her silver light o'er tower and tree,—
>
> When Mary laid her down to sleep,
>
> Her thoughts on Sandy far at sea,

> And soft and low a voice she heard,
> Saying, 'Mary, weep no more for me.'
>
> She from her pillow gently raised
> Her head, to see who there might be;
> She saw young Sandy shivering stand,
> With pallid cheek and hollow ee.
>
> 'O Mary dear, cold is my clay;
> It lies beneath the stormy sea;
> The storm, is past, and I'm at rest;
> So, Mary, weep no more for me.'
>
> Loud crew the cock; the vision fled;
> No more young Sandy could she see;
> But soft a parting whisper said,
> 'Sweet Mary, weep no more for me.'"

I never saw these lines in print any where; I never knew who wrote them; I had only heard them sung at the fireside when a child, to a tune as dreamy and sweet as themselves; but they rose upon me like an enchantment, as I crossed the Dee, in view of that very German Ocean, famed for its storms and shipwrecks.

In this propitious state, disposed to be pleased with every thing, our hearts responded warmly to the greetings of the many friends who were waiting for us at the station house.

The lord provost received us into his carriage, and as we drove along, pointed out to us the various objects of interest in the beautiful town. Among other things, a fine old bridge across the Dee attracted our particular attention.

We were conducted to the house of Mr. Cruikshank, a Friend, and found waiting for us there the thoughtful hospitality which we had ever experienced in all our stopping-places. A snug little quiet supper was laid out upon the table, of which we partook in haste, as we were informed that the assembly at the hall were waiting to receive us.

There arrived, we found the hall crowded, and with difficulty made our way to the platform. Whether owing to the stimulating effect of the air from the ocean, or to the comparatively social aspect of the scene, or perhaps to both, certain it is, that we enjoyed the meeting with great zest. I was surrounded on the stage with blooming young ladies, one of whom put into my hands a beautiful bouquet, some flowers of which I have now dried in my album. The refreshment tables were adorned with some exquisite wax flowers, the work, as I was afterwards told, of a young lady in the place. One of the designs especially interested me. It was a group of water lilies resting on a mirror, which gave them the appearance of growing in the water.

We had some very animated speaking, in which the speakers contrived to blend enthusiastic admiration and love for America with detestation of slavery.

All the afternoon the beautiful coast had reminded me of the State of Maine, and the genius of the meeting confirmed the association. They seemed to me to be a plain, genial, strong, warm-hearted people, like those of Maine.

One of the speakers concluded his address by saying that John Bull and Brother Jonathan, with Paddy and Sandy Scott, should they clasp hands together, might stand against the world; which sentiment was responded to with thunders of applause.

It is because America, like Scotland, has stood for right against oppression, that the Scotch love and sympathize with her. For this reason do they feel it as something taken from the strength of a common cause, when America sides with injustice and oppression. The children of the Covenant and the children of the Puritans are of one blood.

They presented an offering in a beautiful embroidered purse, and after much shaking of hands we went home, and sat down to the supper table, for a little more chat, before going to bed. The next morning,—as we had only till noon to stay in Aberdeen,—our friends, the lord provost, and Mr. Leslie, the architect, came immediately after breakfast to show us the place.

The town of Aberdeen is a very fine one, and owes much of its beauty to the light-colored granite of which most of the houses are built. It has broad, clean, beautiful streets, and many very curious and interesting public buildings. The town exhibits that union of the hoary past with the bustling present which is characteristic of the old world.

It has two parts, the old and the new, as unlike as L'Allegro and Penseroso—the new, clean, and modern; the old, mossy and dreamy. The old town is called Alton, and has venerable houses, standing, many of them, in ancient gardens. And here rises the peculiar, old, gray cathedral. These Scotch cathedrals have a sort of stubbed appearance, and look like the expression in stone of defiant, invincible resolution. This is of primitive granite, in the same heavy, massive style as the cathedral of Glasgow, but having strong individualities of its own.

Whoever located the ecclesiastical buildings of England and Scotland certainly had an exquisite perception of natural scenery; for one notices that they are almost invariably placed on just that point of the landscape, where the poet or the artist would say they should be. These cathedrals, though all having a general similarity of design, seem, each one, to have its own personality, as much as a human being. Looking at nineteen of them is no compensation to you for omitting the twentieth; there will certainly be something new and peculiar in that.

This Aberdeen Cathedral, or Cathedral of St. Machar, is situated on the banks of the River Don; one of those beautiful amber-brown rivers that color the stones and pebbles at the bottom with a yellow light, such as one sees in ancient pictures. Old trees wave and rustle around, and the building itself, though a part of it has fallen into ruins, has, in many parts, a wonderful clearness and sharpness of outline. I cannot describe these things to you; architectural terms convey no picture to the mind. I can only tell you of the character and impression it bears—a character of strong, unflinching endurance, appropriately reminding one of the Scotch people, whom Walter Scott compares to the native sycamore of their hills, "which scorns to be biased in its mode of growth, even by the influence of the prevailing wind, but shooting its branches with equal boldness in every direction, shows no weather side to the storm, and may be broken, but can never be bended."

One reason for the sharpness and distinctness of the architectural preservation of this cathedral is probably that closeness of texture for which Aberdeen granite is remarkable. It bears marks of the hand of violence in many parts. The images of saints and bishops, which lie on their backs with clasped hands, seem to have been wofully maltreated and despoiled, in the fervor of those days, when people fondly thought that breaking down carved work was getting rid of superstition. These granite saints and bishops, with their mutilated fingers and broken noses, seem to be bearing a silent, melancholy witness against that disposition in human nature, which, instead of making clean the cup and platter, breaks them altogether.

The roof of the cathedral is a splendid specimen of carving in black oak, wrought in panels, with leaves and inscriptions in ancient text. The church could once boast in other parts (so says an architectural work) a profusion of carved woodwork of the same character, which must have greatly relieved the massive plainness of the interior.

In 1649, the parish minister attacked the "High Altar," a piece of the most splendid workmanship of any thing of the kind in Europe, and which had to that time remained inviolate; perhaps from the insensible influence of its beauty. It is said that the carpenter employed for the purpose was so struck with the noble workmanship, that he refused to touch it till the minister took the hatchet from his hand and gave the first blow.

These men did not consider that "the leprosy lies deep within," and that when human nature is denied beautiful idols, it will go after ugly ones. There has been just as unspiritual a resting in coarse, bare, and disagreeable adjuncts of religion, as in beautiful and agreeable ones; men have worshipped Juggernaut as pertinaciously as they have Venus or the Graces; so that the good divine might better have aimed a sermon at the heart than an axe at the altar.

We lingered a long time around here, and could scarcely tear ourselves away. We paced up and down under the old trees, looking off on the waters of the Don, listening to the waving branches, and falling into a dreamy state of mind, thought what if it were six hundred years ago! and we were pious simple hearted old abbots! What a fine place that would be to walk up and down at eventide or on a Sabbath morning, reciting the penitential psalms, or reading St. Augustine!

I cannot get over the feeling, that the souls of the dead do somehow connect themselves with the places of their former habitation, and that the hush and thrill of spirit, which we feel in them, may be owing to the overshadowing presence of the invisible. St. Paul says, "We are compassed about with a great cloud of witnesses." How can they be witnesses, if they cannot see and be cognizant?

We left the place by a winding walk, to go to the famous bridge of Balgounie, another dream-land affair, not far from here. It is a single gray stone arch, apparently cut from solid rock, that spans the brown rippling waters, where wild, overhanging banks, shadowy trees, and dipping wild flowers, all conspire to make a romantic picture. This bridge, with the river and scenery, were poetic items that went, with other things, to form the sensitive mind of Byron, who lived here in his earlier days. He has some lines about it:—

> "As 'auld lang syne' brings Scotland, one and all,
>
> Scotch, plaids, Scotch snoods, the blue hills and clear streams,
>
> The Dee, the Don, Balgounie's brig's black wall,

All my boy-feelings, all my gentler dreams,

Of what I then dreamt clothed in their own pall,

Like Banquo's offspring,—floating past me seems

My childhood, in this childishness of mind:

I care not—'tis a glimpse of 'auld lang syne.'"

This old bridge has a prophecy connected with it, which was repeated to us, and you shall have it literatim:—

"Brig of Balgounie, black's your wa',

Wi' a wife's ae son, and a mare's a foal,

Doon ye shall fa'!"

The bridge was built in the time of Robert Bruce, by one Bishop Cheyne, of whom all that I know is, that he evidently had a good eye for the picturesque.

After this we went to visit King's College. The tower of it is surmounted by a massive stone crown, which forms a very singular feature in every view of Aberdeen, and is said to be a perfectly unique specimen of architecture. This King's College is very old, being founded also by a bishop, as far back as the fifteenth century. It has an exquisitely carved roof, and carved oaken seats. We went through the library, the hall, and the museum. Certainly, the old, dark architecture of these universities must tend to form a different style of mind from our plain matter-of-fact college buildings.

Here in Aberdeen is the veritable Marischal College, so often quoted by Dugald Dalgetty. We had not time to go and see it, but I can assure you on the authority of the guide book, that it is a magnificent specimen of architecture.

After this, that we might not neglect the present in our zeal for the past, we went to the marble yards, where they work the Aberdeen granite. This granite, of which we have many specimens in America, is of two kinds, one being gray, the other of a reddish hue. It seems to differ from other granite in the fineness and closeness of its grain, which enables it to receive the most brilliant conceivable polish. I saw some superb columns of the red species, which were preparing to go over the Baltic to Riga, for an Exchange; and a sepulchral monument, which was going to New York. All was busy here, sawing, chipping, polishing; as different a scene from the gray old cathedral as could be imagined. The granite finds its way, I suppose, to countries which the old, unsophisticated abbots never dreamed of.

One of the friends who had accompanied us during the morning tour was the celebrated architect, Mr. Leslie, whose conversation gave us all much enjoyment. He and Mrs. Leslie gave me a most invaluable parting present, to wit, four volumes of engravings, representing the "Baronial and Ecclesiastical Antiquities of Scotland," illustrated by Billings. I cannot tell you what a mine of pleasure it has been to me. It is a proof edition, and the engravings are so vivid, and the drawing so fine, that it is nearly as good as reality. It might almost save one the trouble of a pilgrimage. I consider the book a kind of national poem; for architecture is, in its nature, poetry; especially in these old countries, where it weaves into itself a nation's history, and gives literally the image and body of the times.

LETTER VII

DEAR COUSIN:—

While here in Aberdeen I received a very odd letter, so peculiar and curious that I will give you the benefit of it. The author appears to be, in his way, a kind of Christopher in his cave, or Timon of Athens. I omit some parts which are more expressive than agreeable. It is dated

"STONEHAVEN, N.B., Kincardineshire,
57° N.W. This 21st April, 1853.

"To MRS. HARRIET B. STOWE:—

"My dear Madam: By the time that this gets your length, the fouk o' Aberdeen will be shewin ye off as a rare animal, just arrived frae America; the wife that writ Uncle Tom's Cabin.

"I wad like to see ye mysel, but I canna win for want o' siller, and as I thought ye might be writin a buke about the Scotch when ye get hame, I hae just sent ye this bit auld key to Sawney's Cabin.

"Well then, dinna forget to speer at the Aberdeenians if it be true they ance kidnappet little laddies, and selt them for slaves; that they dang down the Quaker's kirkyard dyke, and houket up dead Quakers out o' their graves; that the young boys at the college printed a buke, and maist naebody wad buy it, and they cam out to Ury, near Stonehaven, and took twelve stots frae Davie Barclay to pay the printer.

"Dinna forget to speer at ——, if it was true that he flogget three laddies in the beginning o' last year, for the three following crimes: first, for the crime of being born of puir, ignorant parents; second, for the crime of being left in ignorance; and, third, for the crime of having nothing to eat.

"Dinna be telling when ye gang hame that ye rode on the Aberdeen railway, made by a hundred men, who

- 140 -

were all in the Stonehaven prison for drunkenness; nor above five could sign their names.

"If the Scotch kill ye with ower feeding and making speeches, be sure to send this hame to tell your fouk, that it was Queen Elizabeth who made the first European law to buy and sell human beings like brute beasts. She was England's glory as a Protestant, and Scotland's shame as the murderer of their bonnie Mary. The auld hag skulked away like a coward in the hour of death. Mary, on the other hand, with calmness and dignity, repeated a Latin prayer to the Great Spirit and Author of her being, and calmly resigned herself into the hands of her murderers.

"In the capital of her ancient kingdom, when ye are in our country, there are eight hundred women, sent to prison every year for the first time. Of fifteen thousand prisoners examined in Scotland in the year 1845, eight thousand could not write at all, and three thousand could not read.

"At present there are about twenty thousand prisoners in Scotland. In Stonehaven they are fed at about seventeen pounds each, annually. The honest poor, outside the prison upon the parish roll, are fed at the rate of five farthings a day, or two pounds a year. The employment of the prisoners is grinding the wind, we ca' it; turning the crank, in plain English. The latest improvement is the streekin board; it's a whig improvement o' Lord Jonnie Russell's.

"I ken brawly ye are a curious wife, and would like to ken a' about the Scotch bodies. Weel, they are a gay, ignorant, proud, drunken pack; they manage to pay ilka year for whiskey one million three hundred and forty-eight thousand pounds.

"But then their piety, their piety; weel, let's luke at it; hing it up by the nape o' the neck, and turn it round atween our finger and thumb on all sides.

"Is there one school in all Scotland where the helpless, homeless poor are fed and clothed at the public expense? None.

"Is there a hame in all Scotland for the cleanly but sick servant maid to go till, until health be restored? Alas! there is none.

"Is there a school in all Scotland for training ladies in the higher branches of learning? None. What then is there for the women of Scotland?

"A weel, be sure and try a cupful of Scottish Kail Broase. See, and get a sup Scotch *lang milk*.

"Hand this bit line yout to the Rev. Mr. ———. Tell him to store out fats nae true.

"God bless you, and set you safe hame, is the prayer of the old Scotch Bachelor."

I think you will agree with me, that the old testifying spirit does not seem to have died out in Scotland, and that the backslidings and abominations of the land do not want for able exponents.

As the indictment runs back to the time of Charles II., to the persecutions of the Quakers in the days of Barclay of Ury, and brings up again the most modern offences, one cannot but feel that there are the most savory indications in it of Scotch thoroughness.

Some of the questions which he wishes to have me "*speer*" at Aberdeen, I fear, alas! would bring but an indifferent answer even in Boston, which gives a high school only to boys, and allows none to girls. On one point, it seems to me, my friend might speer himself to advantage, and that is the very commendable efforts which are being made now in Edinburgh and Aberdeen both, in the way of educating the children of the poor.

As this is one of the subjects which are particularly on my mind, and as all information which we can get upon this subject is peculiarly valuable to us in view of commencing efforts in America, I will abridge for you an account of the industrial schools of Aberdeen, published by the society for improving the condition of the laboring classes, in their paper called the Laborer's Friend.

In June, 1841, it was ascertained that in Aberdeen there were two hundred and eighty children, under fourteen years of age, who maintained themselves professedly by begging, but partly by theft. The first effort to better the moral condition of these children brought with it the discovery which our philanthropists made in New York, that in order to do good to a starving child, we must begin by feeding him; that we must gain his confidence by showing him a benevolence which he can understand, and thus proceed gradually to the reformation of his spiritual nature.

In 1841, therefore, some benevolent individuals in Aberdeen hired rooms and a teacher, and gave out notice among these poor children that they could there be supplied with food, work, and instruction. The general arrangement of the day was four hours of lessons, five hours of work, and three substantial meals. These meals were employed as the incitement to the lessons and the work, since it was made an indispensable condition to each meal that the child should have been present at the work or lessons which preceded it. This arrangement worked admirably; so that they reported that the attendance was more regular than at ordinary schools.

The whole produce of the work of the children goes towards defraying the expense of the establishment, thus effecting several important purposes,— reducing the expense of the school, and teaching the children, practically, the value of their industry,—in procuring for them food and instruction, and fostering in them, from the first, a sound principle of self-dependence; inasmuch as they know, from the moment of their entering school, that they give, or pay, in return for their food and education, all the work they are capable of performing.

The institution did not profess to clothe the children; but by the kindness of benevolent persons who take an interest in the school, there is generally a stock of old clothes on hand, from which the most destitute are supplied.

The following is the daily routine of the school: The scholars assemble every morning at seven in summer, and eight in winter. The school is opened by reading the Scriptures, praise, and prayer, and religious instruction suited to their years; after which there is a lesson in geography, or the more ordinary facts of natural history, taught by means of maps and prints distributed along the walls of the school room; two days in the week they have a singing lesson; at nine they breakfast on porridge and milk, and have half an hour of play; at ten they again assemble in school, and are employed at work till two. At two o'clock they dine; usually on broth, with coarse wheaten bread, but occasionally on potatoes and ox-head soup, &c. The diet is very plain, but nutritious and abundant, and appears to suit the tastes of the pupils completely. It is a pleasing sight to see them assembled, with their youthful appetites sharpened by four hours' work, joining, at least with outward decorum, in asking God's blessing on the food he has provided for them, and most promptly availing themselves of the signal given to commence their dinner.

From dinner till three, the time is spent in exercise or recreation, occasionally working in the garden; from three to four, they work either in the garden or in the work room; from four till seven, they are instructed in reading, writing, and arithmetic. At seven they have supper of porridge and milk; and after short religious exercises, are dismissed to their homes at eight.

On Saturday, they do not return to school after dinner; and occasionally, as a reward of good behavior, they accompany the teacher in a walk to the country or the sea coast.

On Sunday, they assemble at half past eight for devotion; breakfast at nine; attend worship in the school room; after which they dine, and return home, so as, if possible, to go with their parents to church in the afternoon.

At five they again meet, and have *Sabbath school* instruction in Bible and catechism; at seven, supper; and after evening worship are dismissed.

From this detail it will be seen that these schools differ from common day schools. In day schools, neither food nor employment is provided—teaching only is proposed, with a very little moral training.

The principle on which the industrial school proceeds, of giving employment along with instruction—especially as that employment is designed at the same time, if possible, to teach a trade which may be afterwards available—appears of the highest value. It is a practical discipline—a moral training, the importance of which cannot be over-estimated.

In a common school, too, there can be but little moral training, however efficiently the school may be conducted, just because there is little opportunity given for the development and display of individual character. The whole management of a school requires that the pupils be as speedily as possible brought to a uniform outward conduct, and thus an appearance of good behavior and propriety is produced within the school room, which is too often cast aside and forgotten the moment the pupils pass the threshold.

The remark was once made by an experienced teacher, that for the purposes of moral training he valued more the time he spent with his pupils at their games, than that which was spent in the school room.

The pecuniary value of the work done in these schools is not so great as was at first hoped, from the difficulty of procuring employment such as children so neglected could perform to advantage. The real value of the thing, however, they consider lies in the habits of industry and the sense of independence thus imparted.

At the outset the managers of the school regretted extremely their want of ability to furnish lodgings to the children. It was thought and said that the homes, to which the majority of them were obliged to return after school hours, would deprave faster than any instruction could reform. Fortunately it was impossible, at the time, to provide lodging for the children, and thus an experience was wrought out most valuable to all future laborers in this field.

The managers report that after six years' trial, the instances where evil results from the children returning home, are very rare; while there have been most cheering instances of substantial good being carried by the child, from the school, through the whole family. There are few parents, especially mothers, so abandoned as not to be touched by kindness shown to their offspring. It is the direct road to the mother's heart. Show kindness to her child, and she is prepared at once to second your efforts on its behalf. She must be debased, indeed, who will not listen to her child repeating its text from the Bible, or singing a verse of its infant hymn; and by this means the first seeds of a new life may be, and have been, planted in the parent's heart.

In cases where parents are so utterly depraved as to make it entirely hopeless to reform the child at home, they have found it the best course to board them, two or three together, in respectable families; the influences of the family state being held to be essential.

The success which attended the boys' school of industry soon led to the establishment of one for girls, conducted on the same principles; and it is stated that the change wrought among poor, outcast girls, by these means, was even more striking and gratifying than among the boys.

After these schools had been some time in operation, it was discovered that there were still multitudes of depraved children who could not or did not avail themselves of these privileges. It was determined by the authorities of the city of Aberdeen, in conformity with the Scripture injunction, to go out into the highways and hedges and *compel* them to come in. Under the authority of the police act they proposed to lay hold of the whole of the juvenile vagrants, and provide them with food and instruction.

Instructions were given to the police, on the 19th of May, 1845, to convey every child found begging to the soup kitchen; and, in the course of the day, seventy-five were collected, of whom four only could read. The scene which ensued is indescribable. Confusion and uproar, quarrelling and fighting, language of the most hateful description, and the most determined rebellion against every thing like order and regularity, gave the gentlemen engaged in the undertaking of taming them the hardest day's work they had ever encountered. Still, they so far prevailed, that, by evening, their authority was comparatively established. When dismissed, the children were invited to return next day—informed that, of course, they could do so or not, as they pleased, and that, if they did, they should be fed and instructed, but that, whether they came or not, begging would not be tolerated. Next day, the *greater part* returned. The managers felt that they had triumphed, and that a great field of moral usefulness was now secured to them.

The class who were brought to this school were far below those who attend the other two institutions—low as they appeared to be when the schools were first opened; and the scenes of filth, disease, and misery, exhibited even in the school itself, were such as would speedily have driven from the work all merely sentimental philanthropists. Those who undertake this work must have sound, strong principle to influence them, else they will soon turn from it in disgust.

The school went on prosperously; it soon excited public interest; funds flowed in; and, what is most gratifying, the working classes took a lively interest in it; and while the wealthier inhabitants of Aberdeen contributed during the year about one hundred and fifty pounds for its support, the working men collected, and handed over to the committee, no less than two hundred and fifty pounds.

Very few children in attendance at the industrial schools have been convicted of any offence. The regularity of attendance is owing to the children receiving their food in the school; and the school hours being from seven in the morning till seven at night, there is little opportunity for the commission of crime.

The experience acquired in these schools, and the connection which most of the managers had with the criminal courts of the city, led to the opening of a fourth institution—the Child's Asylum. Acting from day to day as judges, these gentlemen had occasionally cases brought before them which gave them extreme pain. Children—nay, infants—were brought up on criminal charges: the facts alleged against them were incontestably proved; and yet, in a moral sense, they could scarcely be held *guilty*, because, in truth, they did not know that they had done wrong.

There were, however, great practical difficulties in the way, which could only be got over indirectly. The magistrate could adjourn the case, directing the child to be cared for in the mean time, and inquiry could be made as to his family and relations, as to his character, and the prospect of his doing better in future; and he could either be restored to his relations, or boarded in the house of refuge, or with a family, and placed at one or other of the industrial schools; the charge of crime still remaining against him, to be made use of at once if he deserted school and returned to evil courses.

The great advantage sought here was to avoid stamping the child for life with the character of a convicted felon before he deserved it. Once thus brand a child in this country, and it is all but impossible for him ever by future good conduct, to efface the mask. How careful ought the law and those who administer it to be, not rashly to impress this stigma on the neglected child!

The Child's Asylum was opened on the 4th of December, 1846; and as a proof of the efficiency of the industrial schools in checking juvenile vagrancy and delinquency, it may be noticed that nearly a week elapsed before a child was brought to the asylum. When a child is apprehended by the police for begging, or other misdemeanor, he is conveyed to this institution, and his case is investigated; for which purpose the committee meets daily. If the child be of destitute parents, he is sent to one of the industrial schools; if the child of a worthless, but not needy, parent, efforts are made to induce the parent to fulfil his duty, and exercise his authority in restraining the evil habits of the child, by sending him to school, or otherwise removing him out of the way of temptation.

From the 4th of December up to the 18th of March, forty-seven cases, several of them more than once, had been brought up and carefully inquired into. Most of them were disposed of in the manner now stated; but a few were either claimed by, or remitted to, the procurator fiscal, as proper objects of punishment.

It is premature to say much of an institution which has existed for so short a time; but if the principle on which it is founded be as correct and sound as it appears, it must prosper and do good. There is, however, one great practical difficulty, which can only be removed by legislative enactment: there is no power at present to *detain* the children in the Asylum, or to force them to attend the schools to which they have been sent.

Such have been the rise and progress of the four industrial schools in Aberdeen, including, as one of them, the Child's Asylum.

All the schools are on the most catholic basis, the only qualification for membership being a subscription of a few shillings a year; and the doors are open to all who require admission, without distinction of sect or party.

The experience, then, of Aberdeen appears to demonstrate the possibility of reclaiming even the most abject and depraved of our juvenile population at a very moderate expense. The schools have been so long in operation, that, if there had been anything erroneous in the principles or the management of them, it must ere now have appeared; and if all the results have been encouraging, why should not the system be extended and established in other places? There is nothing in it which may not easily be copied in any town or village of our land where it is required.

I cannot help adding to this account some directions, which a very experienced teacher in these schools gives to those who are desirous of undertaking this enterprise.

"1. The school rooms and appurtenances ought to be of the plainest and most unpretending description. This is perfectly consistent with the most scrupulous cleanliness and complete ventilation. In like manner, the food should be wholesome, substantial, and abundant, but very plain—such as the boys or girls may soon be able to attain, or even surpass, by their own exertions after leaving school.

"2. The teachers must ever be of the best description, patient and persevering, not easily discouraged, and thoroughly versed in whatever branch they may have to teach; and, above all things, they must be persons of solid and undoubted piety—for without this qualification, all others will, in the end, prove worthless and unavailing.

"Throughout the day, the children must ever be kept in mind that, after all, religion is 'the one thing needful;' that the soul is of more value than the body.

"3. *The schools must be kept of moderate size*: from their nature this is absolutely necessary. It is a task of the greatest difficulty to manage, in a satisfactory manner, a large school of children, even of the higher classes, with all the advantages of careful home-training and superintendence; but with industrial schools it is folly to attempt it.

"From eighty to one hundred scholars is the largest number that ever should be gathered into one institution; when they exceed this, *let additional schools be opened*; in other words, *increase the number, not the size, of the schools*. They should be put down in the localities most convenient for the scholars, so that distance may be no bar to attendance; and if circumstances permit, a garden, either at the school or at no very great distance, will be of great utility.

"4. As soon as practicable, the children should be taught, and kept steadily at, some trade or other, by which they may earn their subsistence on leaving school; for the longer they have pursued this particular occupation at school, the more easily will they be able thereby to support themselves afterwards.

"As to commencing schools in new places, the best way of proceeding is for a few persons, who are of one mind on the subject, to unite, advance from their own purses, or raise among their friends, the small sum necessary at the outset, get their teacher, open their school, and collect a few scholars, gradually extend the number, and when they have made some progress, then tell the public what they have been doing; ask them to come and see; and, if they approve, to give their money and support. Public meetings and eloquent speeches are excellent things for exciting interest and raising funds, but they are of no use in carrying on the every-day work of the school.

"Let not the managers expect impossibilities. There will be crime and distress in spite of industrial schools; but they may be immensely reduced; and let no one be discouraged by the occasional lapse into a crime of a promising pupil. Such things must be while sin reigns in the heart of man; let them only be thereby stirred up to greater and more earnest exertion in their work.

"Let them be most careful as to the parties whom they admit to *act* along with them; for unless *all* the laborers be of one heart and mind, divisions must ensue, and the whole work be marred.

"It is most desirable that as many persons as possible of wealth and influence should lend their aid in supporting these institutions. Patrons and subscribers should be of all ranks and denominations; but they must beware of interfering with the actual daily working of the school, which ought to be left to the unfettered energies of those who, by their zeal, their activity, their sterling principle, and their successful administration, have proved themselves every way competent to the task they have undertaken.

"If the managers wish to carry out the good effect of their schools to the utmost, then they will not confine their labor to the scholars; *they will, through them, get access to the parents.* The good which the ladies of the Aberdeen Female School have already thus accomplished is not to be told; but let none try this work who do not experimentally know the value of the immortal soul."

Industrial schools seem to open a bright prospect to the hitherto neglected outcasts of our cities; for them a new era seems to be commencing: they are no longer to be restrained and kept in order by the iron bars of the prison house, and taught morality by the scourge of the executioner. They are now to be treated as reasonable and immortal beings; and may He who is the God of the poor as well as the rich give his effectual blessing with them, wherever they may be established, so that they may be a source of joy and rejoicing to all ranks of society.

Such is the result of the "speerings" recommended by my worthy correspondent. I have given them much at length, because they are useful to us in the much needed reforms commencing in our cities.

As to the appalling statements about intemperance, I grieve to say that they are confirmed by much which must meet the eye even of the passing stranger. I have said before how often the natural features of this country reminded me of the State of Maine. Would that the beneficent law which has removed, to so great an extent, pauperism and crime from that noble state might also be given to Scotland.

I suppose that the efforts for the benefit of the poorer classes in this city might be paralleled by efforts of a similar nature in the other cities of Scotland, particularly in Edinburgh, where great exertions have been making; but I happened to have a more full account of these in Aberdeen, and so give them as specimens of the whole. I must say, however, that in no city which I visited in Scotland did I see such neatness, order, and thoroughness, as in Aberdeen; and in none did there appear to be more gratifying evidences of prosperity and comfort among that class which one sees along the streets and thoroughfares.

About two o'clock we started from Aberdeen among crowds of friends, to whom we bade farewell with real regret.

Our way at first lay over the course of yesterday, along that beautiful sea coast—beautiful to the eye, but perilous to the navigator. They told us that the winds and waves raged here with an awful power. Not long before we came, the Duke of Sutherland, an iron steamer, was wrecked upon this shore. In one respect the coast of Maine has decidedly the advantage over this, and, indeed, of every other sea coast which I have ever visited; and that is in the richness of the wooding, which veils its picturesque points and capes in luxuriant foldings of verdure.

At Stonehaven station, where we stopped a few minutes, there was quite a gathering of the inhabitants to exchange greetings, and afterwards at successive stations along the road, many a kindly face and voice made our journey a pleasant one.

When we got into old Dundee it seemed all alive with welcome. We went in the carriage with the lord provost, Mr. Thoms, to his residence, where a party had been waiting dinner for us some time.

The meeting in the evening was in a large church, densely crowded, and conducted much as the others had been. When they came to sing the closing hymn, I hoped they would sing Dundee; but they did not, and I fear in Scotland, as elsewhere, the characteristic national melodies are giving way before more modern ones.

On the stage we were surrounded by many very pleasant people, with whom, between the services, we talked without knowing their names. The venerable Dr. Dick, the author of the Christian Philosopher and the Philosophy of the Future State, was there. Gilfillan was also present, and spoke. Together with their contribution to the Scottish offering, they presented me with quite a collection of the works of different writers of Dundee, beautifully bound.

We came away before the exercises of the evening were finished.

The next morning we had quite a large breakfast party, mostly ministers and their wives. Good old Dr. Dick was there, and I had an introduction to him, and had pleasure in speaking to him of the interest with which his works have been read in America. Of this fact I was told that he had received more substantial assurance in a comfortable sum of money subscribed and remitted to him by his American readers. If this be so it is a most commendable movement.

What a pity it was, during Scott's financial embarrassments, that every man, woman, and child in America, who had received pleasure from his writings, had not subscribed something towards an offering justly due to him!

Our host, Mr. Thoms, was one of the first to republish in Scotland Professor Stuart's Letters to Dr. Channing, with a preface of his own. He showed me Professor Stuart's letter in reply, and seemed rather amused that the professor directed it to the Rev. James Thom, supposing, of course, that so much theological zeal could not inhere in a layman. He also showed us many autograph letters of their former pastor, Mr. Cheyne, whose interesting memoirs have excited a good deal of attention in some circles in America.

After breakfast the ladies of the Dundee Antislavery Society called, and then the lord provost took us in his carriage to see the city. Dundee is the third town of Scotland in population, and a place of great antiquity. Its population in 1851 was seventy-eight thousand eight hundred and twenty-nine, and the manufactures consist principally of yarns, linen, with canvas and cotton bagging, great quantities of which are exported to France and North and South America. There are about sixty spinning mills and factories in the town and neighborhood, besides several iron founderies and manufactories of steam engines and machinery.

Dundee has always been a stronghold of liberty and the reformed religion. It is said that in the grammar school of this town William Wallace was educated; and here an illustrious confraternity of noblemen and gentry was formed, who joined to resist the tyranny of England.

Here Wishart preached in the beginning of the reformation, preparatory to his martyrdom. Here flourished some rude historical writers, who devoted their talents to the downfall of Popery. Singularly enough, they accomplished this in part by dramatic representations, in which the vices and absurdities of the Papal establishment were ridiculed before the people. Among others, one James Wedderburn and his brother, John, vicar of Dundee, are mentioned as having excelled in this kind of composition. The same authors composed books of song, denominated "Gude and Godly Ballads," wherein the frauds and deceits of Popery were fully pointed out. A third brother of the family, being a musical genius, it is said, "turned the times and tenor of many profane songs into godly songs and hymns, whereby he stirred up the affections of many," which tunes were called the Psalms of Dundee. Here, perhaps, was the origin of "Dundee's wild warbling measures."

The conjoint forces of tragedy, comedy, ballads, and music, thus brought to bear on the popular mind, was very great.

Dundee has been a great sufferer during the various civil commotions in Scotland. In the time of Charles I. it stood out for the solemn league and covenant, for which crime the Earl of Montrose was sent against it, who took and burned it. It is said that he called Dundee a most seditious town, the securest haunt and receptacle of rebels, and a place that had contributed as much as any other to the rebellion. Yet afterwards, when Montrose was led a captive through Dundee, the historian observes, "It is remarkable of the town of Dundee, in which he lodged one night, that though it had suffered more by his army than any town else within the kingdom, yet were they, amongst all the rest, so far from exulting over him, that the whole town testified a great deal of sorrow for his woful condition; and there was he likewise furnished with clothes suitable to his birth and person."

This town of Dundee was stormed by Monk and the forces of Parliament during the time of the commonwealth, because they had sheltered the fugitive Charles II., and granted him money. When taken by Monk, he committed a great many barbarities.

It has also been once visited by the plague, and once with a seven years' dearth or famine.

Most of these particulars I found in a History of Dundee, which formed one of the books presented to me.

The town is beautifully situated on the Firth of Tay, which here spreads its waters, and the quantity of shipping indicates commercial prosperity.

I was shown no abbeys or cathedrals, either because none ever existed, or because they were destroyed when the town was fired.

In our rides about the city, the local recollections that our friends seemed to recur to with as much interest as any, were those connected with the queen's visit to Dundee, in 1844. The spot where she landed has been commemorated by the erection of a superb triumphal arch in stone. The provost said some of the people were quite astonished at the plainness of the queen's dress, having looked for something very dazzling and overpowering from a queen. They could scarcely believe their eyes, when they saw her riding by in a plain bonnet, and enveloped in a simple shepherd's plaid.

The queen is exceedingly popular in Scotland, doubtless in part because she heartily appreciated the beauty of the country, and the strong and interesting traits of the people. She has a country residence at Balmorrow, where she spends a part of every year; and the impression seems to prevail among her Scottish subjects, that she never appears to feel herself more happy or more at home than in this her Highland dwelling. The legend is, that here she delights to throw off the restraints of royalty; to go about plainly dressed, like a private individual; to visit in the cottages of the poor; to interest herself in the instruction of the children; and to initiate the future heir of England into that practical love of the people which is the best qualification for a ruler.

I repeat to you the things which I hear floating of the public characters of England, and you can attach what degree of credence you may think proper. As a general rule in this censorious world, I think it safe to suppose that the good which is commonly reported of public characters, if not true in the letter of its details, is at least so in its general spirit. The stories which are told about distinguished people generally run in a channel coincident with the facts of their character. On the other hand, with regard to evil reports, it is safe always to allow something for the natural propensity to detraction and slander, which is one of the most undoubted facts of human nature in all lands.

We left Dundee at two o'clock, by cars, for Edinburgh. In the evening we attended another *soirée* of the working men of Edinburgh. As it was similar in all respects to the one at Glasgow, I will not dwell upon it, further than to say how gratifying to me, in every respect, are occasions in which working men, as a class, stand out before the public. *They* are to form, more and more, a new power in society, greater than the old power of helmet and sword, and I rejoice in every indication that they are learning to understand themselves.

We have received letters from the working men, both in Dundee and Glasgow, desiring our return to attend *soirées* in those cities. Nothing could give us greater pleasure, had we time and strength. No class of men are more vitally interested in the conflict of freedom against slavery than working men. The principle upon which slavery is founded touches every interest of theirs. If it be right that one half of the community should deprive the other half of education, of all opportunities to rise in the world, of all property rights and all family ties, merely to make them more convenient tools for their profit and luxury, then every injustice and extortion, which oppresses the laboring man in any country, can be equally defended.

LETTER VIII

Dear Aunt E.:—

You wanted us to write about our visit to Melrose; so here you have it.

On Tuesday morning Mr. S. and C——had agreed to go back to Glasgow for the purpose of speaking at a temperance meeting, and as we were restricted for time, we were obliged to make the visit to Melrose in their absence, much to the regret of us all. G—— thought we would make a little quiet run out in the cars by ourselves, while Mr. S. and C—— were gone back to Glasgow.

It was one of those soft, showery, April days, misty and mystical, now weeping and now shining, that we found ourselves whirled by the cars through this enchanted ground of Scotland. Almost every name we heard spoken along the railroad, every stream we passed, every point we looked at, recalled some line of Walter Scott's poetry, or some event of history. The thought that he was gone forever, whose genius had given the charm to all, seemed to settle itself down like a melancholy mist. To how little purpose seemed the few, short years of his life, compared with the capabilities of such a soul! Brilliant as his success had been, how was it passed like a dream! It seemed sad to think that he had not only passed away himself, but that almost the whole family and friendly circle had passed with him—not a son left to bear his name!

Here we were in the region of the Ettrick, the Yarrow, and the Tweed. I opened the Lay of the Last Minstrel, and, as if by instinct, the first lines my eye fell upon were these:—

> "Call it not vain: they do not err
>
> Who say, that when the poet dies,
>
> Mute nature mourns her worshipper,
>
> And celebrates his obsequies;
>
> Who say, tall cliff and cavern lone
>
> For the departed bard make moan;
>
> That mountains weep in crystal rill;
>
> That flowers in tears of balm distil;
>
> Through his loved groves that breezes sigh,

And oaks, in deeper groan, reply;

And rivers teach their rushing wave

To murmur dirges round his grave."

"Melrose!" said the loud voice of the conductor; and starting, I looked up and saw quite a flourishing village, in the midst of which rose the old, gray, mouldering walls of the abbey. Now, this was somewhat of a disappointment to me. I had been somehow expecting to find the building standing alone in the middle of a great heath, far from all abodes of men, and with no companions more hilarious than the owls. However, it was no use complaining; the fact was, there was a village, and what was more, a hotel, and to this hotel we were to go to get a guide for the places we were to visit; for it was understood that we were to "*do*" Melrose, Dryburgh, and Abbotsford, all in one day. There was no time for sentiment; it was a business affair, that must be looked in the face promptly, if we meant to get through. Ejaculations and quotations of poetry could, of course, be thrown in, as William, of Deloraine pattered his prayers, while riding.

We all alighted at a very comfortable hotel, and were ushered into as snug a little parlor as one's heart could desire.

East Window of Melrose Abbey.

The next thing was to hire a coachman to take us, in the rain,—for the mist had now swelled into a rain,—through the whole appropriate round. I stood by and heard names which I had never heard before, except in song, brought into view in their commercial relations; so much for Abbotsford; and so much for Dryburgh; and then, if we would like to throw in Thomas the Rhymer's Tower, why, that would be something extra.

"Thomas the Rhymer?" said one of the party, not exactly posted up. "Was he any thing remarkable? Well, is it worth while to go to his tower? It will cost something extra, and take more time."

Weighed in such a sacrilegious balance, Thomas was found wanting, of course: the idea of driving three or four miles farther to see an old tower, supposed to have belonged to a man who is supposed to have existed and to have been carried off by a supposititious Queen of the Fairies into Elfland, was too absurd for reasonable people; in fact, I made believe myself that I did not care much about it, particularly as the landlady remarked, that if we did not get home by five o'clock "the chops might be spoiled."

As we all were packed into a tight coach, the rain still pouring, I began to wish mute Nature would not be quite so energetic in distilling her tears. A few sprinkling showers, or a graceful wreath of mist, might be all very well; but a steady, driving rain, that obliged us to shut up the carriage windows, and coated them with mist so that we could not look out, why, I say it is enough to put out the fire of sentiment in any heart. We might as well have been rolled up in a bundle and carried through the country, for all the seeing it was possible to do under such circumstances. It, therefore, should be stated, that we did keep bravely up in our poetic zeal, which kindly Mrs. W. also reënforced, by distributing certain very delicate sandwiches to support the outer man.

At length, the coach stopped at the entrance of Abbotsford grounds, where there was a cottage, out of which, due notice being given, came a trim, little old woman in a black gown, with pattens on; she put up her umbrella, and we all put up ours; the rain poured harder than ever as we went dripping up the gravel walk, looking much, I inly fancied, like a set of discomforted fowls fleeing to covert. We entered the great court yard, surrounded with a high wall, into which were built sundry fragments of curious architecture that happened to please the poet's fancy.

I had at the moment, spite of the rain, very vividly in my mind Washington Irving's graceful account of his visit to Abbotsford while this house was yet building, and the picture which he has given of Walter Scott sitting before his door, humorously descanting on various fragments of sculpture, which lay scattered about, and which he intended to immortalize by incorporating into his new dwelling.

Viewed as a mere speculation, or, for aught I know, as an architectural effort, this building may, perhaps, be counted as a mistake and a failure. I observe, that it is quite customary to speak of it, among some, as a pity that he ever undertook it. But viewed as a development of his inner life, as a working out in wood and stone of favorite fancies and cherished ideas, the building has to me a deep interest. The gentle-hearted poet delighted himself in it; this house was his stone and wood poem, as irregular, perhaps, and as contrary to any established rule, as his Lay of the Last Minstrel, but still wild and poetic. The building has this interest, that it was throughout his own conception, thought, and choice; that he expressed himself in every stone that was laid, and made it a kind of shrine, into which he wove all his treasures of antiquity, and where he imitated, from the beautiful, old, mouldering ruins of Scotland, the parts that had touched him most deeply.

The walls of one room were of carved oak from the Dunfermline Abbey; the ceiling of another imitated from Roslin Castle; here a fireplace was wrought in the image of a favorite niche in Melrose; and there the ancient pulpit of Erskine was wrought into a wall. To him, doubtless, every object in the house was suggestive of poetic fancies; every carving and bit of tracery had its history, and was as truly an expression of something in the poet's mind as a verse of his poetry.

A building wrought out in this way, and growing up like a bank of coral, may very possibly violate all the proprieties of criticism; it may possibly, too, violate one's ideas of mere housewifery utility; but by none of these rules ought such a building to be judged. We should look at it rather as the poet's endeavor to render outward and visible the dream land of his thoughts, and to create for himself a refuge from the cold, dull realities of life, in an architectural romance.

These were thoughts which gave interest to the scene as we passed through the porchway, adorned with petrified stags' horns, into the long entrance hall of the mansion. This porch was copied from one in Linlithgow palace. One side of this hall was lighted by windows of painted glass. The floor was of black and white marble from the Hebrides. Round the whole cornice there was a line of coats armorial, richly blazoned, and the following inscription in old German text:

"These be the coat armories of the clanns and chief men of name wha keepit the marchys of Scotland in the old tyme for the kynge. Trewe men war they in their tyme, and in their defence God them defendyt."

There were the names of the Douglases, the Elliots, the Scotts, the Armstrongs, and others. I looked at this arrangement with interest, because I knew that Scott must have taken a particular delight in it.

The fireplace, designed from a niche in Melrose Abbey, also in this room, and a choice bit of sculpture it is. In it was an old grate, which had its history also, and opposite to it the boards from the pulpit of Erskine were wrought into a kind of side table, or something which served that purpose.

The spaces between the windows were decorated with pieces of armor, crossed swords, and stags' horns, each one of which doubtless had its history. On each side of the door, at the bottom of the hall, was a Gothic shrine, or niche, in both of which stood a figure in complete armor.

Then we went into the drawing room; a lofty saloon, the woodwork of which is entirely of cedar, richly wrought; probably another of the author's favorite poetic fancies. It is adorned with a set of splendid antique ebony furniture; cabinet, chairs, and piano—the gift of George IV. to the poet.

We went into his library; a magnificent room, on which, I suppose, the poet's fancy had expended itself more than any other. The roof is of carved oak, after models from Roslin Castle. Here, in a niche, is a marble bust of Scott, as we understood a present from Chantrey to the poet; it was one of the best and most animated representations of him I ever saw, and very much superior to the one under the monument in Edinburgh. On expressing my idea to this effect, I found I had struck upon a favorite notion of the good woman who showed us the establishment; she seemed to be an ancient servant of the house, and appeared to entertain a regard for the old laird scarcely less than idolatry. One reason why this statue is superior is, that it represents his noble forehead, which the Edinburgh one suffers to be concealed by falling hair: to cover *such* a forehead seems scarcely less than a libel.

The whole air of this room is fanciful and picturesque in the extreme. The walls are entirely filled with the bookcases, there being about twenty thousand volumes. A small room opens from the library, which was Scott's own private study. His writing table stood in the centre, with his inkstand on it, and before it a large, plain, black leather arm chair.

In a glass case, I think in this room, was exhibited the suit of clothes he last wore; a blue coat with large metal buttons, plaid trousers, and broad-brimmed hat. Around the sides of this room there was a gallery of light tracery work; a flight of stairs led up to it, and in one corner of it was a door which the woman said led to the poet's bed room. One seemed to see in all this arrangement how snug, and cozy, and comfortable the poet had thus ensconced himself, to give himself up to his beloved labors and his poetic dreams. But there was a cold and desolate air of order and adjustment about it which reminds one of the precise and chilling arrangements of a room from which has just been carried out a corpse; all is silent and deserted.

The house is at present the property of Scott's only surviving daughter, whose husband has assumed the name of Scott. We could not learn from our informant whether any of the family was in the house. We saw only the rooms which are shown to visitors, and a coldness, like that of death, seemed to strike to my heart from their chilly solitude.

As we went out of the house we passed another company of tourists coming in, to whom we heard our guide commencing the same recitation, "this is," and "this is," &c., just as she had done to us. One thing about the house and grounds had disappointed me; there was not one view from a single window I saw that was worth any thing, in point of beauty; why a poet, with an eye for the beautiful, could have located a house in such an indifferent spot, on an estate where so many beautiful sites were at his command, I could not imagine.

As to the external appearance of Abbotsford, it is as irregular as can well be imagined. There are gables, and pinnacles, and spires, and balconies, and buttresses any where and every where, without rhyme or reason; for wherever the poet wanted a balcony, he had it; or wherever he had a fragment of carved stone, or a bit of historic tracery, to put in, he made a shrine for it forthwith, without asking leave of any rules. This I take to be one of the main advantages of Gothic architecture; it is a most catholic and tolerant system, and any kind of eccentricity may find refuge beneath its mantle.

Here and there, all over the house, are stones carved with armorial bearings and pious inscriptions, inserted at random wherever the poet fancied. Half way up the wall in one place is the door of the old Tolbooth at Edinburgh, with the inscription over it, "The Lord of armeis is my protector; blissit ar thay that trust in the Lord. 1575."

A doorway at the west end of the house is composed of stones which formed the portal of the Tolbooth, given to Sir Walter on the pulling down of the building in 1817.

On the east side of the house is a rude carving of a sword with the words, "Up with ye, sutors of Selkyrke. A.D. 1525." Another inscription, on the same side of the house, runs thus:—

> "By night, by day, remember ay
>
> The goodness of ye Lord;
>
> And thank his name, whose glorious fame
>
> Is spread throughout ye world.—A.C.M.D. 1516."

In the yard, to the right of the doorway of the mansion, we saw the figure of Scott's favorite dog Maida, with a Latin inscription—

> "Maidæ marmorea dormis sub imagine, Maida,
>
> Ad januam domini: sit tibi terra levis."

Which in our less expressive English we might render—

> At thy lord's door, in slumbers light and blest,
>
> Maida, beneath this marble Maida, rest:
>
> Light lie the turf upon thy gentle breast.

One of the most endearing traits of Scott was that sympathy and harmony which always existed between him and the brute creation.

Poor Maida seemed cold and lonely, washed by the rain in the damp grass plat. How sad, yet how expressive is the scriptural phrase for indicating death! "He shall return to his house no more, neither shall his place know him any more." And this is what all our homes are coming to; our buying, our planting, our building, our marrying and giving in marriage, our genial firesides and dancing children, are all like so many figures passing through the magic lantern, to be put out at last in death.

The grounds, I was told, are full of beautiful paths and seats, favorite walks and lounges of the poet; but the obdurate pertinacity of the rain compelled us to choose the very shortest path possible to the carriage. I picked a leaf of the Portugal laurel, which I send you.

Next we were driven to Dryburgh, or rather to the banks of the Tweed, where a ferryman, with a small skiff waits to take passengers over.

The Tweed is a clear, rippling river, with a white, pebbly bottom, just like our New England mountain streams. After we landed we were to walk to the Abbey. Our feet were damp and cold, and our boatman invited us to his cottage. I found him and all his family warmly interested in the fortunes of Uncle Tom and his friends, and for his sake they received me as a long-expected friend. While I was sitting by the ingleside,—that is, a coal grate,—warming my feet, I fell into conversation with my host. He and his family, I noticed, spoke English more than Scotch; he was an intelligent young man, in appearance and style of mind precisely what you might expect to meet in a cottage in Maine. He and all the household, even the old grandmother, had read Uncle Tom's Cabin, and were perfectly familiar with all its details. He told me that it had been universally read in the cottages in the vicinity. I judged from his mode of speaking, that he and his neighbors were in the habit of reading a great deal. I spoke of going to Dryburgh to see the grave of Scott, and inquired if his works were much read by the common people. He said that Scott was not so much a favorite with the people as Burns. I inquired if he took a newspaper. He said that the newspapers were kept at so high a price that working men were not able to take them; sometimes they got sight of them through clubs, or by borrowing. How different, thought I, from America, where a workingman would as soon think of going without his bread as without his newspaper!

The cottages of these laboring people, of which there were a whole village along here, are mostly of stone, thatched with straw. This thatch sometimes gets almost entirely grown over with green moss. Thus moss-covered was the roof of the cottage where we stopped, opposite to Dryburgh grounds.

There was about this time one of those weeping pauses in the showery sky, and a kind of thinning and edging away of the clouds, which gave hope that perhaps the sun was going to look out, and give to our persevering researches the countenance of his presence. This was particularly desirable, as the old woman, who came out with her keys to guide us, said she had a cold and a cough: we begged that she would not trouble herself to go with us at all. The fact is, with all respect to nice old women, and the worthy race of guides in general, they are not favorable to poetic meditation. We promised to be very good if she would let us have the key, and lock up all the gates, and bring it back; but no, she was faithfulness itself, and so went coughing along through the dripping and drowned grass to open the gates for us.

This Dryburgh belongs now to the Earl of Buchan, having been bought by him from a family of the name of Haliburton, ancestral connections of Scott, who, in his autobiography, seems to lament certain mischances of fortune which prevented the estate from coming into his own family, and gave them, he said, nothing but the right of stretching their bones there. It seems a pity, too, because the possession of this rich, poetic ruin would have been a mine of wealth to Scott, far transcending the stateliest of modern houses.

Now, if you do not remember Scott's poem, of the Eve of St. John, you ought to read it over; for it is, I think, the most spirited of all his ballads; nothing conceals the transcendent lustre and beauty of these compositions, but the splendor of his other literary productions. Had he never written any thing but these, they would have made him a name as a poet. As it was, I found the fanciful chime of the cadences in this ballad ringing through my ears. I kept saying to myself—

>"The Dryburgh bells do ring,
>
>And the white monks do sing
>
>For Sir Richard of Coldinghame."

And as I was wandering around in the labyrinth, of old, broken, mossy arches, I thought—

> "There is a nun in Dryburgh bower
>
> Ne'er looks upon the sun;
>
> There is a monk in Melrose tower,
>
> He speaketh word to none.
>
> That nun who ne'er beholds the day,
>
> That monk who speaks to none,
>
> That nun was Smaylhome's lady gay,
>
> That monk the bold Baron."

It seems that there is a vault in this edifice which has had some superstitious legends attached to it, from having been the residence, about fifty years ago, of a mysterious lady, who, being under a vow never to behold the light of the sun, only left her cell at midnight. This little story, of course, gives just enough superstitious chill to this beautiful ruin to help the effect of the pointed arches, the clinging wreaths of ivy, the shadowy pines, and yew trees; in short, if one had not a guide waiting, who had a bad cold, if one could stroll here at leisure by twilight or moonlight, one might get up a considerable deal of the mystic and poetic.

There is a part of the ruin that stands most picturesquely by itself, as if old Time had intended it for a monument. It is the ruin of that part of the chapel called St. Mary's Aisle; it stands surrounded by luxuriant thickets of pine and other trees, a cluster of beautiful Gothic arches supporting a second tier of smaller and more fanciful ones, one or two of which have that light touch of the Moorish in their form which gives such a singular and poetic effect in many of the old Gothic ruins. Out of these wild arches and windows wave wreaths of ivy, and slender harebells shake their blue pendants, looking in and out of the lattices like little capricious fairies. There are fragments of ruins lying on the ground, and the whole air of the thing is as wild, and dreamlike, and picturesque as the poet's fanciful heart could have desired.

Underneath these arches he lies beside his wife; around him the representation of the two things he loved most—the wild bloom and beauty of nature, and the architectural memorial of by-gone history and art. Yet there was one thing I felt I would have had otherwise; it seemed to me that the flat stones of the pavement are a weight too heavy and too cold to be laid on the breast of a lover of nature and the beautiful. The green turf, springing with flowers, that lies above a grave, does not seem, to us so hopeless a barrier between us and what was warm and loving; the springing grass and daisies there seem, types and assurances that the mortal beneath shall put on immortality; they come up to us as kind messages from the peaceful dust, to say that it is resting in a certain hope of a glorious resurrection.

On the cold flagstones, walled in by iron railings, there were no daisies and no moss; but I picked many of both from, the green turf around, which, with some sprigs of ivy from the walls, I send you.

It is strange that we turn away from the grave of this man, who achieved to himself the most brilliant destiny that ever an author did,—raising himself by his own unassisted efforts to be the chosen companions of nobles and princes, obtaining all that heart could desire of riches and honor,—we turn away and say, Poor Walter Scott! How desolately touching is the account in Lockhart, of his dim and indistinct agony the day his wife was brought here to be buried! and the last part of that biography is the saddest history that I know; it really makes us breathe a long sigh of relief when we read of the lowering of the coffin into this vault.

What force does all this give to the passage in his diary in which he records his estimate of life!—"What is this world? a dream within a dream. As we grow older, each step is an awakening. The youth awakes, as he thinks, from childhood; the full-grown man despises the pursuits of youth as visionary; the old man looks on manhood as a feverish dream. The grave the last sleep? No; it is the last and final awakening."

It has often been remarked, that there is no particular moral purpose aimed at by Scott in his writings; he often speaks of it himself in his last days, in a tone of humility. He represents himself as having been employed mostly in the comparatively secondary department of giving innocent amusement. He often expressed, humbly and earnestly, the hope that he had, at least, done no harm; but I am inclined to think, that although moral effect was not primarily his object, yet the influence of his writings and whole existence on earth has been decidedly good.

It is a great thing to have a mind of such power and such influence, whose recognitions of right and wrong, of virtue and vice, were, in most cases, so clear and determined. He never enlists our sympathies in favor of vice, by drawing those seductive pictures, in which it comes so near the shape and form of virtue that the mind is puzzled as to the boundary line. He never makes young ladies feel that they would like to marry corsairs, pirates, or sentimental villains of any description. The most objectionable thing, perhaps, about his influence, is its sympathy with the war spirit. A person Christianly educated can hardly read some of his descriptions in the Lady of the Lake and Marmion without an emotion of disgust, like what is excited by the same things in Homer; and as the world comes more and more under the influence of Christ, it will recede more and more from this kind of literature.

Scott has been censured as being wilfully unjust to the Covenanters and Puritans. I think he meant really to deal fairly by them, and that what *he* called fairness might seem rank injustice to those brought up to venerate them, as we have been. I suppose that in Old Mortality it was Scott's honest intention to balance the two parties about fairly, by putting on the Covenant side his good, steady, well-behaved hero, Mr. Morton, who is just as much of a Puritan as the Puritans would have been had they taken Sir Walter Scott's advice; that is to say, a very nice, sensible, moral man, who takes the Puritan side because he thinks it the *right* side, but contemplates all the devotional enthusiasm and religious ecstasies of his associates from a merely artistic and pictorial point of view. The trouble was, when he got his model Puritan done, nobody ever knew what he was meant for; and then all the young ladies voted steady Henry Morton a bore, and went to falling in love with his Cavalier rival, Lord Evandale, and people talked as if it was a preconcerted arrangement of Scott, to surprise the female heart, and carry it over to the royalist side.

The fact was, in describing Evandale he made a living, effective character, because he was describing something he had full sympathy with, and put his whole life into; but Henry Morton is a laborious arrangement of starch and pasteboard to produce one of those supposititious, just-right men, who are always the stupidest of mortals after they are made. As to why Scott did not describe such a character as the martyr Duke of Argyle, or Hampden, or Sir Harry Vane, where high birth, and noble breeding, and chivalrous sentiment were all united with intense devotional fervor, the answer is, that he could not do it; he had not that in him wherewith to do it; a man cannot create that of which he has not first had the elements in himself; and devotional enthusiasm is a thing which Scott never felt. Nevertheless, I believe that he was perfectly sincere in saying that he would, "if necessary, die a martyr for Christianity." He had calm, firm principle to any extent, but it never was kindled into fervor. He was of too calm and happy a temperament to sound the deepest recesses of souls torn up from their depths by mighty conflicts and sorrows. There are souls like the "alabaster vase of ointment, very precious," which shed no perfume of devotion because a great sorrow has never broken them. Could Scott have been given back to the world again after the heavy discipline of life had passed over him, he would have spoken otherwise of many things. What he vainly struggled to say to Lockhart on his death bed would have been a new revelation, of his soul to the world, could he have lived to unfold it in literature. But so it is: when we have learned to live, life's purpose is answered, and we die!

This is the sum and substance of some conversations held while rambling among these scenes, going in and out of arches, climbing into nooks and through loopholes, picking moss and ivy, and occasionally retreating under the shadow of some arch, while the skies were indulging in a sudden burst of emotion. The poor woman who acted as our guide, ensconcing herself in a dry corner, stood like a literal Patience on a monument, waiting for us to be through; we were sorry for her, but as it was our first and last chance, and she would stay there, we could not help it.

Near by the abbey is a square, modern mansion, belonging to the Earl of Buchan, at present untenanted. There were some black, solemn yew trees there, old enough to have told us a deal of history had they been inclined to speak; as it was, they could only drizzle.

As we were walking through the yard, a bird broke out into a clear, sweet song.

"What bird is that?" said I.

"I think it is the mavis," said the guide. This brought up,—

> "The mavis wild, wie mony a note,
>
> Sings drowsy day to rest."

And also,—

> "Merry it is in wild green wood,
>
> When mavis and merle are singing."

A verse, by the by, dismally suggestive of contrast to this rainy day.

As we came along out of the gate, walking back towards the village of Dryburgh, we began to hope that the skies had fairly wept themselves out; at any rate the rain stopped, and the clouds wore a sulky, leaden-gray aspect, as if they were thinking what to do next.

We saw a knot of respectable-looking laboring men at a little distance, conversing in a group, and now and then stealing glances at us; one of them at last approached and inquired if this was Mrs. Stowe, and being answered in the affirmative, they all said heartily, "Madam, ye're right welcome to Scotland." The chief speaker, then, after a little conversation, asked our party if we would do him the favor to step into his cottage near by, to take a little refreshment after our ramble; to which we assented with alacrity. He led the way to a neat, stone cottage, with a flower garden before the door, and said to a thrifty, rosy-cheeked woman, who met us, "Well, and what do you think, wife, if I have brought Mrs. Stowe and her party to take a cup of tea with us?"

We were soon seated in a neat, clean kitchen, and our hostess hastened to put the teakettle over the grate, lamenting that she had not known of our coming, that she might have had a fire "ben the house," meaning by the phrase what we Yankees mean by "in the best room." We caught a glimpse of the carpet and paper of this room, when the door was opened to bring out a few more chairs.

> "Belyve the bairns cam dropping in,"

rosy-cheeked, fresh from school, with satchel and school books, to whom I was introduced as the mother of Topsy and Eva.

"Ah," said the father, "such a time as we had, when we were reading the book; whiles they were greetin' and whiles in a rage."

My host was quite a young-looking man, with the clear blue eye and glowing complexion which one so often meets here; and his wife, with her blooming cheeks, neat dress, and well-kept house, was evidently one of those fully competent

> "To gar old claes look amaist as weel as new."

I inquired the ages of the several children, to which the father answered with about as much chronological accuracy as men generally display in such points of family history. The gude wife, after correcting his figures once or twice, turned away with a somewhat indignant exclamation about men that didn't know their own bairns' ages, in which many of us, I presume, could sympathize.

I must not omit to say, that a neighbor of our host had been pressed to come in with us; an intelligent-looking man, about fifty. In the course of conversation, I found that they were both masons by trade, and as the rain had prevented their working, they had met to spend their time in reading. They said they were reading a work on America; and thereat followed a good deal of general conversation on our country. I found that, like many others in this old country, they had a tie to connect them with the new—a son in America.

One of our company, in the course of the conversation, says, "They say in America that the working classes of England and Scotland are not so well off as the slaves." The man's eye flashed. "There are many things," he said, "about the working classes, which are not what they should be; there's room for a great deal of improvement in our condition, but," he added with an emphasis, "we are *no slaves!*" There was a, touch, of the

"Scots wha ha' wi' Wallace bled"

about the man, as he spoke, which made the affirmation quite unnecessary.

"But," said I, "you think the affairs of the working classes much improved of late years?"

"O, certainly," said the other; "since the repeal of the corn laws and the passage of the factory bill, and this emigration to America and Australia, affairs have been very much altered."

We asked them what they could make a day by their trade. It was much less, certainly, than is paid for the same labor in our country; but yet the air of comfort and respectability about the cottage, the well-clothed and well-schooled, intelligent children, spoke well for the result of their labors.

While our conversation was carried on, the teakettle commenced singing most melodiously, and by a mutual system of accommodation, a neat tea table was spread in the midst of us, and we soon found ourselves seated, enjoying some delicious bread and butter, with the garniture of cheese, preserves, and tea. Our host before the meal craved a blessing of Him who had made of one blood all the families of the earth; a beautiful and touching allusion, I thought, between Americans and Scotchmen. Our long ramble in the rain had given us something of an appetite, and we did ample justice to the excellence of the cheer.

After tea we walked on down again towards the Tweed, our host and his friends waiting on us to the boat. As we passed through the village of Dryburgh, all the inhabitants of the cottages seemed to be standing in their doors, bowing and smiling, and expressing their welcome in a gentle, kindly way, that was quite touching.

As we were walking towards the Tweed, the Eildon Hill, with its three points, rose before us in the horizon. I thought of the words in the Lay of the Last Minstrel:—

> "Warrior, I could say to thee,
>
> The words that cleft Eildon Hill in three,
>
> And bridled the Tweed with a curb of stone."

I appealed to my friends if they knew any thing about the tradition; I thought they seemed rather reluctant to speak of it. O, there was some foolish story, they believed; they did not well know what it was.

The picturesque age of human childhood is gone by; men and women cannot always be so accommodating as to believe unreasonable stories for the convenience of poets.

At the Tweed the man with the skiff was waiting for us. In parting with my friend, I said, "Farewell. I hope we may meet again some time."

"I am sure we shall, madam," said he; "if not here, certainly hereafter."

After being rowed across I stopped a few moments to admire the rippling of the clear water over the pebbles. "I want some of these pebbles of the Tweed," I said, "to carry home to America." Two hearty, rosy-cheeked Scotch lasses on the shore soon supplied me with as many as I could carry.

We got into our carriage, and drove up to Melrose. After a little negotiation with the keeper, the doors were unlocked. Just at that moment the sun was so gracious as to give a full look through the windows, and touch with streaks of gold the green, grassy floor; for the beautiful ruin is floored with green grass and roofed with sky: even poetry has not exaggerated its beauty, and could not. There is never any end to the charms of Gothic architecture. It is like the beauty of Cleopatra,—

> "Age cannot wither, custom, cannot stale
>
> Her infinite variety."

Here is this Melrose, now, which has been berhymed, bedraggled through infinite guide books, and been gaped at and smoked at by dandies, and been called a "dear love" by pretty young ladies, and been hawked about as a trade article in all neighboring shops, and you know perfectly well that all your raptures are spoken for and expected at the door, and your going off in an ecstasy is a regular part of the programme; and yet, after all, the sad, wild, sweet beauty of the thing comes down on one like a cloud; even for the sake of being original you could not, in conscience, declare you did not admire it.

We went into a minute examination with our guide, a young man, who seemed to have a full sense of its peculiar beauties. I must say here, that Walter Scott's description in the Lay of the Last Minstrel is as perfect in most details as if it had been written by an architect as well as a poet—it is a kind of glorified daguerreotype.

This building was the first of the elaborate and fanciful Gothic which I had seen, and is said to excel in the delicacy of its carving any except Roslin Castle. As a specimen of the exactness of Scott's description, take this verse, where he speaks of the cloisters:—

> "Spreading herbs and flowerets bright,
>
> Glistened with the dew of night,
>
> Nor herb nor floweret glistened there,
>
> But were carved in the cloister arches as fair."

These cloisters were covered porticoes surrounding the garden, where the monks walked for exercise. They are now mostly destroyed, but our guide showed us the remains of exquisite carvings there, in which each group was an imitation of some leaf or flower, such as the curly kail of Scotland; a leaf, by the by, as worthy of imitation as the Greek acanthus, the trefoil oak, and some other leaves, the names of which I do not remember. These Gothic artificers were lovers of nature; they studied at the fountain head; hence the never-dying freshness, variety, and originality of their conceptions.

Another passage, whose architectural accuracy you feel at once, is this:—

> "They entered now the chancel tall;
>
> The darkened, roof rose high, aloof
>
> On pillars lofty, light, and small:
>
> The keystone that locked, each ribbed aisle

> Was a fleur-de-lis, or a quatre-feuille;
>
> The corbels were carved grotesque and grim;
>
> And the pillars, with, clustered shafts so trim,
>
> With, base and with capital flourished around,
>
> Seemed bundles of lances which garlands had bound."

The quatre-feuille here spoken of is an ornament formed by the junction of four leaves. The frequent recurrence of the fleur-de-lis in the carvings here shows traces of French hands employed in the architecture. In one place in the abbey there is a rude inscription, in which a French architect commemorates the part he has borne in constructing the building.

These corbels are the projections from which, the arches spring, usually carved in some fantastic mask or face; and on these the Shakspearian imagination of the Gothic artists seems to have let itself loose to run riot: there is every variety of expression, from, the most beautiful to the most goblin and grotesque. One has the leer of fiendish triumph, with budding horns, showing too plainly his paternity; again you have the drooping eyelids and saintly features of some fair virgin; and then the gasping face of some old monk, apparently in the agonies of death, with his toothless gums, hollow cheeks, and sunken eyes. Other faces have an earthly and sensual leer; some are wrought into expressions of scorn and mockery, some of supplicating agony, and some of grim, despair.

One wonders what gloomy, sarcastic, poetic, passionate mind has thus amused itself, recording in stone all the range of passions—saintly, earthly, and diabolic—on the varying human face. One fancies each corbel to have had its history, its archetype in nature; a thousand possible stories spring into one's mind. They are wrought with such a startling and individual definiteness, that one feels as about Shakspeare's characters, as if they must have had a counterpart in real existence. The pure, saintly nun may have been some sister, or some daughter, or some early love, of the artist, who in an evil hour saw the convent barriers rise between her and all that was loving. The fat, sensual face may have been a sly sarcasm on some worthy abbot, more eminent in flesh than spirit. The fiendish faces may have been wrought out of the author's own perturbed dreams.

An architectural work says that one of these corbels, with an anxious and sinister Oriental countenance, has been made, by the guides, to perform duty as an authentic likeness of the wizard Michael Scott. Now, I must earnestly protest against stating things in that way. Why does a writer want to break up so laudable a poetic design in the guides? He would have been much better occupied in interpreting some of the half-defaced old inscriptions into a corroborative account. No doubt it *was* Michael Scott, and looked just like him.

It were a fine field for a story writer to analyze the conception and growth of an abbey or cathedral as it formed itself, day after day, and year after year, in the soul of some dreamy, impassioned workman, who made it the note book where he wrought out imperishably in stone all his observations on nature and man. I think it is this strong individualism of the architect in the buildings that give the never-dying charm, and variety to the Gothic: each Gothic building is a record of the growth, character, and individualities of its builder's soul; and hence no two can be alike.

I was really disappointed to miss in the abbey the stained glass which gives such a lustre and glow to the poetic description. I might have known better; but somehow I came there fully expecting to see the window, where—

"Full in the midst his cross of red

Triumphant Michael brandished;

The moonbeam kissed the holy pane,

And threw on the pavement the bloody stain."

Alas! the painted glass was all of the poet's own setting; years ago it was shattered by the hands of violence, and the grace of the fashion of it hath perished.

The guide pointed to a broken fragment which commanded a view of the whole interior. "Sir Walter used to sit here," he said. I fancied I could see him sitting on the fragment, gazing around the ruin, and mentally restoring it to its original splendor; he brings back the colored light into the windows, and throws its many-hued reflections over the graves; he ranges the banners along around the walls, and rebuilds every shattered arch and aisle, till we have the picture as it rises on us in his book.

I confess to a strong feeling of reality, when my guide took me to a grave where a flat, green, mossy stone, broken across the middle, is reputed to be the grave of Michael Scott. I felt, for the moment, verily persuaded that if the guide would pry up one of the stones we should see him there, as described:—

"His hoary beard in silver rolled,

He seemed some seventy winters old;

A palmer's amice wrapped, him round,

> With a wrought Spanish baldric bound,
>
> Like a pilgrim from beyond the sea:
>
> His left hand held his book of might;
>
> A silver cross was in his right;
>
> The lamp was placed beside his knee;
>
> High and majestic was his look,
>
> At which, the fellest fiends had shook,
>
> And all unruffled, was his face:
>
> They trusted his soul had gotten grace."

I never knew before how fervent a believer I had been in the realities of these things.

There are two graves that I saw, which correspond to those mentioned in these lines:—

> "And there the dying lamps did burn
>
> Before thy lone and lowly urn,
>
> O gallafit chief of Otterburne,
>
> And thine, dark knight of Liddesdale."

The Knight of Otterburne was one of the Earls Douglas, killed in a battle with Henry Percy, called Hotspur, in 1388. The Knight of Liddesdale was another Douglas, who lived in the reign of David II., and was called the "Flower of Chivalry." One performance of this "Flower" is rather characteristic of the times. It seems the king made one Ramsey high sheriff of Teviotdale. The Earl of Douglas chose to consider this as a personal affront, as he wanted the office himself. So, by way of exhibiting his own qualifications for administering justice, he one day came down on Ramsey, *vi et armis*, took him off his judgment seat, carried him to one of his castles, and without more words tumbled him and his horse into a deep dungeon, where they both starved to death. There's a "Flower" for you, peculiar to the good old times. Nobody could have doubted after this his qualifications to be high sheriff.

Having looked all over the abbey from below, I noticed a ruinous winding staircase; so up I went, rustling along through the ivy, which matted and wove itself around the stones. Soon I found myself looking down on the abbey from a new point of view—from a little narrow stone gallery, which threads the whole inside of the building. There I paced up and down, looking occasionally through the ivy-wreathed arches on the green, turfy floor below.

It seems as if silence and stillness had become a real presence in these old places. The voice of the guide and the company beneath had a hushed and muffled sound; and when I rustled the ivy leaves, or, in trying to break off a branch, loosened some fragment of stone, the sound affected me with a startling distinctness. I could not but inly muse and wonder on the life these old monks and abbots led, shrined up here as they were in this lovely retirement.

In ruder ages these places were the only retreat for men of a spirit too gentle to take force and bloodshed for their life's work; men who believed that pen and parchment were better than sword and steel. Here I suppose multitudes of them lived harmless, dreamy lives—reading old manuscripts, copying and illuminating new ones.

It is said that this Melrose is of very ancient origin, extending back to the time of the Culdees, the earliest missionaries who established religion in Scotland, and who had a settlement in this vicinity. However, a royal saint, after a while, took it in hand to patronize, and of course the credit went to him, and from, him Scott calls it "St. David's lonely pile." In time a body of Cistercian monks were settled there.

According to all accounts the abbey has raised some famous saints. We read of trances, illuminations, and miraculous beatifications; and of one abbot in particular, who exhibited the odor of sanctity so strongly that it is said the mere opening of his grave, at intervals, was sufficient to perfume the whole establishment with odors of paradise. Such stories apart, however, we must consider that for all the literature, art, and love of the beautiful, all the humanizing influences which hold society together, the world was for many ages indebted to these monastic institutions.

In the reformation, this abbey was destroyed amid the general storm, which attacked the ecclesiastical architecture of Scotland. "Pull down the nest, and the rooks will fly away," was the common saying of the mob; and in those days a man was famous according as he had lifted up axes upon the carved work.

Melrose was considered for many years merely a stone quarry, from which materials were taken for all sorts of buildings, such as constructing tolbooths, repairing mills and sluices; and it has been only till a comparatively recent period that its priceless value as an architectural remain has led to proper efforts for its preservation. It is now most carefully kept.

After wandering through the inside we walked out into the old graveyard, to look at the outside. The yard is full of old, curious, mouldering gravestones; and on one of them there is an inscription sad and peculiar enough to have come from the heart of the architect who planned the abbey; it runs as follows:—

"The earth walks on the earth, glittering with gold;

The earth goes to the earth sooner than it wold;

The earth, builds on the earth, castles and towers;

The earth, says to the earth, All shall be ours."

Here, also, we were interested in a plain marble slab, which marks the last resting-place of Scott's faithful Tom Purdie, his zealous factotum. In his diary, when he hears of the wreck of his fortunes, Scott says of this serving man, "Poor Tom Purdie, such news will wring your heart, and many a poor fellow's beside, to whom my prosperity was daily bread."

One fancies again the picture described by Lockhart, the strong, lank frame, hard features, sunken eyes, and grizzled eyebrows, the green jacket, white hat, and gray trousers—the outer appointments of the faithful serving man. One sees Scott walking familiarly by his side, staying himself on Tom's shoulder, while Tom talks with glee of "*our* trees," and "*our* bukes." One sees the little skirmishing, when master wants trees planted one way and man sees best to plant them another; and the magnanimity with which kindly, cross-grained Tom at last agrees, on reflection, to "take his honor's advice" about the management of his honor's own property. Here, between master and man, both freemen, is all that beauty of relation sometimes erroneously considered as the peculiar charm of slavery. Would it have made the relation any more picturesque and endearing had Tom been stripped of legal rights, and made liable to sale with the books and furniture of Abbotsford? Poor Tom is sleeping here very quietly, with a smooth coverlet of green grass. Over him is the following inscription: "Here lies the body of Thomas Purdie, wood forester at Abbotsford, who died 29th October, 1829, aged sixty-two years. Thou hast been faithful over a few things, I will make thee ruler over many things." Matt. xxv. 21.

We walked up, and down, and about, getting the best views of the building. It is scarcely possible for description to give you the picture. The artist, in whose mind the conception of this building arose, was a Mozart in architecture; a plaintive and ethereal lightness, a fanciful quaintness, pervaded his composition. The building is not a large one, and it has not that air of solemn massive grandeur, that plain majesty, which impresses you in the cathedrals of Aberdeen and Glasgow. As you stand looking at the wilderness of minarets and flying buttresses, the multiplied shrines, and mouldings, and cornices, all incrusted with carving as endless in its variety as the frostwork on a window pane; each shrine, each pinnace, each moulding, a study by itself, yet each contributing, like the different strains of a harmony, to the general effect of the whole; it seems to you that for a thing so airy and spiritual to have sprung up by enchantment, and to have been the product of spells and fairy fingers, is no improbable account of the matter.

Speaking of gargoyles—you are no architect, neither am I, but you may as well get used to this descriptive term; it means the water-spouts which conduct the water from the gutters at the eaves of these buildings, and which are carved in every grotesque and fanciful device that can be imagined. They are mostly goblin and fiendish faces, and look as if they were darting out of the church in a towering passion, or a fit of diabolic disgust and malice. Besides these gargoyles, there are in many other points of the external building representations of fiendish faces and figures, as if in the act of flying from the building, under the influence of a terrible spell: by this, as my guide said, was expressed the idea that the holy hymns and worship of the church put Satan and all his forces to rout, and made all that was evil flee.

One remark on this building, in Billings's architectural account of it, interested me; and that is, that it is finished with the most circumstantial elegance and minuteness in those concealed portions which are excluded, from public view, and which can only be inspected by laborious climbing or groping; and he accounts for this by the idea that the whole carving and execution was considered as an act of solemn worship and adoration, in which the artist offered up his best faculties to the praise of the Creator.

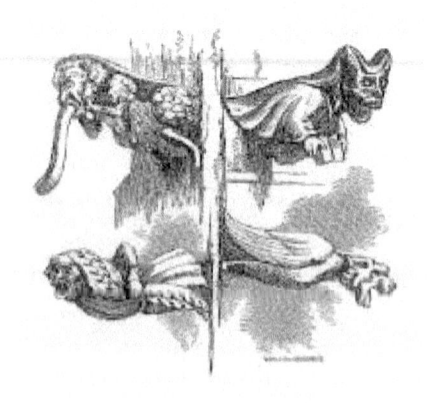

After lingering a while here, we went home to our inn or hotel. Now, these hotels in the small towns of England, if this is any specimen, are delightful affairs for travellers, they are so comfortable and home-like. Our snug little parlor was radiant with the light of the coal grate; our table stood before it, with its bright silver, white cloth, and delicate china cups; and then such a dish of mutton chops! My dear, we are all mortal, and emotions of the beautiful and sublime tend especially to make one hungry. We, therefore, comforted ourselves over the instability of earthly affairs, and the transitory nature of all human grandeur, by consolatory remarks on the present whiteness of the bread, the sweetness of the butter; and as to the chops, all declared, with one voice, that such mutton was a thing unknown in America. I moved an emendation, except on the sea coast of Maine. We resolved to cherish the memory of our little hostess in our heart of hearts, and as we gathered round the cheery grate, drying our cold feet, we voted that poetry was a humbug, and damp, old, musty cathedrals a bore. Such are the inconsistencies of human nature!

"Nevertheless," said I to S——, after dinner, "I am going back again to-night, to see that abbey by moonlight. I intend to walk the whole figure while I am about it."

Just on the verge of twilight I stepped out, to see what the town afforded in the way of relics. To say the truth, my eye had been caught by some cunning little tubs and pails in a window, which I thought might be valued in the home department. I went into a shop, where an auld wife soon appeared, who, in reply to my inquiries, told me, that the said little tubs and pails were made of plum tree wood from Dryburgh Abbey, and, of course, partook of the sanctity of relics. She and her husband seemed to be driving a thriving trade in the article, and either plum trees must be very abundant at Dryburgh, or what there are must be gifted with that power of self-multiplication which inheres in the wood of the true Cross. I bought them in blind faith, however, suppressing all rationalistic doubts, as a good relic hunter should.

I went up into a little room where an elderly woman professed to have quite a collection of the Melrose relics. Some years ago extensive restorations and repairs were made in the old abbey, in which Walter Scott took a deep interest. At that time, when the scaffolding was up for repairing the building, as I understood, Scott had the plaster casts made of different parts, which he afterwards incorporated into his own dwelling at Abbotsford. I said to the good woman that I had understood by Washington Irving's account, that Scott appropriated *bona fide* fragments of the building, and alluded to the account which he gives of the little red sandstone lion from Melrose. She repelled the idea with great energy, and said she had often heard Sir Walter say, that he would not carry off a bit of the building as big as his thumb. She showed me several plaster casts that she had in her possession, which were taken at this time. There were several corbels there; one was the head of an old monk, and looked as if it might have been a mask taken of his face the moment after death; the eyes were hollow and sunken, the cheeks fallen in, the mouth lying helplessly open, showing one or two melancholy old stumps of teeth. I wondered over this, whether it really was the fac-simile of some poor old Father Ambrose, or Father Francis, whose disconsolate look, after his death agony, had so struck the gloomy fancy of the artist as to lead him to immortalize him in a corbel, for a lasting admonition to his fat worldly brethren; for if we may trust the old song, these monks of Melrose had rather a suspicious reputation in the matter of worldly conformity. The impudent ballad says,—

"O, the monks of Melrose, they made good, kail

On Fridays, when they fasted;

They never wanted beef or ale

As long as their neighbors' lasted."

Naughty, roistering fellows! I thought I could perceive how this poor Father Francis had worn his life out exhorting them to repentance, and given up the ghost at last in despair, and so been made at once into a saint and a corbel.

There were fragments of tracery, of mouldings and cornices, and grotesque bits of architecture there, which I would have given a good deal to be the possessor of. Stepping into a little cottage hard by to speak to the guide about unlocking the gates, when we went out on our moonlight excursion at midnight, I caught a glimpse, in an inner apartment, of a splendid, large, black dog. I gave one exclamation and jump, and was into the room after him.

"Ah," said the old man, "that was just like Sir Walter; he always had an eye for a dog."

It gave me a kind of pain to think of him and his dogs, all lying in the dust together; and yet it was pleasant to hear this little remark of him, as if it were made by those who had often seen, and were fond of thinking of him. The dog's name was Coal, and he was black enough, and remarkable enough, to make a figure in a story—a genuine Melrose Abbey dog. I should not wonder if he were a descendant, in a remote degree, of the "mauthe doog," that supernatural beast, which Scott commemorates in his notes. The least touch in the world of such blood in his veins would be, of course, an appropriate circumstance in a dog belonging to an old ruined abbey.

Well, I got home, and narrated my adventures to my friends, and showed them my reliquary purchases, and declared my strengthening intention to make my ghostly visit by moonlight, if there was any moon to be had that night, which was a doubtful possibility.

In the course of the evening came in Mr. ——, who had volunteered his services as guide and attendant during the interesting operation.

"When does the moon rise?" said one.

"O, a little after eleven o'clock, I believe," said Mr. ——.

Some of the party gaped portentously.

"You know," said I, "Scott says we must see it by moonlight; it is one of the proprieties of the place, as I understand."

"How exquisite that description is, of the effect of moonlight!" says another.

"I think it probable," says Mr. ——, dryly, "that Scott never saw it by moonlight himself. He was a man of very regular habits, and seldom went out evenings."

The blank amazement with which this communication was received set S——— into an inextinguishable fit of laughter.

"But do you really believe he never saw it?" said I, rather crestfallen.

"Well," said the gentleman, "I have heard him charged with never having seen it, and he never denied it."

Knowing that Scott really was as practical a man as Dr. Franklin, and as little disposed to poetic extravagances, and an exceedingly sensible, family kind of person, I thought very probably this might be true, unless he had seen it some time in his early youth. Most likely good Mrs. Scott never would have let him commit the impropriety that we were about to, and run the risk of catching the rheumatism by going out to see how an old abbey looked at twelve o'clock at night.

We waited for the moon to rise, and of course it did not rise; nothing ever does when it is waited for. We went to one window, and went to another, half past eleven came, and no moon. "Let us give it up," said I, feeling rather foolish. However, we agreed to wait another quarter of an hour, and finally Mr. —— announced that the moon *was* risen; the only reason we did not see it was, because it was behind the Eildon Hills. So we voted to consider her risen at any rate, and started out in the dark, threading the narrow streets of the village with the comforting reflection that we were doing what Sir Walter would think rather a silly thing. When we got out before the abbey there was enough light behind the Eildon Hills to throw their three shadowy cones out distinctly to view, and to touch with a gloaming, uncertain ray the ivy-clad walls. As we stood before the abbey, the guide fumbling with his keys, and finally heard the old lock clash as the door slowly opened to admit us, I felt a little shiver of the ghostly come over me, just enough to make it agreeable.

In the daytime we had criticized Walter Scott's moonlight description in the lines which say,—

> "The distant Tweed is heard, to rave,
>
> And the owlet to hoot o'er the dead man's grave."

"We hear nothing of the Tweed, at any rate," said we; "that must be a poetic license." But now at midnight, as we walked silently through the mouldering aisles, the brawl of the Tweed was so distinctly heard that it seemed as if it was close by the old, lonely pile; nor can any term describe the sound more exactly than the word "rave," which the poet has chosen. It was the precise accuracy of this little item of description which made me feel as if Scott must have been here in the night. I walked up into the old chancel, and sat down where William of Deloraine and the monk sat, on the Scottish monarch's tomb, and thought over the words

> "Strange sounds along the chancel passed,
>
> And banners wave without a blast;
>
> Still spake the monk when the bell tolled one."

And while we were there the bell tolled twelve.

And then we went to Michael Scott's grave, and we looked through the east oriel, with its

> "Slender shafts of shapely stone,
>
> By foliage tracery combined."

The fanciful outlines showed all the more distinctly for the entire darkness within, and the gloaming moonlight without. The tall arches seemed higher in their dimness, and vaster than they did in the daytime. "Hark!" said I; "what's that?" as we heard a rustling and flutter of wings in the ivy branches over our heads. Only a couple of rooks, whose antiquarian slumbers were disturbed by the unwonted noise there at midnight, and who rose and flew away, rattling down some fragments of the ruin as they went. It was somewhat odd, but I could not help fancying, what if these strange, goblin rooks were the spirits of old monks coming back to nestle and brood among their ancient cloisters! Rooks are a ghostly sort of bird. I think they were made on purpose to live in old yew trees and ivy, as much as yew trees and ivy were to grow round old churches and abbeys. If we once could get inside of a rook's skull, to find out what he is thinking of, I'll warrant that we should know a great deal more about these old buildings than we do now. I should not wonder if there were long traditionary histories handed down from one generation of rooks to another, and that these are what they are talking about when we think they are only chattering. I imagine I see the whole black fraternity the next day, sitting, one on a gargoyle, one on a buttress, another on a shrine, gossiping over the event of our nightly visit.

We walked up and down the long aisles, and groped out into the cloisters; and then I thought, to get the full ghostliness of the thing, we would go up the old, ruined staircase into the long galleries, that

"Midway thread the abbey wall."

We got about half way up, when there came into our faces one of those sudden, passionate puffs of mist and rain which Scotch clouds seem to have the faculty of getting up at a minute's notice. Whish! came the wind in our faces, like the rustling of a whole army of spirits down the staircase; whereat we all tumbled back promiscuously on to each other, and concluded we would not go up. In fact we had done the thing, and so we went home; and I dreamed of arches, and corbels, and gargoyles all night. And so, farewell to Melrose Abbey.

LETTER IX

Edinburgh, April.

My Dear Sister:—

Mr. S. and C—— returned from their trip to Glasgow much delighted with the prospects indicated by the results of the temperance meetings they attended there.

They were present at the meeting of the Scottish Temperance League, in an audience of about four thousand people. The reports were encouraging, and the feeling enthusiastic. One hundred and eighty ministers are on the list of the League, forming a nucleus of able, talented, and determined operators. It is the intention to make a movement for a law which shall secure to Scotland some of the benefits of the Maine law.

It appears to me that on the questions of temperance and antislavery, the religious communities of the two countries are in a situation mutually to benefit each other. Our church and ministry have been through a long struggle and warfare on this temperance question, in which a very valuable experience has been, elaborated. The religious people of Great Britain, on the contrary, have led on to a successful result a great antislavery experiment, wherein their experience and success can be equally beneficial and encouraging to us.

The day after we returned from Melrose we spent in resting and riding about, as we had two engagements in the evening—one at a party at the house of Mr. Douglas, of Cavers, and the other at a public temperance *soirée*. Mr. Douglas is the author of several works which have excited attention; but perhaps you will remember him best by his treatise on the Advancement of Society in Religion and Knowledge. He is what is called here a "laird," a man of good family, a large landed proprietor, a zealous reformer, and a very devout man.

We went early to spend a short time with the family. I was a little surprised, as I entered the hall, to find myself in the midst of a large circle of well-dressed men and women, who stood apparently waiting to receive us, and who bowed, courtesied, and smiled as we came in. Mrs. D. apologized to me afterwards, saying that these were the servants of the family, that they were exceedingly anxious to see me, and so she had allowed them all to come into the hall. They were so respectable in their appearance, and so neatly dressed, that I might almost have mistaken them for visitors.

We had a very pleasant hour or two with the family, which I enjoyed exceedingly. Mr. and Mrs. Douglas were full of the most considerate kindness, and some of the daughters had intimate acquaintances in America. I enjoy these little glimpses into family circles more than any thing else; there is no warmth like fireside warmth.

In the evening the rooms were filled. I should think all the clergymen of Edinburgh must have been there, for I was introduced to ministers without number. The Scotch have a good many little ways that are like ours; they call their clergy ministers, as we do. There were many persons from ancient families, distinguished in Scottish history both for rank and piety; among others, Lady Carstairs, Sir Henry Moncrief and lady. There was also the Countess of Gainsborough, one of the ladies of the queen's household, a very beautiful woman with charming manners, reminding one of the line of Pope—

"Graceful ease, and sweetness void of pride."

I was introduced to Dr. John Brown, who is reckoned one of the best exegetial scholars in Europe. He is small of stature, sprightly, and pleasant in manners, but with a high bald forehead and snow-white hair.

There were also many members of the faculty of the university. I talked a little with Dr. Guthrie, whom I described in a former letter. I told him that one thing which had been an agreeable disappointment to me was, the apparent cordiality between the members of the Free and the National church. He seemed to think that the wounds of the old conflict were, to a great extent, healed. He spoke in high terms of the Duchess of Sutherland, her affability, kindness, and considerateness to the poor. I forget from whom I received the anecdote, but somebody told me this of her—that, one of her servants having lost a relative, she had left a party where she was engaged, and gone in the plainest attire and quietest way to attend the funeral. It was remarked upon as showing her considerateness for the feelings of those in inferior positions.

About nine o'clock we left to go to the temperance *soirée*. It was in the same place, and conducted in the same way, with the others which I have described. The lord provost presided, and one or two of the working men who spoke in the former *soirée* made speeches, and very good ones too. The meeting was greatly enlivened by the presence and speech of the jovial Lord Conynghame, who amused us all by the gallant manner in which he expressed the warmth of Scottish welcome towards "our American guests." If it had been in the old times of Scottish hospitality, he said, he should have proposed a *bumper* three times three; but as that could not be done in a temperance meeting, he proposed three cheers, in which he led off with a hearty good will.

All that the Scotch people need now for the prosperity of their country is the temperance reformation; and undoubtedly they will have it. They have good sense and strength of mind enough to work out whatever they choose.

We went home tired enough.

The next day we had a few calls to make, and an invitation from Lady Drummond to visit "classic Hawthornden." Accordingly, in the forenoon, Mr. S. and I called first on Lord and Lady Gainsborough; though, she is one of the queen's household, she is staying here at Edinburgh, and the queen at Osborne. I infer therefore that the appointment includes no very onerous duties. The Earl of Gainsborough is the eldest brother of Rev. Baptist W. Noel.

Lady Gainsborough is the daughter of the Earl of Roden, who is an Irish lord of the very strictest Calvinistic persuasion: He is a devout man, and for many years, we were told, maintained a Calvinistic church of the English establishment in Paris. While Mr. S. talked with Lord Gainsborough, I talked with his lady, and Lady Roden, who was present. Lady Gainsborough inquired about our schools for the poor, and how they were conducted. I reflected a moment, and then answered that we had no schools for the poor as such, but the common school was open alike to all classes.[11]

In England and Scotland, in all classes, from the queen downward, no movements are so popular as those for the education and elevation of the poor; one is seldom in company without hearing the conversation turn upon them.

The conversation generally turned upon the condition of servants in America. I said that one of the principal difficulties in American housekeeping proceeded from the fact that there were so many other openings of profit that very few were found willing to assume the position of the servant, except as a temporary expedient; in fact, that the whole idea of service was radically different, it being a mere temporary contract to render certain services, not differing essentially from the contract of the mechanic or tradesman. The ladies said they thought there could be no family feeling among servants if that was the case; and I replied that, generally speaking, there was none; that old and attached family servants in the free states were rare exceptions.

This, I know, must look, to persons in old countries, like a hard and discouraging feature of democracy. I regard it, however, as only a temporary difficulty. Many institutions among us are in a transition state. Gradually the whole subject of the relations of labor and the industrial callings will assume a new form in America, and though we shall never be able to command the kind of service secured in aristocratic countries, yet we shall have that which will be as faithful and efficient. If domestic service can be made as pleasant, profitable, and respectable as any of the industrial callings, it will soon become as permanent.

Our next visit was to Sir William Hamilton and lady. Sir William is the able successor of Dugald Stewart and Dr. Brown in the chair of intellectual philosophy. His writings have had a wide circulation in America. He is a man of noble presence, though we were sorry to see that he was suffering from ill health. It seems to me that Scotland bears that relation to England, with regard to metaphysical inquiry, that New England does to the rest of the United States. If one counts over the names of distinguished metaphysicians, the Scotch, as compared with the English, number three to one—Reid, Stewart, Brown, all Scotchmen.

Sir William still writes and lectures. He and Mr. S. were soon discoursing on German, English, Scotch, and American metaphysics, while I was talking with Lady Hamilton and her daughters. After we came away Mr. S. said, that no man living had so thoroughly understood and analyzed the German philosophy. He said that Sir William spoke of a call which he had received from Professor Park, of Andover, and expressed himself in high terms of his metaphysical powers.

After that we went to call on George Combe, the physiologist. We found him and Mrs. Combe in a pleasant, sunny parlor, where, among other objects of artistic interest, we saw a very fine engraving of Mrs. Siddons. I was not aware until after leaving that Mrs. Combe is her daughter. Mr. Combe, though somewhat advanced, seems full of life and animation, and conversed with a great deal of warmth and interest on America, where he made a tour some years since. Like other men in Europe who sympathize in our progress, he was sanguine in the hope that the downfall of slavery must come at no distant date.

After a pleasant chat here we came home; and after an interval of rest the carriage was at the door for Hawthornden. It is about seven miles out from Edinburgh. It is a most romantic spot, on the banks of the River Esk, now the seat of Mr. James Walker Drummond. Scott has sung in the ballad of the Gray Brother,—

> Sweet are the paths, O, passing sweet,
>
> By Esk's fair streams that run,

O'er airy steep, through copse-woods deep,

Impervious to the sun.

Who knows not Melville's beechy grove,

And Roslin's rocky glen,

Dalkeith, which all the virtues love,

And classic Hawthornden?

"Melville's beechy grove" is an allusion to the grounds of Lord Melville, through which we drove on our way. The beech trees here are magnificent; fully equal to any trees of the sort which I have seen in our American forests, and they were in full leaf. They do not grow so high, but have more breadth and a wider sweep of branches; on the whole they are well worthy of a place in song.

I know in my childhood I often used to wish that I could live in a ruined castle; and this Hawthornden would be the very beau ideal of one as a romantic dwelling-place. It is an old castellated house, perched on the airy verge of a precipice, directly over the beautiful River Esk, looking down one of the most romantic glens in Scotland. Part of it is in ruins, and, hung with wreaths of ivy, it seems to stand just to look picturesque. The house itself, with its quaint, high gables, and gray, antique walls, appears old enough to take you back to the times of William Wallace. It is situated within an hour's walk of Roslin Castle and Chapel, one of the most beautiful and poetic architectural remains in Scotland.

Our drive to the place was charming. It was a showery day; but every few moments the sun blinked out, smiling through the falling rain, and making the wet leaves glitter, and the raindrops wink at each other in the most sociable manner possible. Arrived at the house, our friend, Miss S———, took us into a beautiful parlor overhanging the glen, each window of which commanded a picture better than was ever made on canvas.

We had a little chat with Lady Drummond, and then we went down to examine the caverns,—for there are caverns under the house, with long galleries and passages running from them through the rocks, some way down the river. Several apartments are hollowed out here in the rock on which the house is founded, which they told us belonged to Bruce; the tradition being, that he was hidden here for some months. There was his bed room, dining room, sitting room, and a very curious apartment where the walls were all honeycombed into little partitions, which they called his library, these little partitions being his book shelves. There are small loophole windows in these apartments, where you can look up and down the glen, and enjoy a magnificent prospect. For my part, I thought if I were Bruce, sitting there with a book in my lap, listening to the gentle brawl of the Esk, looking up and down the glen, watching the shaking raindrops on the oaks, the birches and beeches, I should have thought that was better than fighting, and that my pleasant little cave was as good an arbor on the Hill Difficulty as ever mortal man enjoyed.

There is a ponderous old two-handed sword kept here, said to have belonged to Sir William Wallace. It is considerably shorter than it was originally, but, resting on its point, it reached to the chin of a good six foot gentleman of our party. The handle is made of the horn of a sea-horse, (if you know what that is,) and has a heavy iron ball at the end. It must altogether have weighed some ten or twelve pounds. Think of a man hewing away *on men* with this!

There is a well in this cavern, down which we were directed to look and observe a hole in the side; this we were told was the entrance to another set of caverns and chambers under those in which we were, and to passages which extended down and opened out into the valley. In the olden days the approach to these caverns was not through the house, but through the side of a deep well sunk in the court yard, which communicates through a subterranean passage with this well. Those seeking entrance were let down by a windlass into the well in the court yard, and drawn up by a windlass into this cavern. There was no such accommodation at present, but we were told some enterprising tourists had explored the lower caverns. Pleasant kind of times those old days must have been, when houses had to be built like a rabbit burrow, with all these accommodations for concealment and escape.

After exploring the caverns we came up into the parlors again, and Miss S. showed me a Scottish album, in which were all sorts of sketches, memorials, autographs, and other such matters. What interested me more, she was making a collection of Scottish ballads, words and tunes. I told her that I had noticed, since I had been in Scotland, that the young ladies seemed to take very little interest in the national Scotch airs, and were all devoted to Italian; moreover, that the Scotch ballads and memories, which so interested me, seemed to have very little interest for people generally in Scotland. Miss S. was warm enough in her zeal to make up a considerable account, and so we got on well together.

While we were sitting, chatting, two young ladies came in, who had walked up the glen despite the showery day. They were protected by good, substantial outer garments, of a kind of shag or plush, and so did not fear the rain. I wanted to walk down to Roslin Castle, but the party told me there would not be time this afternoon, as we should have to return at a certain hour. I should not have been reconciled to this, had not another excursion been proposed for the purpose of exploring Roslin.

However, I determined to go a little way down the glen, and get a distant view of it, and my fair friends, the young ladies, offered to accompany me; so off we started down the winding paths, which were cut among the banks overhanging the Esk. The ground was starred over with patches of pale-yellow primroses, and for the first time I saw the heather, spreading over rocks and matting itself around the roots of trees. My companions, to whom it was the commonest thing in the world, could hardly appreciate the delight which I felt in looking at it; it was not in flower; I believe it does not blossom till some time in July or August. We have often seen it in greenhouses, and it is so hardy that it is singular it will not grow wild in America.

We walked, ran, and scrambled to an eminence which commanded a view of Roslin Chapel, the only view, I fear, which will ever gladden my eyes, for the promised expedition to it dissolved itself into mist. When on the hill top, so that I could see the chapel at a distance, I stood thinking over the ballad of Harold, in the Lay of the Last Minstrel, and the fate of the lovely Rosabel, and saying over to myself the last verses of the ballad:—

> "O'er Roslin, all that dreary night,
>
> A wondrous blaze was seen to gleam;
>
> 'Twas broader than the watchfire's light,
>
> And redder than the bright moonbeam.
>
> It glared on Roslin's castled rock,
>
> It ruddied, all the copsewood glen;

'Twas seen from Deyden's groves of oak,
And seen from cavern'd Hawthornden.

Seemed all on fire that chapel proud,
Where Roslin's chiefs uncoffined lie,
Each baron, for a sable shroud,
Sheathed in his iron panoply.

Seemed all on fire within, around,
Deep sacristy and altar's pale;
Shone every pillar foliage-bound,
And glimmered, all the dead men's mail.

Blazed battlement and pinnet high,
Blazed every rose-carved buttress fair,
So will they blaze, when fate is nigh
The lordly line of high St. Clair.

There are twenty of Roslin's barons bold
Lie buried, within that proud chapelle;
Each one the holy vault doth hold;
But the sea holds lovely Rosabelle!

And each St. Clair was buried there,
With candle, with book, and with knell;
But the sea caves rung, and the wild winds sung,
The dirge of lovely Rosabelle."

There are many allusions in this which show Scott's minute habits of observation; for instance, these two lines:—

"Blazed battlement and pinnet high,
Blazed every rose-carved buttress fair."

Every buttress, battlement, and projection of the exterior is incrusted with the most elaborate floral and leafy carving, among which the rose is often repeated, from its suggesting, by similarity of sound, Roslin.

Again, this line—

"Shone every pillar foliage-bound"—

suggests to the mind the profusion and elaborateness of the leafy decorations in the inside. Among these, one pillar, garlanded with spiral wreaths of carved foliage, is called the "Apprentice's Pillar;" the tradition being, that while the master was gone to Rome to get some further hints on executing the plan, a precocious young mason, whom he left at home, completed it in his absence. The master builder summarily knocked him on the head, as a warning to all progressive young men not to grow wiser than their teachers. Tradition points out the heads of the master and workmen among the corbels. So you see, whereas in old Greek times people used to point out their celebrities among the stars, and gave a defunct hero a place in the constellations, in the middle ages he only got a place among the corbels.

I am increasingly sorry that I was beguiled out of my personal examination of this chapel, since I have seen the plates of it in my Baronial Sketches. It is the rival of Melrose, but more elaborate; in fact, it is a perfect cataract of architectural vivacity and ingenuity, as defiant of any rules of criticism and art as the leaf-embowered arcades and arches of our American forest cathedrals. From the comparison of the plates of the engravings, I should judge there was less delicacy of taste, and more exuberance of invention, than in Melrose. One old prosaic commentator on it says that it is quite remarkable that there are no two cuts in it precisely alike; each buttress, window, and pillar is unique, though with such a general resemblance to each other as to deceive the eye.

It was built in 1446, by William St. Clair, who was Prince of Orkney, Duke of Oldenburgh, Lord of Roslin, Earl of Caithness and Strathearn, and so on *ad infinitum*. He was called the "Seemly St. Clair," from his noble deportment and elegant manners; resided in royal splendor at this Castle of Roslin, and kept a court there as Prince of Orkney. His table was served with vessels of gold and silver, and he had one lord for his master of household, one for his cup bearer, and one for his carver. His princess, Elizabeth Douglas, was served by seventy-five gentlewomen, fifty-three of whom were daughters of noblemen, and they were attended in all their excursions by a retinue of two hundred gentlemen.

These very woods and streams, which now hear nothing but the murmurs of the Esk, were all alive with the bustle of a court in those days.

The castle was now distinctly visible; it stands on an insulated rock, two hundred and twenty yards from the chapel. It has under it a set of excavations and caverns almost equally curious with those of Hawthornden; there are still some tolerably preserved rooms in it, and Mrs. W. informed me that they had once rented these rooms for a summer residence. What a delightful idea! The barons of Roslin were all buried under this Chapel, in their armor, as Scott describes in the poem. And as this family were altogether more than common folks, it is perfectly credible that on the death of one of them a miraculous light should illuminate the castle, chapel, and whole neighborhood.

It appears, by certain ancient documents, that this high and mighty house of St. Clair were in a particular manner patrons of the masonic craft. It is known that the trade of masonry was then in the hands of a secret and mysterious order, from whom probably our modern masons have descended.

The St. Clair family, it appears, were at the head of this order, with power to appoint officers and places of meeting, to punish transgressors, and otherwise to have the superintendence of all their affairs. This fact may account for such a perfect Geyser of architectural ingenuity as has been poured out upon their family chapel, which was designed for a *chef-d'oeuvre*, a concentration of the best that could be done to the honor of their patron's family. The documents which authenticate this statement are described in Billings's Baronial Antiquities. So much for "the lordly line of high St. Clair."

When we came back to the house, and after taking coffee in the drawing room, Miss S. took me over the interior, a most delightful place, full of all sorts of out-of-the-way snuggeries, and comfortable corners, and poetic irregularities. There she showed me a picture of one of the early ancestors of the family, the poet Drummond, hanging in a room, which tradition has assigned to him. It represents a man with a dark, Spanish-looking face, with the broad Elizabethan ruff, earnest, melancholy eyes, and an air half cavalier, half poet, bringing to mind the chivalrous, graceful, fastidious bard, accomplished scholar, and courtier of his time, the devout believer in the divine right of kings, and of the immunities and privileges of the upper class generally. This Drummond, it seems, was early engaged to a fair young lady, whose death rendered his beautiful retreat of Hawthornden insupportable to him, and of course, like other persons of romance, he sought refuge in foreign travel, went abroad, and remained eight years. Afterwards he came back, married, and lived here for some time.

Among other traditions of the place, it is said that Ben Jonson once walked all the way from London to visit the poet in this retreat; and a tree is still shown on the grounds under which they are said to have met. It seems that Ben's habits were rather too noisy and convivial to meet altogether the taste of his fastidious and aristocratic host; and so he had his own thoughts of him, which, being written down in a diary, were published by some indiscreet executor, after they were both dead.

We were shown an old, original edition of the poems. I must confess I never read them. Since I have seen the material the poet and novelist has on this ground, all I wonder at is, that there have not been a thousand poets to one. I should have thought they would have been as plenty as the mavis and merle, and sprouting out every where, like the primroses and heather bells.

Our American literature is unfortunate in this respect—that our nation never had any childhood, our day never had any dawn; so we have very little traditionary lore to work over.

We came home about five o'clock, and had some company in the evening. Some time to-day I had a little chat with Mrs. W. on the Quakers. She is a cultivated and thoughtful woman, and seemed to take quite impartial views, and did not consider her own sect as by any means the only form of Christianity, but maintained—what every sensible person must grant, I think—that it has had an important mission in society, even in its peculiarities. I inferred from her conversation that the system of plain dress, maintained with the nicety which they always use, is by no means a saving in a pecuniary point of view. She stated that one young friend, who had been brought up in this persuasion, gave it as her reason for not adopting its peculiar dress, that she could not afford it; that is to say, that for a given sum of money she could make a more creditable appearance were she allowed the range of form, shape, and trimming, which the ordinary style of dressing permits.

I think almost any lady, who knows the magical value of bits of trimming, and bows of ribbon judiciously adjusted in critical locations, of inserting, edging, and embroidery, considered as economic arts, must acknowledge that there is some force in the young lady's opinion. Nevertheless the Doric simplicity of a Quaker lady's dress, who is in circumstances to choose her material, has a peculiar charm. As at present advised, the Quaker ladies whom I have seen very judiciously adhere to the spirit of plain attire, without troubling themselves to maintain the exact letter. For instance, a plain straw cottage, with its white satin ribbon, is sometimes allowed to take the place of the close silk bonnet of Fox's day.

For my part, while I reverence the pious and unworldly spirit which dictated the peculiar forms of the Quaker sect, I look for a higher development of religion still, when all the beautiful artistic faculties of the soul being wholly sanctified and offered up to God, we shall no longer shun beauty in any of its forms, either in dress or household adornment, as a temptation, but rather offer it up as a sacrifice to Him who has set us the example, by making every thing beautiful in its season.

As to art and letters, I find many of my Quaker friends sympathizing in those judicious views which were taken by the society of Friends in Philadelphia, when Benjamin West developed a talent for painting, regarding such talent as an indication of the will of Him who had bestowed it. So I find many of them taking pleasure in the poetry of Scott, Longfellow, and Whittier, as developments of his wisdom who gives to the human soul its different faculties and inspirations.

More delightful society than a cultivated Quaker family cannot be found: the truthfulness, genuineness, and simplicity of character, albeit not wanting, at proper times, a shrewd dash of worldly wisdom, are very refreshing.

Mrs. W. and I went to the studio of Hervey, the Scotch artist. Both he and his wife received us with great kindness. I saw there his Covenanters celebrating the Lord's Supper—a picture which I could not look at critically on account of the tears which kept blinding my eyes. It represents a bleak hollow of a mountain side, where a few trembling old men and women, a few young girls and children, with one or two young men, are grouped together, in that moment of hushed prayerful repose which precedes the breaking of the sacramental bread. There is something touching always about that worn, weary look of rest and comfort with which a sick child lies down on a mother's bosom, and like this is the expression with which these hunted fugitives nestle themselves beneath the shadow of their Redeemer; mothers who had seen their sons "tortured, not accepting deliverance"— wives who had seen the blood of their husbands poured out on their doorstone—children with no father but God—and bereaved old men, from whom, every child had been rent—all gathering for comfort round the cross of a suffering Lord. In such hours they found strength to suffer, and to say to every allurement of worldly sense and pleasure as the drowning Margaret Wilson said to the tempters in her hour of martyrdom, "I am *Christ's child*—let me go."

Another most touching picture of Hervey's commemorates a later scene of Scottish devotion and martyr endurance scarcely below that of the days of the Covenant. It is called Leaving the Manse.

We in America all felt to our heart's core a sympathy with that high endurance which led so many Scottish ministers to forsake their churches, their salaries, the happy homes where their children were born and their days passed, rather than violate a principle.

This picture is a monument of this struggle. There rises the manse overgrown with its flowering vines, the image of a lovely, peaceful home. The minister's wife, a pale, lovely creature, is just locking the door, out of which her husband and family have passed—leaving it forever. The husband and father is supporting on his arm an aged, feeble mother, and the weeping children are gathering sorrowfully round him, each bearing away some memorial of their home; one has the bird cage. But the unequalled look of high, unshaken patience, of heroic faith, and love which seems to spread its light over every face, is what I cannot paint. The painter told me that the faces were *portraits*, and the scene by no means imaginary.

But did not these sacrifices bring with them, even in their bitterness, a joy the world knoweth not? Yes, they did. I know it full well, not vainly did Christ say, There is no man that hath left houses or lands for my sake and the gospel's but he shall receive manifold more *in this life*.

Mr. Hervey kindly gave me the engraving of his Covenanters' Sacrament, which I shall keep as a memento of him and of Scotland.

His style of painting is forcible and individual. He showed us the studies that he has taken with his palette and brushes out on the mountains and moors of Scotland, painting moss, and stone, and brook, just as it is. This is the way to be a national painter.

One pleasant evening, not long before we left Edinburgh, C., S., and I walked out for a quiet stroll. We went through the Grass Market, where so many defenders of the Covenant have suffered, and turned into the churchyard of the Gray Friars; a gray, old Gothic building, with multitudes of graves around it. Here we saw the tombs of Allan Ramsay and many other distinguished characters. The grim, uncouth sculpture on the old graves, and the quaint epitaphs, interested me much; but I was most moved by coming quite unexpectedly on an ivy-grown slab, in the wall, commemorating the martyrs of the Covenant. The inscription struck me so much, that I got C—— to copy it in his memorandum book.

> "Halt, passenger! take heed what you do see.
>
> Here lies interred the dust of those who stood
>
> 'Gainst perjury, resisting unto blood,
>
> Adhering to the Covenant, and laws

Establishing the same; which was the cause
Their lives were sacrificed unto the last
Of prelatists abjured, though here their dust
Lies mixed with murderers and other crew
Whom justice justly did to death pursue;
But as for them, no cause was to be found
Worthy of death, but only they were found
Constant and steadfast, witnessing
For the prerogatives of Christ their King;
Which truths were sealed, by famous Guthrie's head,
And all along to Mr. Renwick's blood
They did endure the wrath of enemies,
Reproaches, torments, deaths, and injuries;
But yet they're those who from such troubles came
And triumph now in glory with the Lamb.

> "From May 27, 1681, when the Marquis of Argyle was beheaded, to February 17, 1688, when James Renwick suffered, there were some eighteen thousand one way or other murdered, of whom were executed at Edinburgh about one hundred noblemen, ministers, and gentlemen, and others, noble martyrs for Christ."

Despite the roughness of the verse, there is a thrilling power in these lines. People in gilded houses, on silken couches, at ease among books, and friends, and literary pastimes, may sneer at the Covenanters; it is much easier to sneer than to die for truth and right, as they died. Whether they were right in all respects is nothing to the purpose; but it is to the purpose that in a crisis of their country's history they upheld a great principle vital to her existence. Had not these men held up the heart of Scotland, and kept alive the fire of liberty on her altars, the very literature which has been used to defame them could not have had its existence. The very literary celebrity of Scotland has grown out of their grave; for a vigorous and original literature is impossible, except to a strong, free, self-respecting people. The literature of a people must spring from the sense of its nationality; and nationality is impossible without self-respect, and self-respect is impossible without liberty.

It is one of the trials of our mortal state, one of the disciplines of our virtue, that the world's benefactors and reformers are so often without form or comeliness. The very force necessary to sustain the conflict makes them appear unlovely; they "tread the wine press alone, and of the people there is none with them." The shrieks, and groans, and agonies of men wrestling in mortal combat are often not graceful or gracious; but the comments that the children of the Puritans, and the children of the Covenanters, make on the ungraceful and severe elements which marked the struggles of their great fathers, are as ill-timed as if a son, whom a mother had just borne from a burning dwelling, should criticize the shrieks with which she sought him, and point out to ridicule the dishevelled hair and singed garments which show how she struggled for his life. But these are they which are "sown in weakness, but raised in power; which are sown in dishonor, but raised in glory:" even in this world they will have their judgment day, and their names which went down in the dust like a gallant banner trodden in the mire, shall rise again all glorious in the sight of nations.

The evening sky, glowing red, threw out the bold outline of the castle, and the quaint old edifices as they seemed to look down on us silently from their rocky heights, and the figure of Salisbury Crags marked itself against the red sky like a couchant lion.

The time of our sojourn in Scotland had drawn towards its close. Though feeble in health, this visit to me has been full of enjoyment; full of lofty, but sad memories; full of sympathies and inspirations. I think there is no nobler land, and I pray God that the old seed here sown in blood and tears may never be rooted out of Scotland.

LETTER X

My Dear H.:—

It was a rainy, misty morning when I left my kind retreat and friends in Edinburgh. Considerate as every body had been about imposing on my time or strength, still you may well believe that I was much exhausted.

We left Edinburgh, therefore, with the determination to plunge at once into some hidden and unknown spot, where we might spend two or three days quietly by ourselves; and remembering your Sunday at Stratford-on-Avon, I proposed that we should go there. As Stratford, however, is off the railroad line we determined to accept the invitation, which was lying by us, from our friend Joseph Sturge, of Birmingham, and take sanctuary with him. So we wrote on, intrusting him with the secret, and charging him on no account to let any one know of our arrival.

Well in the rail car, we went whirling along by Preston Pans, where was fought the celebrated battle in which Colonel Gardiner was killed; by Dunbar, where Cromwell told his army to "trust in God and keep their powder dry;" through Berwick-on-the-Tweed and Newcastle-on-Tyne; by the old towers and gates of York, with its splendid cathedral; getting a view of Durham Cathedral in the distance.

The country between Berwick and Newcastle is one of the greatest manufacturing districts of England, and for smoke, smut, and gloom, Pittsburg and Wheeling bear no comparison to it. The English sky, always paler and cooler in its tints than ours, here seems to be turned into a leaden canopy; tall chimneys belch forth gloom and confusion; houses, factories, fences, even trees and grass, look grim and sooty.

It is true that people with immense wealth can live in such regions in cleanliness and elegance; but how must it be with the poor? I know of no one circumstance more unfavorable to moral purity than the necessity of being physically dirty. Our nature is so intensely symbolical, that where the outward sign of defilement becomes habitual, the inner is too apt to correspond. I am quite sure that before there can be a universal millennium, trade must be pursued in such a way as to enable the working classes to realize something of beauty and purity in the circumstances of their outward life.

I have heard there is a law before the British Parliament, whose operation is designed to purify the air of England by introducing chimneys which shall consume all the sooty particles which now float about, obscuring the air and carrying defilement with them. May that day be hastened!

At Newcastle-on-Tyne and some other places various friends came out to meet us, some of whom presented us with most splendid bouquets of hothouse flowers. This region has been the seat of some of the most zealous and efficient antislavery operations in England.

About night our cars whizzed into the depot at Birmingham; but just before we came in a difficulty was started in the company. "Mr. Sturge is to be there waiting for us, but he does not know us, and we don't know him; what is to be done?" C—— insisted that he should know him by instinct; and so after we reached the depot, we told him to sally out and try. Sure enough, in a few moments he pitched upon a cheerful, middle-aged gentleman, with a moderate but not decisive broad brim to his hat, and challenged him as Mr. Sturge; the result verified the truth that "instinct is a great matter." In a few moments our new friend and ourselves were snugly encased in a fly, trotting off as briskly as ever we could to his place at Edgbaston, nobody a whit the wiser. You do not know how snug we felt to think we had done it so nicely.

The carriage soon drove in upon a gravel walk, winding among turf, flowers, and shrubs, where we found opening to us another home as warm and kindly as the one we had just left, made doubly interesting by the idea of entire privacy and seclusion.

After retiring to our chambers to repair the ravages of travel, we united in the pleasant supper room, where the table was laid before a bright coal fire: no unimportant feature this fire, I can assure you, in a raw cloudy evening. A glass door from the supper room opened into a conservatory, brilliant with pink and yellow azalias, golden calceolarias, and a profusion of other beauties, whose names I did not know.

The side tables were strewn with books, and the ample folds of the drab curtains, let down over the windows, shut out the rain, damp, and chill. When we were gathered round the table, Mr. Sturge said that he had somewhat expected Elihu Burritt that evening, and we all hoped he would come. I must not omit to say, that the evening circle was made more attractive and agreeable in my eyes by the presence of two or three of the little people, who were blessed with the rosy cheek of English children.

Mr. Sturge is one of the most prominent and efficient of the philanthropists of modern days. An air of benignity and easy good nature veils and conceals in him the most unflinching perseverance and energy of purpose. He has for many years been a zealous advocate of the antislavery cause in England, taking up efficiently the work begun by Clarkson and

Wilberforce. He, with a friend of the same denomination, made a journey at their own expense, to investigate the workings of the apprentice system, by which the act of immediate emancipation in the West Indies was for a while delayed. After his return he sustained a rigorous examination of seven days before a committee of the House of Commons, the result of which successfully demonstrated the abuses of that system, and its entire inutility for preparing either masters or servants for final emancipation. This evidence went as far as any thing to induce Parliament to declare immediate and entire emancipation.

Mr. Sturge also has been equally zealous and engaged in movements for the ignorant and perishing classes at home. At his own expense he has sustained a private Farm School for the reformation of juvenile offenders, and it has sometimes been found that boys, whom no severity and no punishment seemed to affect, have been entirely melted and subdued by the gentler measures here employed. He has also taken a very ardent and decided part in efforts for the extension of the principles of peace, being a warm friend and supporter of Elihu Burritt.

The next morning it was agreed that we should take our drive to Stratford-on-Avon. As yet this shrine of pilgrims stands a little aloof from the bustle of modern progress, and railroad cars do not run whistling and whisking with brisk officiousness by the old church and the fanciful banks of the Avon.

The country that we were to pass over was more peculiarly old English; that phase of old English which is destined soon to pass away, under the restless regenerating force of modern progress.

Our ride along was a singular commixture of an upper and under current of thought. Deep down in our hearts we were going back to English days; the cumbrous, quaint, queer, old, picturesque times; the dim, haunted times between cock-crowing and morning; those hours of national childhood, when popular ideas had the confiding credulity, the poetic vivacity, and versatile life, which distinguish children from grown people.

No one can fail to feel, in reading any of the plays of Shakspeare, that he was born in an age of credulity and marvels, and that the materials out of which his mind was woven were dyed in the grain, in the haunted springs of tradition. It would have been as absolutely impossible for even himself, had he been born in the daylight of this century, to have built those quaint, Gothic structures of imagination, and tinted them with their peculiar coloring of marvellousness and mystery, as for a modern artist to originate and execute the weird designs of an ancient cathedral. Both Gothic architecture and this perfection of Gothic poetry were the springing and efflorescence of that age, impossible to grow again. They were the forest primeval; other trees may spring in their room, trees as mighty and as fair, but not such trees.

So, as we rode along, our speculations and thoughts in the under current were back in the old world of tradition. While, on the other hand, for the upper current, we were keeping up a brisk conversation on the peace question, on the abolition of slavery, on the possibility of ignoring slave-grown produce, on Mr. Cobden and Mr. Bright, and, in fact, on all the most wide-awake topics of the present day.

One little incident occurred upon the road. As we were passing by a quaint old mansion, which stood back from the road, surrounded by a deep court, Mr. S. said to me, "There is a friend here who would like to see thee, if thou hast no objections," and went on to inform me that she was an aged woman, who had taken a deep interest in the abolition of slavery since the time of its first inception under Clarkson and Wilberforce, though now lying very low on a sick bed. Of course we all expressed our willingness to stop, and the carriage was soon driving up the gravelled walk towards the house. We were ushered into a comfortable sitting room, which looked out on beautiful grounds, where the velvet grass, tall, dark trees, and a certain quaint air of antiquity in disposition and arrangement, gave me a singular kind of pleasure; the more so, that it came to me like a dream; that the house and the people were unknown to me, and the whole affair entirely unexpected.

I was soon shown into a neat chamber, where an aged woman was lying in bed. I was very much struck and impressed by her manner of receiving me. With deep emotion and tears, she spoke of the solemnity and sacredness of the cause which had for years lain near her heart. There seemed to be something almost prophetic in the solemn strain of assurance with which she spoke of the final extinction of slavery throughout the world.

I felt both pleased and sorrowful. I felt sorrowful because I knew, if all true Christians in America had the same feelings, that men, women, and children, for whom Christ died, would no more be sold in my country on the auction block.

There have been those in America who have felt and prayed thus nobly and sincerely for the heathen in Burmah and Hindostan, and that sentiment was a beautiful and an ennobling one; but, alas! the number has been few who have felt and prayed for the heathenism, and shame of our own country; for the heathenism which sells the very members of the body of Christ as merchandise.

When we were again on the road, we were talking on the change of times in England since railroads began; and Mr. S. gave an amusing description of how the old lords used to travel in state, with their coaches and horses, when they went up once a year on a solemn pilgrimage to London, with postilions and outriders, and all the country gaping and wondering after them.

"I wonder," said one of us, "if Shakspeare were living, what he would say to our times, and what he would think of all the questions that are agitating the world now." That he did have thoughts whose roots ran far beyond the depth of the age in which he lived, is plain enough from numberless indications in his plays; but whether he would have taken any practical interest in the world's movements is a fair question. The poetic mind is not always the progressive one; it has, like moss and ivy, a need for something old to cling to and germinate upon. The artistic temperament, too, is soft and sensitive; so there are all these reasons for thinking that perhaps he would have been for keeping out of the way of the heat and dust of modern progress. It does not follow because a man has penetration to see an evil, he has energy to reform it.

Erasmus saw all that Luther saw just as clearly, but he said that he had rather never have truth at all, than contend for it with the world in such a tumult. However, on the other hand, England did, in Milton, have one poet who girt himself up to the roughest and stormiest work of reformation; so it is not quite certain, after all, that Shakspeare might not have been a reformer in our times. One thing is quite certain, that he would have said very shrewd things about all the matters that move the world now, as he certainly did about all matters that he was cognizant of in his own day.

It was a little before noon when we drove into Stratford, by which time, with our usual fatality in visiting poetic shrines, the day had melted off into a kind of drizzling mist, strongly suggestive of a downright rain. It is a common trick these English days have; the weather here seems to be possessed of a water spirit. This constant drizzle is good for ivies, and hawthorns, and ladies' complexions, as whoever travels here will observe, but it certainly is very bad for tourists.

This Stratford is a small town, of between three and four thousand inhabitants, and has in it a good many quaint old houses, and is characterized (so I thought) by an air of respectable, stand-still, and meditative repose, which, I am afraid, will entirely give way before the railroad demon, for I understand that it is soon to be connected by the Oxford, Worcester, and Wolverhampton line with all parts of the kingdom. Just think of that black little screeching imp rushing through these fields which have inspired so many fancies; how every thing poetical will fly before it! Think of such sweet snatches as these set to the tune of a railroad whistle:—

> "Hark! hark! the lark at heaven's gate sings,
> And Phoebus 'gins to rise,
> His steeds to water at those springs
> On chaliced flowers that lies.
>
> And winking Mary-buds begin
> To ope their golden eyes,
> With everything that pretty bid
> My lady sweet to rise."

And again:—

> "Philomel with melody sing in our sweet lullaby,
> Lulla, lulla, lullaby.
> Never harm, nor spell, nor charm,
> Come our lovely lady nigh."

I suppose the meadows, with their "winking Mary-buds," will be all cut up into building lots in the good times coming, and Philomel caught and put in a cage to sing to tourists at threepence a head.

We went to the White Lion, and soon had a little quiet parlor to ourselves, neatly carpeted, with a sofa drawn up to the cheerful coal fire, a good-toned piano, and in short every thing cheerful and comfortable.

At first we thought we were too tired to do any thing till after dinner; we were going to take time to rest ourselves and proceed leisurely; so, while the cloth was laying, C—— took possession of the piano, and I of the sofa, till Mr. S. came in upon us, saying, "Why, Shakspeare's house is right the next door here!" Upon that we got up, just to take a peep, and from peeping we proceeded to looking, and finally put on our things and went over *seriatim*. The house has recently been bought by a Shakspearian club, who have taken upon themselves the restoration and preservation of the premises.

Shakspeare's father, it seems, was a man of some position and substance in his day, being high sheriff and justice of the peace for the borough; and this house, therefore, I suppose, may be considered a specimen of the respectable class of houses in the times of Queen Elizabeth. This cut is taken from an old print, and is supposed to represent the original condition of the house.

We saw a good many old houses somewhat similar to this on the road, particularly resembling it in this manner of plastering, which shows all the timber on the outside. Parts of the house have been sold, altered, and used for various purposes; a butcher's stall having been kept in a part of it, and a tavern in another portion, being new-fronted with brick.

The object of this Shakspeare Club has been to repurchase all these parts, and restore them as nearly as possible to their primeval condition. The part of the house which is shown consists of a lower room, which is floored with flat stones very much broken. It has a wide, old-fashioned chimney on one side, and opens into a smaller room back of it. From thence you go up a rude flight of stairs to a low-studded room, with rough-plastered walls, where the poet was born.

The prints of this room, which are generally sold, allow themselves in considerable poetic license, representing it in fact as quite an elegant apartment, whereas, though it is kept scrupulously neat and clean, the air of it is ancient and rude. This is a somewhat flattered likeness. The roughly-plastered walls are so covered with names that it seemed impossible to add another. The name of almost every modern genius, names of kings, princes, dukes, are shown here; and it is really curious to see by what devices some very insignificant personages have endeavored to make their own names conspicuous in the crowd. Generally speaking the inscription books and walls of distinguished places tend to give great force to the Vulgate rendering of Ecclesiastes i. 15, "The number of fools is infinite."

To add a name in a private, modest way to walls already so crowded, is allowable; but to scrawl one's name, place of birth, and country, half across a wall, covering scores of names under it, is an operation which speaks for itself. No one would ever want to know more of a man than to see his name there and thus.

Back of this room were some small bed rooms, and what interested me much, a staircase leading up into a dark garret. I could not but fancy I saw a bright-eyed, curly-headed boy creeping up those stairs, zealous to explore the mysteries of that dark garret. There perhaps he saw the cat, with "eyne of burning coal, crouching 'fore the mouse's hole." Doubtless in this old garret were wonderful mysteries to him, curious stores of old cast-off goods and furniture, and rats, and mice, and cobwebs. I fancied the indignation of some belligerent grandmother or aunt, who finds Willie up there watching a mouse hole, with the cat, and has him down straightway, grumbling that Mary did not govern that child better.

We know nothing who this Mary was that was his mother; but one sometimes wonders where in that coarse age, when queens and ladies talked familiarly, as women would blush to talk now, and when the broad, coarse wit of the Merry Wives of Windsor was gotten up to suit the taste of a virgin queen,—one wonders, I say, when women were such and so, where he found those models of lily-like purity, women so chaste in soul and pure in language that they could not even bring their lips to utter a word of shame. Desdemona cannot even bring herself to speak the coarse word with which her husband taunts her; she cannot make herself believe that there are women in the world who could stoop-to such grossness.[12]

For my part I cannot believe that, in such an age, such deep heart-knowledge of pure womanhood could have come otherwise than by the impression on the child's soul of a mother's purity. I seem to have a vision of one of those women whom the world knows not of, silent, deep-hearted, loving, whom the coarser and more practically efficient jostle aside and underrate for their want of interest in the noisy chitchat and commonplace of the day; but who yet have a sacred power, like that of the spirit of peace, to brood with dovelike wings over the childish heart, and quicken into life the struggling, slumbering elements of a sensitive nature.

I cannot but think, in that beautiful scene, where he represents Desdemona as amazed and struck dumb with the grossness and brutality of the charges which had been thrown upon her, yet so dignified in the consciousness of her own purity, so magnanimous in the power of disinterested, forgiving love, that he was portraying no ideal excellence, but only reproducing, under fictitious and supposititious circumstances, the patience, magnanimity, and enduring love which had shone upon him in the household words and ways of his mother.

It seemed to me that in that bare and lowly chamber I saw a vision of a lovely face which was the first beauty that dawned on those childish eyes, and heard that voice whose lullaby tuned his ear to an exquisite sense of cadence and rhythm. I fancied that, while she thus serenely shone upon, him like a benignant star, some rigorous grand-aunt took upon her the practical part of his guidance, chased up his wanderings to the right and left, scolded him for wanting to look out of the window because his little climbing toes left their mark on the neat wall, or rigorously arrested him when his curly head was seen bobbing off at the bottom of the street, following a bird, or a dog, or a showman; intercepting him in some happy hour when he was aiming to strike off on his own account to an adjoining field for "winking Mary-buds;" made long sermons to him on the wickedness of muddying his clothes and wetting his new shoes, (if he had any,) and told him that something dreadful would come out of the graveyard and catch him if he was not a better boy, imagining that if it were not for her bustling activity Willie would go straight to destruction.

I seem, too, to have a kind of perception of Shakspeare's father; a quiet, God-fearing, thoughtful man, given to the reading of good books, avoiding quarrels with a most Christian-like fear, and with but small talent, either in the way of speech making or money getting; a man who wore his coat with an easy slouch, and who seldom knew where his money went to.

All these things I seemed to perceive as if a sort of vision had radiated from the old walls; there seemed to be the rustling of garments and the sound of voices in the deserted rooms; the pattering of feet on the worm-eaten staircase; the light of still, shady summer afternoons, a hundred years ago, seemed to fall through the casements and lie upon the floor. There was an interest to every thing about the house, even to the quaint iron fastenings about the windows; because those might have arrested that child's attention, and been dwelt on in some dreamy hour of infant thought. The fires that once burned in those old chimneys, the fleeting sparks, the curling smoke, and glowing coals, all may have inspired their fancies. There is a strong tinge of household coloring in many parts of Shakspeare, imagery that could only have come from such habits of quiet, household contemplation. See, for example, this description of the stillness of the house, after all are gone to bed at night:—

> "Now sleep yslaked hath the rout;
>
> No din but snores, the house about,
>
> Made louder by the o'er-fed breast

> Of this most pompous marriage feast.
> The cat, with, eyne of burning coal,
> Now crouches 'fore the mouse's hole;
> And, crickets sing at th' oven's mouth,
> As the blither for their drouth."

Also this description of the midnight capers of the fairies about the house, from Midsummer Night's Dream:—

PUCK.:

> "Now the hungry lion roars,
> And the wolf behowls the moon;
> Whilst the heavy ploughman snores,
> All with, weary task fordone.
> Now the wasted brands do glow,
> Whilst the scritch-owl, scritching loud,
> Puts the wretch, that lies in woe,
> In remembrance of a shroud.
> Now it is the time of night,
> That the graves all gaping wide,
> Every one lets forth his sprite,
> In the churchway paths to glide:
> And we fairies that do run
> By the triple Hecate's team,
> From the presence of the sun,
> Following darkness like a dream,
> Now are frolic; not a mouse
> Shall disturb this hallowed house:
> I am sent with, broom, before,
> To sweep the dust behind the door.

OBE.:

> Through this house give glimmering light,
>
> By the dead and drowsy fire:
>
> Every elf, and fairy sprite,
>
> Hop as light as bird, from brier;
>
> And this ditty after me
>
> Sing, and dance it trippingly."

By the by, one cannot but be struck with the resemblance, in the spirit and coloring of these lines, to those very similar ones in the Penseroso of Milton:—

> "Far from all resort of mirth,
>
> Save the cricket on the hearth,
>
> Or the bellman's drowsy charm,
>
> To bless the doors from nightly harm;
>
> While glowing embers, through the room,
>
> Teach light to counterfeit a gloom."

I have often noticed how much the first writings of Milton resemble in their imagery and tone of coloring those of Shakspeare, particularly in the phraseology and manner of describing flowers. I think, were a certain number of passages from Lycidas and Comus interspersed with a certain number from Midsummer Night's Dream, the imagery, tone of thought, and style of coloring, would be found so nearly identical, that it would be difficult for one not perfectly familiar to distinguish them. You may try it.

That Milton read and admired Shakspeare is evident from his allusion to him in L'Allegro. It is evident, however, that Milton's taste had been so formed by the Greek models, that he was not entirely aware of all that was in Shakspeare; he speaks of him as a sweet, fanciful warbler, and it is exactly in sweetness and fancifulness that he seems to have derived benefit from him. In his earlier poems, Milton seems, like Shakspeare, to have let his mind run freely, as a brook warbles over many-colored pebbles; whereas in his great poem he built after models. Had he known as little Latin and Greek as Shakspeare, the world, instead of seeing a well-arranged imitation of the ancient epics from his pen, would have seen inaugurated a new order of poetry.

An unequalled artist, who should build after the model of a Grecian temple, would doubtless produce a splendid and effective building, because a certain originality always inheres in genius, even when copying; but far greater were it to invent an entirely new style of architecture, as different as the Gothic from the Grecian. This merit was Shakspeare's. He was a superb Gothic poet; Milton, a magnificent imitator of old forms, which by his genius were wrought almost into the energy of new productions.

I think Shakspeare is to Milton precisely what Gothic architecture is to Grecian, or rather to the warmest, most vitalized reproductions of the Grecian; there is in Milton a calm, severe majesty, a graceful and polished inflorescence of ornament, that produces, as you look upon it, a serene, long, strong ground-swell of admiration and approval. Yet there is a cold unity of expression, that calls into exercise only the very highest range of our faculties: there is none of that wreathed involution of smiles and tears, of solemn earnestness and quaint conceits; those sudden uprushings of grand and magnificent sentiment, like the flame-pointed arches of cathedrals; those ranges of fancy, half goblin, half human; those complications of dizzy magnificence with fairy lightness; those streamings of many-colored light; those carvings wherein every natural object is faithfully reproduced, yet combined into a kind of enchantment: the union of all these is in Shakspeare, and not in Milton. Milton had one most glorious phase of humanity in its perfection; Shakspeare had all united; from the "deep and dreadful" sub-bass of the organ to the most aerial warbling of its highest key, not a stop or pipe was wanting.

But, in fine, at the end of all this we went back to our hotel to dinner. After dinner we set out to see the church. Even Walter Scott has not a more poetic monument than this church, standing as it does amid old, embowering trees, on the beautiful banks of the Avon. A soft, still rain was falling on the leaves of the linden trees, as we walked up the avenue to the church. Even rainy though it was, I noticed that many little birds would occasionally break out into song. In the event of such a phenomenon as a bright day, I think there must be quite a jubilee of birds here, even as he sung who lies below:—

> "The ousel-cock, so black of hue,
>
> With orange-tawny bill,
>
> The throstle with his note so true,
>
> The wren with little quill;
>
> The finch, the sparrow, and the lark,
>
> The plain-song cuckoo gray."

The church has been carefully restored inside, so that it is now in excellent preservation, and Shakspeare lies buried under a broad, flat stone in the chancel. I had full often read, and knew by heart, the inscription on this stone; but somehow, when I came and stood over it, and read it, it affected me as if there were an emanation from the grave beneath. I have often wondered at that inscription, that a mind so sensitive, that had thought so much, and expressed thought with such startling power on all the mysteries of death, the grave, and the future world, should have found nothing else to inscribe on his own grave but this:—

> Good Friend for Iesus SAKE forbare
>
> To digg T-E Dust EncloAsed HERe
>
> Blese be T-E Man T/Y spares T-Es Stones
>
> And curst be He T/Y moves my Bones

It seems that the inscription has not been without its use, in averting what the sensitive poet most dreaded; for it is recorded in one of the books sold here, that some years ago, in digging a neighboring grave, a careless sexton broke into the side of Shakspeare's tomb, and looking in saw his bones, and could easily have carried away the skull had he not been deterred by the imprecation.

There is a monument in the side of the wall, which has a bust of Shakspeare upon it, said to be the most authentic likeness, and supposed to have been taken by a cast from his face after death. This statement was made to us by the guide who showed it, and he stated that Chantrey had come to that conclusion by a minute examination of the face. He took us into a room, where was an exact plaster cast of the bust, on which he pointed out various little minutiae on which this idea was founded. The two sides of the face are not alike; there is a falling in and depression of the muscles on one side which does not exist on the other, such as probably would never have occurred in a fancy bust, where the effort always is to render the two sides of the face as much alike as possible. There is more fulness about the lower part of the face than is consistent with the theory of an idealized bust, but is perfectly consistent with the probabilities of the time of life at which he died, and perhaps with the effects of the disease of which he died.

All this I set down as it was related to me by our guide; it had a very plausible and probable sound, and I was bent on believing, which is a great matter in faith of all kinds.

It is something in favor of the supposition that this is an authentic likeness, that it was erected in his own native town within seven years of his death, among people, therefore, who must have preserved the recollection of his personal appearance. After the manner of those times it was originally painted, the hair and beard of an auburn color, the eyes hazel, and the dress was represented as consisting of a scarlet doublet, over which was a loose black gown without sleeves; all which looks like an attempt to preserve an exact likeness. The inscription upon it, also, seemed to show that there were some in the world by no means unaware of who and what he was.

Next to the tomb of Shakspeare in the chancel is buried his favorite daughter, over whom somebody has placed the following quaint inscription:—

> "Witty above her sex, but that's not all,
>
> Wise to salvation was good Mistress Hall.
>
> Something of Shakspeare was in that, but this
>
> Wholly of him, with whom she is now in bliss;
>
> Then, passenger, hast ne'er a tear,
>
> To weep with her that wept with, all—
>
> That wept, yet set herself to cheer
>
> Them, up with comfort's cordial?
>
> Her lore shall live, her mercy spread,
>
> When thou hast ne'er a tear to shed."

This good Mistress Hall, it appears, was Shakspeare's favorite among his three children. His son, Hamet, died at twelve years of age. His daughter Judith, as appears from some curious document still extant, could not write her own name, but signed with her mark; so that the "wit" of the family must have concentrated itself in Mistress Hall. To her, in his last will, which is still extant, Shakspeare bequeathed an amount of houses, lands, plate, jewels, and other valuables, sufficient to constitute quite a handsome estate. It would appear, from this, that the poet deemed her not only "wise unto salvation," but wise in her day and generation, thus intrusting her with the bulk of his worldly goods.

His wife, Ann Hathaway, is buried near by, under the same pavement. From the slight notice taken of her in the poet's will, it would appear that there was little love between them. He married her when he was but eighteen; most likely she was a mere rustic beauty, entirely incapable either of appreciating or adapting herself to that wide and wonderful mind in its full development.

As to Mistress Hall, though the estate was carefully entailed, through her, to heirs male through all generations, it was not her good fortune to become the mother of a long line, for she had only one daughter, who became Lady Barnard, and in whom, dying childless, the family became extinct. Shakspeare, like Scott, seems to have had the desire to perpetuate himself by founding a family with an estate, and the coincidence in the result is striking. Genius must be its own monument.

After we had explored the church we went out to walk about the place. We crossed the beautiful bridge over the Avon, and thought how lovely those fields and meadows would look, if they only had sunshine to set them out. Then we went to the town hall, where we met the mayor, who had kindly called and offered to show us the place.

It seems, in 1768, that Garrick set himself to work in good earnest to do honor to Shakspeare's memory, by getting up a public demonstration at Stratford; and the world, through the talents of this actor, having become alive and enthusiastic, liberal subscriptions were made by the nobility and gentry, the town hall was handsomely repaired and adorned, and a statue of Shakspeare, presented by Garrick, was placed in a niche at one end. Then all the chief men and mighty men of the nation came and testified their reverence for the poet, by having a general jubilee. A great tent was spread on the banks of the Avon, where they made speeches and drank wine, and wound up all with a great dance in the town hall; and so the manes of Shakspeare were appeased, and his position settled for all generations. The room in the town hall is a very handsome one, and has pictures of Garrick, and the other notables who figured on that occasion.

After that we were taken to see New Place. "And what is New Place?" you say; "the house where Shakspeare lived?" Not exactly; but a house built where his house was. This drawing is taken from an old print, and is supposed to represent the house as Shakspeare fitted it up.

We went out into what was Shakspeare's garden, where we were shown his mulberry—not the one that he planted though, but a veritable mulberry planted on the same spot; and then we went back to our hotel very tired, but having conscientiously performed every jot and tittle of the duty of good pilgrims.

As we sat, in the drizzly evening, over our comfortable tea table, C—— ventured to intimate pretty decidedly that he considered the whole thing a bore; whereat I thought I saw a sly twinkle around the eyes and mouth of our most Christian and patient friend, Joseph Sturge. Mr. S. laughingly told him that he thought it the greatest exercise of Christian tolerance, that he should have trailed round in the mud with us all day in our sightseeing, bearing with our unreasonable raptures. He smiled, and said, quietly, "I must confess that I was a little pleased that our friend Harriet was so zealous to see Shakspeare's house, when it wasn't his house, and so earnest to get sprigs from his mulberry, when it wasn't his mulberry." We were quite ready to allow the foolishness of the thing, and join the laugh at our own expense.

As to our bed rooms, you must know that all the apartments in this house are named after different plays of Shakspeare, the name being printed conspicuously over each door; so that the choosing of our rooms made us a little sport.

"What rooms will you have, gentlemen?" says the pretty chamber maid.

"Rooms," said Mr. S.; "why, what are there to have?"

"Well, there's Richard III., and there's Hamlet," says the girl.

"O, Hamlet, by all means," said I; "that was always my favorite. Can't sleep in Richard III., we should have such bad dreams."

"For my part," said C——, "I want All's well that ends well."

"I think," said the chamber maid, hesitating, "the bed in Hamlet isn't large enough for two. Richard III. is a very nice room, sir."

In fact, it became evident that we were foreordained to Richard; so we resolved to embrace the modern historical view of this subject, which will before long turn him out a saint, and not be afraid of the muster roll of ghosts which Shakspeare represented as infesting his apartment.

Well, for a wonder, the next morning arose a genuine sunny, beautiful day. Let the fact be recorded that such things do sometimes occur even in England. C—— was mollified, and began to recant his ill-natured heresies of the night before, and went so far as to walk, out of his own proper motion, to Ann Hathaway's Cottage before breakfast—he being one of the brethren described by Longfellow,

> "Who is gifted with most miraculous powers
>
> Of getting up at all sorts of hours;"

and therefore he came in to breakfast table with that serenity of virtuous composure which generally attends those who have been out enjoying the beauties of nature while their neighbors have been ingloriously dozing.

The walk, he said, was beautiful; the cottage damp, musty, and fusty; and a supposititious old bedstead, of the age of Queen Elizabeth, which had been obtruded upon his notice because it *might* have belonged to Ann Hathaway's mother, received a special malediction. For my part, my relic-hunting propensities were not in the slightest degree appeased, but rather stimulated, by the investigations of the day before.

It seemed to me so singular that of such a man there should not remain one accredited relic! Of Martin Luther, though he lived much earlier, how many things remain! Of almost any distinguished character how much more is known than of Shakspeare! There is not, so far as I can discover, an authentic relic of any thing belonging to him. There are very few anecdotes of his sayings or doings; no letters, no private memoranda, that should let us into the secret of what he was personally who has in turns personated all minds. The very perfection of his dramatic talent has become an impenetrable veil: we can no more tell from his writings what were his predominant tastes and habits than we can discriminate among the variety of melodies what are the native notes of the mocking bird. The only means left us for forming an opinion of what he was personally are inferences of the most delicate nature from, the slightest premises.

The common idea which has pervaded the world, of a joyous, roving, somewhat unsettled, and dissipated character, would seem, from many well-authenticated facts, to be incorrect. The gayeties and dissipations of his life seem to have been confined to his very earliest days, and to have been the exuberance of a most extraordinary vitality, bursting into existence with such force and vivacity that it had not had time to collect itself, and so come to self-knowledge and control. By many accounts it would appear that the character he sustained in the last years of his life was that of a judicious, common-sense sort of man; a discreet, reputable, and religious householder.

The inscription on his tomb is worthy of remark, as indicating the reputation he bore at the time: "*Judicio Pylium, genio Socratem, arte Maronem*" (In judgment a Nestor, in genius a Socrates, in art a Virgil.)

The comparison of him in the first place to Nestor, proverbially famous for practical judgment and virtue of life, next to Socrates, who was a kind of Greek combination of Dr. Paley and Dr. Franklin, indicates a very different impression of him from what would generally be expressed of a poet, certainly what would not have been placed on the grave of an eccentric, erratic will-o'-the-wisp genius, however distinguished. Moreover, the pious author of good Mistress Hall's epitaph records the fact of her being "wise to salvation," as a more especial point of resemblance to her father than even her being "witty above her sex," and expresses most confident hope of her being with him in bliss. The Puritan tone of the epitaph, as well as the quality of the verse, gives reason to suppose that it was not written by one who was seduced into a tombstone lie by any superfluity of poetic sympathy.

The last will of Shakspeare, written by his own hand and still preserved, shows several things of the man.

The introduction is as follows:—

"In the name of God. Amen. I, William Shakspeare, at Stratford-upon-Avon, in the county of Warwick, gentleman, in perfect health and memory, (God be praised,) do make and ordain this my last will and testament in manner and form following; that is to say,—

"First, I commend my soul into the hands of God my Creator, hoping, and assuredly believing, through the only merits of Jesus Christ, my Savior, to be made partaker of life everlasting; and my body to the earth, whereof it is made."

The will then goes on to dispose of an amount of houses, lands, plate, money, jewels, &c., which showed certainly that the poet had possessed some worldly skill and thrift in accumulation, and to divide them with a care and accuracy which would indicate that he was by no means of that dreamy and unpractical habit of mind which cares not what becomes of worldly goods.

We may also infer something of a man's character from the tone and sentiments of others towards him. Glass of a certain color casts on surrounding objects a reflection of its own hue, and so the tint of a man's character returns upon us in the habitual manner in which he is spoken of by those around him. The common mode of speaking of Shakspeare always savored of endearment. "Gentle Will" is an expression that seemed oftenest repeated. Ben Jonson inscribed his funeral verses "To the Memory of *my beloved* Mr. William Shakspeare;" he calls him the "sweet swan of Avon." Again, in his lines under a bust of Shakspeare, he says,—

> "The figure that thou seest put,
>
> It was for gentle Shakspeare cut."

In later times Milton, who could have known him only by tradition, calls him "my Shakspeare," "dear son of memory," and "sweetest Shakspeare." Now, nobody ever wrote of sweet John Milton, or gentle John Milton, or gentle Martin Luther, or even sweet Ben Jonson.

Rowe says of Shakspeare, "The latter part of his life was spent, as all men of good sense would wish theirs may be, in ease, retirement, and the conversation of his friends. His pleasurable wit and good nature engaged him in the acquaintance, and entitled him to the friendship, of the gentlemen of the neighborhood." And Dr. Drake says, "He was high in reputation as a poet, favored by the great and the accomplished, and beloved by all who knew him."

That Shakspeare had religious principle, I infer not merely from the indications of his will and tombstone, but from those strong evidences of the working of the religious element which are scattered through his plays. No man could have a clearer perception of God's authority and man's duty; no one has expressed more forcibly the strength of God's government, the spirituality of his requirements, or shown with more fearful power the struggles of the "law in the members warring against the law of the mind."

These evidences, scattered through his plays, of deep religious struggles, make probable the idea that, in the latter, thoughtful, and tranquil years of his life, devotional impulses might have settled into habits, and that the solemn language of his will, in which he professes his faith, in Christ, was not a mere form. Probably he had all his life, even in his gayest hours, more real religious principle than the hilarity of his manner would give reason to suppose. I always fancy he was thinking of himself when he wrote this character: "For the man doth fear God, howsoever it seem not in him by reason of some large jests he doth make."

Neither is there any foundation for the impression that he was undervalued in his own times. No literary man of his day had more success, more flattering attentions from the great, or reaped more of the substantial fruits of popularity, in the form of worldly goods. While his contemporary, Ben Jonson, sick in a miserable alley, is forced to beg, and receives but a wretched pittance from Charles I., Shakspeare's fortune steadily increases from year to year. He buys the best place in his native town, and fits it up with great taste; he offered to lend, on proper security, a sum of money for the use of the town of Stratford; he added to his estate in Stratford a hundred and seventy acres of land; he bought half the great and small tithes of Stratford; and his annual income is estimated to have been what would at the present time be nearly four thousand dollars.

Queen Elizabeth also patronized him after her ordinary fashion of patronizing literary men,—that is to say, she expressed her gracious pleasure that he should burn incense to her, and pay his own bills: economy was not one of the least of the royal graces. The Earl of Southampton patronized him in a more material fashion.

Queen Elizabeth even so far condescended to the poet as to perform certain hoidenish tricks while he was playing on the stage, to see if she could not disconcert his speaking by the majesty of her royal presence. The poet, who was performing the part of King Henry IV., took no notice of her motions, till, in order to bring him to a crisis, she dropped her glove at his feet; whereat he picked it up, and presented it her, improvising these two lines, as if they had been a part of the play:—

"And though, now bent on this high embassy,

Yet stoop we to take up our cousin's glove."

I think this anecdote very characteristic of them both; it seems to me it shows that the poet did not so absolutely crawl in the dust before her, as did almost all the so called men of her court; though he did certainly flatter her after a fashion in which few queens can be flattered. His description of the belligerent old Gorgon as the "Fair Vestal throned by the West" seems like the poetry and fancy of the beautiful Fairy Queen wasted upon the half-brute clown:—

"Come, sit thee down upon this flowery bed,

While I thy amiable cheeks do coy,

And stick musk roses in thy sleek, smooth, head,

And kiss thy fair, large ears, my gentle joy."

Elizabeth's understanding and appreciation of Shakspeare was much after the fashion of Nick Bottom's of the Fairy Queen. I cannot but believe that the men of genius who employed their powers in celebrating this most repulsive and disagreeable woman must sometimes have comforted themselves by a good laugh in private.

In order to appreciate Shakspeare's mind from his plays, we must discriminate what expressed the gross tastes of his age, and what he wrote to please himself. The Merry Wives of Windsor was a specimen of what he wrote for the "Fair Vestal;" a commentary on the delicacy of her maiden meditations. The Midsummer Night's Dream he wrote from his own inner dream world.

In the morning we took leave of our hotel. In leaving we were much touched with the simple kindliness of the people of the house. The landlady and her daughters came to bid us farewell, with much feeling; and the former begged my acceptance of a bead purse, knit by one of her daughters, she said, during the winter evenings while they were reading Uncle Tom. In this town one finds the simple-hearted, kindly English people corresponding to the same class which we see in our retired New England towns. We received many marks of kindness from different residents in Stratford; in the expression of them, they appreciated and entered into our desire for privacy with a delicacy which touched us sensibly.

We had little time to look about us to see Stratford in the sunshine. So we went over to a place on the banks of the Avon, where, it was said, we could gain a very perfect view of the church. The remembrance of this spot is to me like a very pleasant dream. The day was bright, the air was soft and still, as we walked up and down the alleys of a beautiful garden that extended quite to the church; the rooks were dreamily cawing, and wheeling in dark, airy circles round the old buttresses and spire. A funeral train had come into the graveyard, and the passing bell was tolling. A thousand undefined emotions struggled in my mind.

That loving heart, that active fancy, that subtile, elastic power of appreciating and expressing all phases, all passions of humanity, are they breathed out on the wind? are they spent like the lightning? are they exhaled like the breath of flowers? or are they still living, still active? and if so, where and how? Is it reserved for us, in that "undiscovered country" which he spoke of, ever to meet the great souls whose breath has kindled our souls?

I think we forget the consequences of our own belief in immortality, and look on the ranks of prostrate dead as a mower on fields of prostrate flowers, forgetting that activity is an essential of souls, and that every soul which has passed away from this world must ever since have been actively developing those habits of mind and modes of feeling which it began here.

The haughty, cruel, selfish Elizabeth, and all the great men of her court, are still living and acting somewhere; but where? For my part I am often reminded, when dwelling on departed genius, of Luther's ejaculation for his favorite classic poet: "I hope God will have mercy on such."

We speak of the glory of God as exhibited in natural landscape making; what is it, compared with the glory of God as shown in the making of souls, especially those souls which seem to be endowed with a creative power like his own?

There seems, strictly speaking, to be only two classes of souls—the creative and the receptive. Now, these creators seem to me to have a beauty and a worth about them entirely independent of their moral character. That ethereal power which shows itself in Greek sculpture and Gothic architecture, in Rubens, Shakspeare, and Mozart, has a quality to me inexpressibly admirable and lovable. We may say, it is true, that there is no moral excellence in it; but none the less do we admire it. God has made us so that we cannot help loving it; our souls go forth to it with an infinite longing, nor can that longing be condemned. That mystic quality that exists in these souls is a glimpse and intimation of what exists in Him in full perfection. If we remember this we shall not lose ourselves in admiration of worldly genius, but be led by it to a better understanding of what He is, of whom all the glories of poetry and art are but symbols and shadows.

LETTER XI

Dear H.:—

From Stratford we drove to Warwick, (or "Warrick," as they call it here.) This town stands on a rocky hill on the banks of the Avon, and is quite a considerable place, for it returns two members to Parliament, and has upwards of ten thousand inhabitants; and also has some famous manufactories of wool combing and spinning. But what we came to see was the castle. We drove up to the Warwick Arms, which is the principal hotel in the place; and, finding that we were within the hours appointed for exhibition, we went immediately.

With my head in a kind of historical mist, full of images of York and Lancaster, and Red and White Roses, and Warwick the king maker, I looked up to the towers and battlements of the old castle. We went in through a passage way cut in solid rock, about twenty feet deep, and I should think fifty long. These walls were entirely covered with ivy, hanging down like green streamers; gentle and peaceable pennons these are, waving and whispering that the old war times are gone.

At the end of this passage there is a drawbridge over what was formerly the moat, but which is now grassed and planted with shrubbery. Up over our heads we saw the great iron teeth of the portcullis. A rusty old giant it seemed up there, like Pope and Pagan in Pilgrim's Progress, finding no scope for himself in these peaceable times.

When we came fairly into the court yard of the castle, a scene of magnificent beauty opened before us. I cannot describe it minutely. The principal features are the battlements, towers, and turrets of the old feudal castle, encompassed by grounds on which has been expended all that princely art of landscape gardening for which England is famous—leafy thickets, magnificent trees, openings, and vistas of verdure, and wide sweeps of grass, short, thick, and vividly green, as the velvet moss we sometimes see growing on rocks in New England. Grass is an art and a science in England—it is an institution. The pains that are taken in sowing, tending, cutting, clipping, rolling, and otherwise nursing and coaxing it, being seconded by the misty breath and often falling tears of the climate, produce results which must be seen to be appreciated.

So again of trees in England. Trees here are an order of nobility; and they wear their crowns right kingly. A few years ago, when Miss Sedgwick was in this country, while admiring some splendid trees in a nobleman's park, a lady standing by said to her encouragingly, "O, well, I suppose your trees in America will be grown up after a while!" Since that time another style of thinking of America has come up, and the remark that I most generally hear made is, "O, I suppose we cannot think of showing you any thing in the way of trees, coming as you do from America!" Throwing out of account, however, the gigantic growth of our western river bottoms, where I have seen sycamore trunks twenty feet in diameter—leaving out of account, I say, all this mammoth arboria, these English parks have trees as fine and as effective, of their kind, as any of ours; and when I say their trees are an order of nobility, I mean that they pay a reverence to them such as their magnificence deserves. Such elms as adorn the streets of New Haven, or overarch the meadows of Andover, would in England be considered as of a value which no money could represent; no pains, no expense would be spared to preserve their life and health; they would never be shot dead by having gas pipes laid under them, as they have been in some of our New England towns; or suffered to be devoured by canker worms for want of any amount of money spent in their defence.

Some of the finest trees in this place are magnificent cedars of Lebanon, which bring to mind the expression in Psalms, "Excellent as the cedars." They are the very impersonation of kingly majesty, and are fitted to grace the old feudal stronghold of Warwick the king maker. These trees, standing as they do amid magnificent sweeps and undulations of lawn, throwing out their mighty arms with such majestic breadth and freedom of outline, are themselves a living, growing, historical epic. Their seed was brought from Holy Land in the old days of the crusades; and a hundred legends might be made up of the time, date, and occasion of their planting. These crusades have left their mark every where through Europe, from the cross panel on the doors of common houses to the oriental touches and arabesques of castles and cathedrals.

In the reign of Stephen there was a certain Roger de Newburg, second Earl of Warwick, who appears to have been an exceedingly active and public-spirited character; and, besides conquering part of Wales, founded in this neighborhood various priories and hospitals, among which was the house of the Templars, and a hospital for lepers. He made several pilgrimages to Holy Land; and so I think it as likely as most theories that he ought to have the credit of these cedars.

These Earls of Warwick appear always to have been remarkably stirring men in their day and generation, and foremost in whatever was going on in the world, whether political or religious. To begin, there was Guy, Earl of Warwick, who lived somewhere in the times of the old dispensation, before King Arthur, and who distinguished himself, according to the fashion of those days, by killing giants and various colored dragons, among which a green one especially figures. It appears that he slew also a notable dun cow, of a kind of mastodon breed, which prevailed in those early days, which was making great havoc in the neighborhood. In later times, when the giants, dragons, and other animals of that sort were somewhat brought under, we find the Earls of Warwick equally busy burning and slaying to the right and left; now crusading into Palestine, and now fighting the French, who were a standing resort for activity when nothing else was to be done; with great versatility diversifying these affairs with pilgrimages to the holy sepulchre, and founding monasteries and hospitals. One stout earl, after going to Palestine and laying about him like a very dragon for some years, brought home a live Saracen king to London, and had him baptized and made a Christian of, *vi et armis*.

During the scuffle of the Roses, it was a Warwick, of course, who was uppermost. Stout old Richard, the king maker, set up first one party and then the other, according to his own sovereign pleasure, and showed as much talent at fighting on both sides, and keeping the country in an uproar, as the modern politicians of America.

When the times of the Long Parliament and the Commonwealth came, an Earl of Warwick was high admiral of England, and fought valiantly for the Commonwealth, using the navy on the popular side; and his grandson married the youngest daughter of Oliver Cromwell. When the royal family was to be restored, an Earl of Warwick was one of the six lords who were sent to Holland for Charles II. The earls of this family have been no less distinguished for movements which have favored the advance of civilization and letters than for energy in the battle field. In the reign of Queen Elizabeth an Earl of Warwick founded the History Lecture at Cambridge, and left a salary for the professor. This same earl was general patron of letters and arts, assisting many men of talents, and was a particular and intimate friend of Sir Philip Sidney.

What more especially concerns us as New Englanders is, that an earl of this house was the powerful patron and protector of New England during the earlier years of our country. This was Robert Greville, the high admiral of England before alluded to, and ever looked upon as a protector of the Puritans. Frequent allusion is made to him in Winthrop's Journal as performing various good offices for them.

The first grant of Connecticut was made to this earl, and by him assigned to Lord Say and Seal, and Lord Brooke. The patronage which this earl extended to the Puritans is more remarkable because in principle he was favorable to Episcopacy. It appears to have been prompted by a chivalrous sense of justice; probably the same which influenced old Guy of Warwick in the King Arthur times, of whom the ancient chronicler says, "This worshipful knight, in his acts of warre, ever consydered what parties had wronge, and therto would he drawe."

The present earl has never taken a share in public or political life, but resided entirely on his estate, devoting himself to the improvement of his ground and tenants. He received the estate much embarrassed, and the condition of the tenantry was at that time quite depressed. By the devotion of his life it has been rendered one of the most flourishing and prosperous estates in this part of England. I have heard him spoken of as a very exemplary, excellent man. He is now quite advanced, and has been for some time in failing health. He sent our party a very kind and obliging message, desiring that we would consider ourselves fully at liberty to visit any part of the grounds or castle, there being always some reservation as to what tourists may visit.

We caught glimpses of him once or twice, supported by attendants, as he was taking the air in one of the walks of the grounds, and afterwards wheeled about in a garden chair.

The family has thrice died out in the direct line, and been obliged to resuscitate through collateral branches; but it seems the blood holds good notwithstanding. As to honors there is scarcely a possible distinction in the state or army that has not at one time or other been the property of this family.

Under the shade of these lofty cedars they have sprung and fallen, an hereditary line of princes. One cannot but feel, in looking on these majestic trees, with the battlements, turrets, and towers of the old castle every where surrounding him, and the magnificent parks and lawns opening through dreamy vistas of trees into what seems immeasurable distance, the force of the soliloquy which Shakspeare puts into the mouth of the dying old king maker, as he lies breathing out his soul in the dust and blood of the battle field:—

"Thus yields the cedar to the axe's edge,

> Whose arms gave shelter to the princely eagle,
> Under whose shade the rampant lion slept;
> Whose top branch overpeered Jove's spreading tree,
> And kept low shrubs from, winter's powerful wind.
> These eyes, that now are dimmed with death's black veil,
> Have been as piercing as the midday sun
> To search, the secret treasons of the world:
> The wrinkles in my brow, now filled with blood,
> Were likened oft to kingly sepulchres;
> For who lived king but I could dig his grave?
> And who durst smile when Warwick bent his brow?
> Lo, now my glory smeared in dust and blood!
> My parks, my walks, my manors that I had,
> Even now forsake me; and of all my lands
> Is nothing left me but my body's length!
> Why, what is pomp, rule, reign, but earth and dust?
> And live we how we can, yet die we must."

During Shakspeare's life Warwick was in the possession of Greville, the friend of Sir Philip Sidney, and patron of arts and letters. It is not, therefore, improbable that Shakspeare might, in his times, often have been admitted to wander through the magnificent grounds, and it is more than probable that the sight of these majestic cedars might have suggested the noble image in this soliloquy. It is only about eight miles from Stratford, within the fair limits of a comfortable pedestrian excursion, and certainly could not but have been an object of deep interest to such a mind as his.

I have described the grounds first, but, in fact, we did not look at them first, but went into the house where we saw not only all the state rooms, but, through the kindness of the noble proprietor, many of those which are not commonly exhibited; a bewildering display of magnificent apartments, pictures, gems, vases, arms and armor, antiques, all, in short, that the wealth of a princely and powerful family had for centuries been accumulating.

The great hall of the castle is sixty-two feet in length and forty in breadth, ornamented with a richly carved Gothic roof, in which figures largely the family cognizance of the bear and ragged staff. There is a succession of shields, on which are emblazoned the quarterings of successive Earls of Warwick. The sides of the wall are ornamented with lances, corselets, shields, helmets, and complete suits of armor, regularly arranged as in an armory. Here I learned what the buff coat is, which had so often puzzled me in reading Scott's descriptions, as there were several hanging up here. It seemed to be a loose doublet of chamois leather, which was worn under the armor, and protected the body from its harshness.

Here we saw the helmet of Cromwell, a most venerable relic. Before the great, cavernous fireplace was piled up on a sled a quantity of yew tree wood. The rude simplicity of thus arranging it on the polished floor of this magnificent apartment struck me as quite singular. I suppose it is a continuation of some ancient custom.

Opening from this apartment on either side are suits of rooms, the whole series being three hundred and thirty-three feet in length. These rooms are all hung with pictures, and studded with antiques and curiosities of immense value. There is, first, the red drawing room, and then the cedar drawing room, then the gilt drawing room, the state bed room, the boudoir, &c., &c., hung with pictures by Vandyke, Rubens, Guido, Sir Joshua Reynolds, Paul Veronese, any one of which would require days of study; of course, the casual glance that one could give them in a rapid survey would not amount to much.

We were shown one table of gems and lapis lazuli, which cost what would be reckoned a comfortable fortune in New England. For matters of this kind I have little sympathy. The canvas, made vivid by the soul of an inspired artist, tells me something of God's power in creating that soul; but a table of gems is in no wise interesting to me, except so far as it is pretty in itself.

I walked to one of the windows of these lordly apartments, and while the company were examining buhl cabinets, and all other deliciousness of the place, I looked down the old gray walls into the amber waters of the Avon, which flows at their base, and thought that the most beautiful of all was without. There is a tiny fall that crosses the river just above here, whose waters turn the wheels of an old mossy mill, where for centuries the family grain has been ground. The river winds away through the beautiful parks and undulating foliage, its soft, grassy banks dotted here and there with sheep and cattle, and you catch farewell gleams and glitters of it as it loses itself among the trees.

Gray moss, wall flowers, ivy, and grass were growing here and there out of crevices in the castle walls, as I looked down, sometimes trailing their rippling tendrils in the river. This vegetative propensity of walls is one of the chief graces of these old buildings.

In the state bed room were a bed and furnishings of rich, crimson velvet, once belonging to Queen Anne, and presented by George III. to the Warwick family. The walls are hung with Brussels tapestry, representing the gardens of Versailles as they were at the time. The chimney-piece, which is sculptured of verde antique and white marble, supports two black marble vases on its mantel. Over the mantel-piece is a full-length portrait of Queen Anne, in a rich brocade dress, wearing the collar and jewels of the Garter, bearing in one hand a sceptre, and in the other a globe. There are two splendid buhl cabinets in the room, and a table of costly stone from Italy; it is mounted on a richly carved and gilt stand.

The boudoir, which adjoins, is hung with pea-green satin and velvet. In this room is one of the most authentic portraits of Henry VIII., by Holbein, in which that selfish, brutal, unfeeling tyrant is veritably set forth, with all the gold and gems which, in his day, blinded mankind; his fat, white hands were beautifully painted. Men have found out Henry VIII. by this time; he is a dead sinner, and nothing more is to be expected of him, and so he gets a just award; but the disposition which bows down and worships any thing of any character in our day which is splendid and successful, and excuses all moral delinquencies, if they are only available, is not a whit better than that which cringed before Henry.

In the same room was a boar hunt, by Rubens, a disagreeable subject, but wrought with wonderful power. There were several other pictures of Holbein's in this room; one of Martin Luther.

We passed through a long corridor, whose sides were lined with pictures, statues, busts, &c. Out of the multitude, three particularly interested me; one was a noble but melancholy bust of the Black Prince, beautifully chiselled in white marble; another was a plaster cast, said to have been taken of the face of Oliver Cromwell immediately after death. The face had a homely strength amounting almost to coarseness. The evidences of its genuineness appear in glancing at it; every thing is authentic, even to the wart on his lip; no one would have imagined such a one, but the expression was noble and peaceful, bringing to mind the oft-quoted words,—

"After life's fitful fever, he sleeps well."

At the end of the same corridor is a splendid picture of Charles I. on horseback, by Vandyke, a most masterly performance, and appearing in its position almost like a reality. Poor Charles had rather hard measure, it always seemed to me. He simply did as all other princes had done before him; that is to say, he lied steadily, invariably, and conscientiously, in every instance where he thought he could gain any thing by it, just as Charles V., and Francis IV., and Catharine de Medicis, and Henry VIII., and Elizabeth, and James, and all good royal folks had always done; and lo! *he* must lose his head for it. His was altogether a more gentlemanly and respectable performance than that of Henry, not wanting in a sort of ideal magnificence, which his brutal predecessor, or even his shambling old father never dreamed of. But so it is; it is not always on those who are sinners above all men that the tower of Siloam falls, but only on those who happen to be under it when its time comes. So I intend to cherish a little partiality for gentlemanly, magnificent Charles I.; and certainly one could get no more splendid idea of him than by seeing him stately, silent, and melancholy on his white horse, at the end of this long corridor. There he sits, facing the calm, stony, sleeping face of Oliver, and neither question or reply passes between them.

From this corridor we went into the chapel, whose Gothic windows, filled with rich, old painted glass, cast a many-colored light over the oak-carved walls and altar-piece. The ceiling is of fine, old oak, wrought with the arms of the family. The window over the altar is the gift of the Earl of Essex. This room is devoted to the daily religious worship of the family. It has been the custom of the present earl in former years to conduct the devotions of the family here himself.

About this time my head and eyes came to that point which Solomon intimates to be not commonly arrived at by mortals—when the eye is satisfied with seeing. I remember a confused ramble through apartment after apartment, but not a single thing in them, except two pictures of

Salvator Rosa's, which I thought extremely ugly, and was told, as people always are when they make such declarations, that the difficulty was entirely in myself, and that if I would study them two or three months in faith, I should perceive something very astonishing. This may be, but it holds equally good of the coals of an evening fire, or the sparks on a chimney back; in either of which, by resolute looking, and some imagination, one can see any thing he chooses. I utterly distrust this process, by which old black pictures are looked into shape; but then I have nothing to lose, being in the court of the Gentiles in these matters, and obstinately determined not to believe in any real presence in art which I cannot perceive by my senses.

After having examined all the upper stories, we went down into the vaults underneath—vaults once grim and hoary, terrible to captives and feudal enemies, now devoted to no purpose more grim than that of coal cellars and wine vaults. In Oliver's time, a regiment was quartered there: they are extensive enough, apparently, for an army.

The kitchen and its adjuncts are of magnificent dimensions, and indicate an amplitude in the way of provision for good cheer worthy an ancient house; and what struck me as a still better feature was a library of sound, sensible, historical, and religious works for the servants.

We went into the beer vaults, where a man drew beer into a long black jack, such as Scott describes. It is a tankard, made of black leather, I should think half a yard deep. He drew the beer from a large hogshead, and offered us some in a glass. It looked very clear, but, on tasting, I found it so exceedingly bitter that it struck me there would be small virtue for me in abstinence.

In passing up to go out of the house, we met in the entry two pleasant-looking young women, dressed in white muslin. As they passed us, a door opened where a table was handsomely set out, at which quite a number of well-dressed people were seating themselves. I withdrew my eyes immediately, fearing lest I had violated some privacy. Our conductor said to us, "That is the upper servants' dining room."

Once in the yard again, we went to see some of the older parts of the building. The oldest of these, Caesar's Tower, which is said to go back to the time of the Romans, is not now shown to visitors. Beneath it is a dark, damp dungeon, where prisoners used to be confined, the walls of which are traced all over with inscriptions and rude drawings.

Then you are conducted to Guy's Tower, named, I suppose, after the hero of the green dragon and dun cow. Here are five tiers of guard rooms, and by the ascent of a hundred and thirty-three steps you reach the battlements, where you gain a view of the whole court and grounds, as well as of the beautiful surrounding landscape.

In coming down from this tower, we somehow or other got upon the ramparts, which connect it with the great gate. We walked on the wall four abreast, and played that we were knights and ladies of the olden time, walking on the ramparts. And I picked a bough from an old pine tree that grew over our heads; it much resembled our American yellow pitch pine.

Then we went down and crossed the grounds to the greenhouse, to see the famous Warwick vase. The greenhouse is built with a Gothic stone front, situated on a fine point in the landscape. And there, on a pedestal, surrounded by all manner of flowering shrubs, stands this celebrated antique. It is of white marble, and was found at the bottom of a lake near Adrian's villa, in Italy. They say that it holds a hundred and thirty-six gallons; constructed, I suppose, in the roistering old drinking times of the Roman emperors, when men seem to have discovered that the grand object for which they were sent into existence was to perform the functions of wine skins. It is beautifully sculptured with grape leaves, and the skin and claws of the panther—these latter certainly not an inappropriate emblem of the god of wine, beautiful, but dangerous.

Well, now it was all done. Merodach Baladan had not a more perfect *exposé* of the riches of Hezekiah than we had of the glories of Warwick. One always likes to see the most perfect thing of its kind; and probably this is the most perfect specimen of the feudal ages yet remaining in England.

As I stood with Joseph Sturge under the old cedars of Lebanon, and watched the multitude of tourists, and parties of pleasure, who were thronging the walks, I said to him, "After all, this establishment amounts to a public museum and pleasure grounds for the use of the people." He assented. "And," said I, "you English people like these things; you like these old magnificent seats, kept up by old families." "That is what I tell them," said Joseph Sturge. "I tell them there is no danger in enlarging the suffrage, for the people would not break up these old establishments if they could." On that point, of course, I had no means of forming an opinion.

One cannot view an institution so unlike any thing we have in our own country without having many reflections excited, for one of these estates may justly be called an institution; it includes within itself all the influence on a community of a great model farm, of model housekeeping, of a general museum of historic remains, and of a gallery of fine arts.

It is a fact that all these establishments through England are, at certain fixed hours, thrown open for the inspection of whoever may choose to visit them, with no other expense than the gratuity which custom requires to be given to the servant who shows them. I noticed, as we passed from one part of the ground to another, that our guides changed—one part apparently being the perquisite of one servant, and one of another. Many of the servants who showed them appeared to be superannuated men, who probably had this post as one of the dignities and perquisites of their old age.

The influence of these estates on the community cannot but be in many respects beneficial, and should go some way to qualify the prejudice with which republicans are apt to contemplate any thing aristocratic; for although the legal title to these things inheres in but one man, yet in a very important sense they belong to the whole community, indeed, to universal humanity. It may be very undesirable and unwise to wish to imitate these institutions in America, and yet it may be illiberal to undervalue them as they stand in England. A man would not build a house, in this nineteenth century, on the pattern of a feudal castle; and yet where the feudal castle is built, surely its antique grace might plead somewhat in its favor, and it may be better to accommodate it to modern uses, than to level it, and erect a modern mansion in its place.

Nor, since the world is wide, and now being rapidly united by steam into one country, does the objection to these things, on account of the room they take up, seem so great as formerly. In the million of square miles of the globe there is room enough for all sorts of things.

With such reflections the lover of the picturesque may comfort himself, hoping that he is not sinning against the useful in his admiration of the beautiful.

One great achievement of the millennium, I trust, will be in uniting these two elements, which have ever been contending. There was great significance in the old Greek fable which represented Venus as the divinely-appointed helpmeet of Vulcan, and yet always quarrelling with him.

We can scarce look at the struggling, earth-bound condition of useful labor through the world without joining in the beautiful aspiration of our American poet,—

> "Surely, the wiser time shall come
>
> When this fine overplus of might,
>
> No longer sullen, slow, and dumb,
>
> Shall leap to music and to light.
>
> In that new childhood of the world

Life of itself shall dance and play,

Fresh blood through Time's shrunk veins be hurled,

And labor meet delight half way."[13]

In the new state of society which we are trying to found in America, it must be our effort to hasten the consummation. These great estates of old countries may keep it for their share of the matter to work out perfect models, while we will seize the ideas thus elaborated, and make them the property of the million.

As we were going out, we stopped a little while at the porter's lodge to look at some relics.

Now, I dare say that you have been thinking, all the while, that these stories about the wonderful Guy are a sheer fabrication, or, to use a convenient modern term, a myth. Know, then, that the identical armor belonging to him is still preserved here; to wit, the sword, about seven feet long, a shield, helmet, breastplate, and tilting pole, together with his porridge pot, which holds one hundred and twenty gallons, and a large fork, as they call it, about three feet long; I am inclined to think this must have been his toothpick! His sword weighs twenty pounds.

There is, moreover, a rib of the mastodon cow which he killed, hung up for the terror of all refractory beasts of that name in modern days.

Furthermore, know, then, that there are authentic documents in the Ashmolean Museum, at Oxford, showing that the family run back to within four years after the birth of Christ, so that there is abundance of time for them to have done a little of almost every thing. It appears that they have been always addicted to exploits, since we read of one of them, soon after the Christian era, encountering a giant, who ran upon him with a tree which he had snapped off for the purpose, for it seems giants were not nice in the choice of weapons; but the chronicler says, "The Lord had grace with him, and overcame the giant," and in commemoration of this event the family introduced into their arms the ragged staff.

It is recorded of another of the race, that he was one of seven children born at a birth, and that all the rest of his brothers and sisters were, by enchantment, turned into swans with gold collars. This remarkable case occurred in the time of the grandfather of Sir Guy, and of course, if we believe this, we shall find no difficulty in the case of the cow, or any thing else.

There is a very scarce book in the possession of a gentleman of Warwick, written by one Dr. John Kay, or caius, in which he gives an account of the rare and peculiar animals of England in 1552. In this he mentioned seeing the bones of the head and the vertebrae of the neck of an enormous animal at Warwick Castle. He states that the shoulder blade was hung up by chains from the north gate of Coventry, and that a rib of the same animal was hanging up in the chapel of Guy, Earl of Warwick, and that the people fancied it to be the rib of a cow which haunted a ditch near Coventry, and did injury to many persons; and he goes on to imagine that this may be the bone of a bonasus or a urus. He says, "It is probable many animals of this kind formerly lived in our England, being of old an island full of woods and forests, because even in our boyhood the horns of these animals were in common use at the table." The story of Sir Guy is furthermore quite romantic, and contains some circumstances very instructive to all ladies. For the chronicler asserts, "that Dame Felye, daughter and heire to Erle Rohand, for her beauty called Fely le Belle, or Felys the Fayre, by true enheritance, was Countesse of Warwyke, and lady and wyfe to the most victoriouse Knight, Sir Guy, to whom in his woing tyme she made greate straungeres, and caused him, for her sake, to put himself in meny greate distresses, dangers, and perills; but when they were wedded, and b'en but a little season together, he departed from her, to her greate hevynes, and never was conversant with her after, to her understandinge." That this may not appear to be the result of any revengeful spirit on the part of Sir Guy, the chronicler goes on further to state his motives—that, after his marriage, considering what he had done for a woman's sake, he thought to spend the other part of his life for God's sake, and so departed from his lady in pilgrim weeds, which raiment he kept to his life's end. After wandering about a good many years he settled in a hermitage, in a place not far from the castle, called Guy's Cliff, and when his lady distributed food to beggars at the castle gate, was in the habit of coming among them to receive alms, without making himself known to her. It states, moreover, that two days before his death an angel informed him of the time of his departure, and that his lady would die a fortnight after him, which happening accordingly, they were both buried in the grave together. A romantic cavern, at the place called Guy's Cliff, is shown as the dwelling of the recluse. The story is a curious relic of the religious ideas of the times.

On our way from the castle we passed by Guy's Cliff, which is at present the seat of the Hon. C.B. Percy. The establishment looked beautifully from the road, as we saw it up a long avenue of trees; it is one of the places travellers generally examine, but as we were bound for Kenilworth we were content to take it on trust. It is but a short drive from there to Kenilworth. We got there about the middle of the afternoon. Kenilworth has been quite as extensive as Warwick, though now entirely gone to ruins. I believe Oliver Cromwell's army have the credit of finally dismantling it. Cromwell seems literally to have left his mark on his generation, for I never saw a ruin in

England when I did not hear that he had something to do with it. Every broken arch and ruined battlement seemed always to find a sufficient account of itself by simply enunciating the word Cromwell. And when we see how much the Puritans arrayed against themselves all the æsthetic principles of our nature, we can somewhat pardon those who did not look deeper than the surface, for the prejudice with which they regarded the whole movement; a movement, however, of which we, and all which is most precious to us, are the lineal descendants and heirs.

We wandered over the ruins, which are very extensive, and which Scott, with his usual vivacity and accuracy, has restored and repeopled. We climbed up into Amy Robsart's chamber; we scrambled into one of the arched windows of what was formerly the great dining hall, where Elizabeth feasted in the midst of her lords and ladies, and where every stone had rung to the sound of merriment and revelry. The windows are broken out; it is roofless and floorless, waving and rustling with pendent ivy, and vocal with the song of hundreds of little birds.

We wandered from room to room, looking up and seeing in the walls the desolate fireplaces, tier over tier, the places where the beams of the floors had gone into the walls, and still the birds continued their singing every where.

Nothing affected me more than this ceaseless singing and rejoicing of birds in these old gray ruins. They seemed so perfectly joyous and happy amid the desolations, so airy and fanciful in their bursts of song, so ignorant and careless of the deep meaning of the gray desolation around them, that I could not but be moved. It was nothing to them how these stately, sculptured walls became lonely and ruinous, and all the weight of a thousand thoughts and questionings which arise to us is never even dreamed by them. They sow not, neither do they reap, but their heavenly Father feeds them; and so the wilderness and the desolate place is glad in them, and they are glad in the wilderness and desolate place.

It was a beautiful conception, this making of birds. Shelley calls them "imbodied joys;" and Christ says, that amid the vaster ruins of man's desolation, ruins more dreadfully suggestive than those of sculptured frieze and architrave, we can yet live a bird's life of unanxious joy; or, as Martin Luther beautifully paraphrases it, "We can be like a bird, that sits singing on his twig and lets God think for him."

The deep consciousness that we are ourselves ruined, and that this world is a desolation more awful, and of more sublime material, and wrought from stuff of higher temper than ever was sculptured in hall or cathedral, this it must be that touches such deep springs of sympathy in the presence of ruins. We, too, are desolate, shattered, and scathed; there are traceries and columns of celestial workmanship; there are heaven-aspiring arches, splendid colonnades and halls, but fragmentary all. Yet above us bends an all-pitying Heaven, and spiritual voices and callings in our hearts, like these little singing birds, speak of a time when almighty power shall take pleasure in these stones, and favor the dust thereof.

We sat on the top of the strong tower, and looked off into the country, and talked a good while. Some of the ivy that mantles this building has a trunk as large as a man's body, and throws out numberless strong arms, which, interweaving, embrace and interlace half-falling towers, and hold them up in a living, growing mass of green.

The walls of one of the oldest towers are sixteen feet thick. The lake, which Scott speaks of, is dried up and grown over with rushes. The former moat presents only a grassy hollow. What was formerly a gate house is still inhabited by the family who have the care of the building. The land around the gate house is choicely and carefully laid out, and has high, clipped hedges of a species of variegated holly.

Thus much of old castles and ivy. Farewell to Kenilworth.

LETTER XII

My Dear H.:—

After leaving Kenilworth we drove to Coventry, where we took the cars again. This whole ride from Stratford to Warwick, and on to Coventry, answers more to my ideas of old England than any thing I have seen; it is considered one of the most beautiful parts of the kingdom. It has quaint old houses, and a certain air of rural, picturesque quiet, which is very charming.

Coventry is old and queer, with narrow streets and curious houses, famed for the ancient legend of Godiva, one of those beautiful myths that grow, like the mistletoe, on the bare branches of history, and which, if they never were true in the letter, have been a thousand times true in the spirit.

The evening came on raw and chilly, so that we rejoiced to find ourselves once more in the curtained parlor by the bright, sociable fire.

As we were drinking tea Elihu Burritt came in. It was the first time I had ever seen him, though I had heard a great deal of him from our friends in Edinburgh. He is a man in middle life, tall and slender, with fair complexion, blue eyes, an air of delicacy and refinement, and manners of great gentleness. My ideas of the "Learned Blacksmith" had been of something altogether more ponderous and peremptory. Elihu has been, for some years, operating in England and on the continent in a movement which many, in our half-Christianized times, regard with as much incredulity as the grim, old, warlike barons did the suspicious imbecilities of reading and writing. The sword now, as then, seems so much more direct a way to terminate controversies, that many Christian men, even, cannot conceive how the world is to get along without it.

Burritt's mode of operation has been by the silent organization of circles of ladies in all the different towns of the United Kingdom, who raise a certain sum for the diffusion of the principles of peace on earth and good will to men. Articles, setting forth the evils of war, moral, political, and social, being prepared, these circles pay for their insertion in all the principal newspapers of the continent. They have secured to themselves in this way a continual utterance in France, Spain, Italy, Switzerland, Austria, and Germany; so that from week to week, and month to month, they can insert articles upon these subjects. Many times the editors insert the articles as editorial, which still further favors their design. In addition to this, the ladies of these circles in England correspond with the ladies of similar circles existing in other countries; and in this way there is a mutual kindliness of feeling established through these countries.

When recently war was threatening between England and France, through the influence of these societies conciliatory addresses were sent from many of the principal towns of England to many of the principal towns of France; and the effect of these measures in allaying irritation and agitation was very perceptible.

Furthermore, these societies are preparing numerous little books for children, in which the principles of peace, kindness, and mutual forbearance are constantly set forth, and the evil and unchristian nature of the mere collision of brute force exemplified in a thousand ways. These tracts also are reprinted in the other modern languages of Europe, and are becoming a part of family literature.

The object had in view by those in this movement is, the general disbandment of standing armies and warlike establishments, and the arrangement, in their place, of some settled system of national arbitration. They suggest the organization of some tribunal of international law, which shall correspond to the position of the Supreme Court of the United States with reference to the several states. The fact that the several states of our Union, though each a distinct sovereignty, yet agree in this arrangement, is held up as an instance of its practicability. These ideas are not to be considered entirely chimerical, if we reflect that commerce and trade are as essentially opposed to war as is Christianity. War is the death of commerce, manufactures, agriculture, and the fine arts. Its evil results are always certain and definite, its good results scattered and accidental. The whole current of modern society is as much against war as against slavery; and the time must certainly come when some more rational and humane mode of resolving national difficulties will prevail.

When we ask these reformers how people are to be freed from the yoke of despotism without war, they answer, "By the diffusion of ideas among the masses—by teaching the bayonets to think." They say, "If we convince every individual soldier of a despot's army that war is ruinous, immoral, and unchristian, we take the instrument out of the tyrant's hand. If each individual man would refuse to rob and murder for the Emperor of Austria, and the Emperor of Russia, where would be their power to hold Hungary? What gave power to the masses in the French revolution, but that the army, pervaded by new ideas, refused any longer to keep the people down?"

These views are daily gaining strength in England. They are supported by the whole body of the Quakers, who maintain them with that degree of inflexible perseverance and never-dying activity which have rendered the benevolent actions of that body so efficient. The object that they are aiming at is one most certain to be accomplished, infallible as the prediction that swords are to be beaten into ploughshares, and spears into pruning-hooks, and that nations shall learn war no more.

This movement, small and despised in its origin, has gained strength from year to year, and now has an effect on the public opinion of England which is quite perceptible.

We spent the evening in talking over these things, and also various topics relating to the antislavery movement. Mr. Sturge was very confident that something more was to be done than had ever been done yet, by combinations for the encouragement of free, in the place of slave-grown, produce; a question which has, ever since the days of Clarkson, more or less deeply occupied the minds of abolitionists in England.

I should say that Mr. Sturge in his family has for many years conscientiously forborne the use of any article produced by slave labor. I could scarcely believe it possible that there could be such an abundance and variety of all that is comfortable and desirable in the various departments of household living within these limits. Mr. Sturge presents the subject with very great force, the more so from the consistency of his example.

From what I have since observed, as well as from what they said, I should imagine that the Quakers generally pursue this course of entire separation from all connection with slavery, even in the disuse of its products. The subject of the disuse of slave-grown produce has obtained currency in the same sphere in which Elihu Burritt operates, and has excited the attention of the Olive Leaf Circles. Its prospects are not so weak as on first view might be imagined, if we consider that Great Britain has large tracts of cotton-growing land at her disposal in India. It has been calculated that, were suitable railroads and arrangements for transportation provided for India, cotton could be raised in that empire sufficient for the whole wants of England, at a rate much cheaper than it can be imported from America. Not only so, but they could then afford to furnish cotton cheaper at Lowell than the same article could be procured from the Southern States.

It is consolatory to know that a set of men have undertaken this work whose perseverance in any thing once begun has never been daunted. Slave labor is becoming every year more expensive in America. The wide market which has been opened for it has raised it to such an extravagant price as makes the stocking of a plantation almost ruinous. If England enters the race with free labor, which has none of these expenses, and none of the risk, she will be sure to succeed. All the forces of nature go with free labor; and all the forces of nature resist slave labor. The stars in their courses fight against it; and it cannot but be that ere long some way will be found to bring these two forces to a decisive issue.

Mr. Sturge seemed exceedingly anxious that the American states should adopt the theory of immediate, and not gradual, emancipation. I told him the great difficulty was to persuade them to think of any emancipation at all; that the present disposition was to treat slavery as the pillar and ground of the truth, the ark of religion, the summary of morals, and the only true millennial form of modern society.

He gave me, however, a little account of their antislavery struggles in England, and said, what was well worthy of note, that they made no apparent progress in affecting public opinion until they firmly advocated the right of every innocent being to immediate and complete freedom, without any conditions. He said that a woman is fairly entitled to the credit of this suggestion. Elizabeth Heyrick of Leicester, a member of the society of Friends, published a pamphlet entitled Immediate, not Gradual Emancipation. This little pamphlet contains much good sense; and, being put forth at a time when men were really anxious to know the truth, produced a powerful impression.

She remarked, very sensibly, that the difficulty had arisen from indistinct ideas in respect to what is implied in emancipation. She went on to show that emancipation did not imply freedom from government and restraint; that it properly brought a slave under the control of the law, instead of that of an individual; and that it was possible so to apply law as perfectly to control the emancipated. This is an idea which seems simple enough when pointed out; but men often stumble a long while before they discover what is most obvious.

The next day was Sunday; and, in order to preserve our incognito, and secure an uninterrupted rest, free from conversation and excitement, we were obliged to deprive ourselves of the pleasure of hearing our friend Rev. John Angell James, which we had much desired to do.

It was a warm, pleasant day, and we spent much of our time in a beautiful arbor constructed in a retired place in the garden, where the trees and shrubbery were so arranged as to make a most charming retreat.

The grounds of Mr. Sturge are very near to those of his brother—only a narrow road interposing between them. They have contrived to make them one by building under this road a subterranean passage, so that the two families can pass and repass into each other's grounds in perfect privacy.

These English gardens delight me much; they unite variety, quaintness, and an imitation of the wildness of nature with the utmost care and cultivation. I was particularly pleased with the rockwork, which at times formed the walls of certain walks, the hollows and interstices of which were filled with every variety of creeping plants. Mr. Sturge told me that the substance of which these rockeries are made is sold expressly for the purpose.

On one side of the grounds was an old-fashioned cottage, which one of my friends informed me Mr. Sturge formerly kept fitted up as a water cure hospital, for those whose means did not allow them to go to larger establishments. The plan was afterwards abandoned. One must see that such an enterprise would have many practical difficulties.

At noon we dined in the house of the other brother, Mr. Edmund Sturge. Here I noticed a full-length engraving of Joseph Sturge. He is represented as standing with his hand placed protectingly on the head of a black child.

We enjoyed our quiet season with these two families exceedingly. We seemed to feel ourselves in an atmosphere where all was peace and good will to man. The little children, after dinner, took us through the walks, to show us their beautiful rabbits and other pets. Every thing seemed in order, peaceable and quiet. Towards evening we went back through the arched passage to the other house again. My Sunday here has always seemed to me a pleasant kind of pastoral, much like the communion of Christian and Faithful with the shepherds on the Delectable Mountains.

What is remarkable of all these Friends is, that, although they have been called, in the prosecution of philanthropic enterprises, to encounter so much opposition, and see so much of the unfavorable side of human nature, they are so habitually free from any tinge of uncharitableness or evil speaking in their statements with regard to the character and motives of others. There is also an habitual avoidance of all exaggerated forms of statement, a sobriety of diction, which, united with great affectionateness of manner, inspires the warmest confidence.

C. had been, with Mr. Sturge, during the afternoon, to a meeting of the Friends, and heard a discourse from Sibyl Jones, one of the most popular of their female preachers. Sibyl is a native of the town of Brunswick, in the State of Maine. She and her husband, being both preachers, have travelled extensively in the prosecution of various philanthropic and religious enterprises.

In the evening Mr. Sturge said that she had expressed a desire to see me. Accordingly I went with him to call upon her, and found her in the family of two aged Friends, surrounded by a circle of the same denomination. She is a woman of great delicacy of appearance, betokening very frail health. I am told that she is most of her time in a state of extreme suffering from neuralgic complaints. There was a mingled expression of enthusiasm and tenderness in her face which was very interesting. She had had, according to the language of her sect, a concern upon her mind for me.

To my mind there is something peculiarly interesting about that primitive simplicity and frankness with which the members of this body express themselves. She desired to caution me against the temptations of too much flattery and applause, and against the worldliness which might beset me in London. Her manner of addressing me was like one who is commissioned with a message which must be spoken with plainness and sincerity. After this the whole circle kneeled, and she offered prayer. I was somewhat painfully impressed with her evident fragility of body, compared with the enthusiastic workings of her mind.

In the course of the conversation she inquired if I was going to Ireland. I told her, yes, that was my intention. She begged that I would visit the western coast, adding, with great feeling, "It was the miseries which I saw there which have brought my health to the state it is." She had travelled extensively in the Southern States, and had, in private conversation, been able very fully to bear her witness against slavery, and had never been heard with unkindness.

The whole incident afforded me matter for reflection. The calling of women to distinct religious vocations, it appears to me, was a part of primitive Christianity; has been one of the most efficient elements of power in the Romish church; obtained among the Methodists in England; and has, in all these cases, been productive of great good. The deaconesses whom the apostle mentions with honor in his epistle, Madame Guyon in the Romish church, Mrs. Fletcher, Elizabeth Fry, are instances which show how much may be done for mankind by women who feel themselves impelled to a special religious vocation.

The Bible, which always favors liberal development, countenances this idea, by the instances of Deborah, Anna the prophetess, and by allusions in the New Testament, which plainly show that the prophetic gift descended upon women. St. Peter, quoting from the prophetic writings, says, "Upon your sons and upon your daughters I will pour out my spirit, and they shall prophesy." And St. Paul alludes to women praying and prophesying in the public assemblies of the Christians, and only enjoins that it should be done with becoming attention to the established usages of female delicacy. The example of the Quakers is a sufficient proof that acting upon this idea does not produce discord and domestic disorder. No class of people are more remarkable for quietness and propriety of deportment, and for household order and domestic excellence. By the admission of this liberty, the world is now and then gifted with a woman like Elizabeth Fry, while the family state loses none of its security and sacredness. No one in our day can charge the ladies of the Quaker sect with boldness or indecorum; and they have demonstrated that even public teaching, when performed under the influence of an overpowering devotional spirit, does not interfere with feminine propriety and modesty.

The fact is, that the number of women to whom this vocation is given will always be comparatively few: they are, and generally will be, exceptions; and the majority of the religious world, ancient and modern, has decided that these exceptions are to be treated with reverence.

The next morning, as we were sitting down to breakfast, our friends of the other house sent in to me a plate of the largest, finest strawberries I have ever seen, which, considering that it was only the latter part of April, seemed to me quite an astonishing luxury.

On the morning before we left we had agreed to meet a circle of friends from Birmingham, consisting of the Abolition Society there, which is of long standing, extending back in its memories to the very commencement of the agitation under Clarkson and Wilberforce. It was a pleasant morning, the 1st of May. The windows of the parlor were opened to the ground; and the company invited filled not only the room, but stood in a crowd on the grass around the window. Among the peaceable company present was an admiral in the navy, a fine, cheerful old gentleman, who entered with hearty interest into the scene.

The lady secretary of the society read a neatly-written address, full of kind feeling and Christian sentiment. Joseph Sturge made a few sensible and practical remarks on the present aspects of the antislavery cause in the world, and the most practical mode of assisting it among English Christians. He dwelt particularly on the encouragement of free labor. The Rev. John Angell James followed with some extremely kind and interesting remarks, and Mr. S. replied. As we were intending to return to this city to make a longer visit, we felt that this interview was but a glimpse of friends whom we hoped to know more perfectly hereafter.

A throng of friends accompanied us to the depot. We had the pleasure of the company of Elihu Burritt, and enjoyed a delightful run to London, where we arrived towards evening.

LETTER XIII

Dear Sister:—

At the station house in London, we found Rev. Messrs. Binney and Sherman waiting for us with carriages. C. went with Mr. Sherman, and Mr. S. and I soon found ourselves in a charming retreat called Rose Cottage, in Walworth, about which I will tell you more anon. Mrs. B. received us with every attention which the most thoughtful hospitality could suggest.

S. and W., who had gone on before us, and taken lodgings very near, were there waiting to receive us. One of the first things S. said to me, after we got into our room, was, "O, H——, we are so glad you have come, for we are all going to the lord mayor's dinner to night, and you are invited."

"What!" said I, "the lord mayor of London, that I used to read about in Whittington and his Cat?" And immediately there came to my ears the sound of the old chime, which made so powerful an impression on my childish memory, wherein all the bells of London were represented as tolling.

> "Turn again, Whittington,
>
> Thrice lord mayor of London."

It is curious what an influence these old rhymes have on our associations.

S. went on to tell me that the party was the annual dinner given to the judges of England by the lord mayor, and that there we should see the whole English bar, and hosts of *distingués* besides. So, though I was tired, I hurried to dress in all the glee of meeting an adventure, as Mr. and Mrs. B. and the rest of the party were ready. Crack went the whip, round went the wheels, and away we drove.

We alighted at the Mansion House, and entered a large illuminated hall, supported by pillars. Chandeliers were glittering, servants with powdered heads and gold lace coats were hurrying to and fro in every direction, receiving company and announcing names. Do you want to know how announcing is done? Well, suppose a staircase, a hall, and two or three corridors, intervening between you and the drawing room. At all convenient distances on this route are stationed these grave, powdered-headed gentlemen, with their embroidered coats. You walk up to the first one, and tell him confidentially that you are Miss Smith. He calls to the man on the first landing, "Miss Smith." The man on the landing says to the man in the corridor, "Miss Smith." The man in the corridor shouts to the man at the drawing room door, "Miss Smith." And thus, following the sound of your name, you hear it for the last time shouted aloud, just before you enter the room.

We found a considerable throng, and I was glad to accept a seat which was offered me in the agreeable vicinity of the lady mayoress, so that I might see what would be interesting to me of the ceremonial.

The titles in law here, as in every thing else, are manifold; and the powdered-headed gentleman at the door pronounced them with an evident relish, which was joyous to hear—Mr. Attorney, Mr. Solicitor, and Mr. Sergeant; Lord Chief Baron, Lord Chief Justice, and Lord this, and Lord that, and Lord the other, more than I could possibly remember, as in they came dressed in black, with smallclothes and silk stockings, with swords by their sides, and little cocked hats under their arms, bowing gracefully before the lady mayoress.

I saw no big wigs, but some wore the hair tied behind with a small black silk bag attached to it. Some of the principal men were dressed in black velvet, which became them finely. Some had broad shirt frills of point or Mechlin lace, with wide ruffles of the same round their wrists.

Poor C., barbarian that he was, and utterly unaware of the priceless gentility of the thing, said to me, *sotto voce*, "How can men wear such dirty stuff? Why don't they wash it?" I expounded to him what an ignorant sinner he was, and that the dirt of ages was one of the surest indications of value. Wash point lace! it would be as bad as cleaning up the antiquary's study.

The ladies were in full dress, which here in England means always a dress which exposes the neck and shoulders. This requirement seems to be universal, since ladies of all ages conform to it. It may, perhaps, account for this custom, to say that the bust of an English lady is seldom otherwise than fine, and develops a full outline at what we should call quite an advanced period of life.

A very dignified gentleman, dressed in black velvet, with a fine head, made his way through the throng, and sat down by me, introducing himself as Lord Chief Baron Pollock. He told me he had just been reading the legal part of the Key to Uncle Tom's Cabin, and remarked especially on the opinion of Judge Ruffin, in the case of State *v.* Mann, as having made a deep impression on his mind. Of the character of the decision, considered as a legal and literary document, he spoke in terms of high admiration; said that nothing had ever given him so clear a view of the essential nature of slavery. We found that this document had produced the same impression on the minds of several others present. Mr. S. said that one or two distinguished legal gentlemen mentioned it to him in similar terms. The talent and force displayed in it, as well as the high spirit and scorn of dissimulation, appear to have created a strong interest in its author. It always seemed to me that there was a certain severe strength and grandeur about it which approached to the heroic. One or two said that they were glad such a man had retired from the practice of such a system of law.

But there was scarce a moment for conversation amid the whirl and eddy of so many presentations. Before the company had all assembled, the room was a perfect jam of legal and literary notabilities. The dinner was announced between nine and ten o'clock. We were conducted into a splendid hall, where the tables were laid. Four long tables were set parallel with the length of the hall, and one on a raised platform across the upper end. In the midst of this sat the lord mayor and lady mayoress, on their right hand the judges, on their left the American minister, with other distinguished guests. I sat by a most agreeable and interesting young lady, who seemed to take pleasure in enlightening me on all those matters about which a stranger would naturally be inquisitive.

Directly opposite me was Mr. Dickens, whom I now beheld for the first time, and was surprised to see looking so young. Mr. Justice Talfourd, known as the author of Ion, was also there with his lady. She had a beautiful antique cast of head.

The lord mayor was simply dressed in black, without any other adornment than a massive gold chain.

I asked the lady if he had not robes of state. She replied, yes; but they were very heavy and cumbersome, and that he never wore them when he could, with any propriety, avoid it. It seems to me that this matter of outward parade and state is gradually losing its hold even here in England. As society becomes enlightened, men care less and less for mere shows, and are apt to neglect those outward forms which have neither beauty nor convenience on their side, such as judges' wigs and lord mayors' robes.

As a general thing the company were more plainly dressed than I had expected. I am really glad that there is a movement being made to carry the doctrine of plain dress into our diplomatic representation. Even older nations are becoming tired of mere shows; and, certainly, the representatives of a republic ought not to begin to put on the finery which monarchies are beginning to cast off.

The present lord mayor is a member of the House of Commons—a most liberal-minded man; very simple, but pleasing in his appearance and address; one who seems to think more of essentials than of show.

He is a dissenter, being a member of Rev. Mr. Binney's church, a man warmly interested in the promotion of Sabbath schools, and every worthy and benevolent object.

The ceremonies of the dinner were long and weary, and, I thought, seemed to be more fully entered into by a flourishing official, who stood at the mayor's back, than by any other person present.

The business of toast-drinking is reduced to the nicest system. A regular official, called a toast master, stood behind the lord mayor with a paper, from which he read the toasts in their order. Every one, according to his several rank, pretensions, and station, must be toasted in his gradation; and every person toasted must have his name announced by the official,—the larger dignitaries being proposed alone in their glory, while the smaller fry are read out by the dozen,—and to each toast somebody must get up and make a speech.

First, after the usual loyal toasts, the lord mayor proposed the health of the American minister, expressing himself in the warmest terms of friendship towards our country; to which Mr. Ingersoll responded very handsomely. Among the speakers I was particularly pleased with Lord Chief Baron Pollock, who, in the absence of Lord Chief Justice Campbell, was toasted as the highest representative of the legal profession. He spoke with great dignity, simplicity, and courtesy, taking occasion to pay very flattering compliments to the American legal profession, speaking particularly of Judge Story. The compliment gave me great pleasure, because it seemed a just and noble-minded appreciation, and not a mere civil fiction. We are always better pleased with appreciation than flattery, though perhaps he strained a point when he said, "Our brethren on the other side of the Atlantic, with whom we are now exchanging legal authorities, I fear largely surpass us in the production of philosophic and comprehensive forms."

Speaking of the two countries he said, "God forbid that, with a common language, with common laws which we are materially improving for the benefit of mankind, with one common literature, with one common religion, and above all with one common love of liberty, God forbid that any feeling should arise between the two countries but the desire to carry through the world these advantages."

Mr. Justice Talfourd proposed the literature of our two countries, under the head of "Anglo-Saxon Literature." He made allusion to the author of Uncle Tom's Cabin and Mr. Dickens, speaking of both as having employed fiction as a means of awakening the attention of the respective countries to the condition of the oppressed and suffering classes. Mr. Talfourd appears to be in the prime of life, of a robust and somewhat florid habit. He is universally beloved for his nobleness of soul and generous interest in all that tends to promote the welfare of humanity, no less than for his classical and scholarly attainments.

Mr. Dickens replied to this toast in a graceful and playful strain. In the former part of the evening, in reply to a toast on the chancery department, Vice-Chancellor Wood, who spoke in the absence of the lord chancellor, made a sort of defence of the Court of Chancery, not distinctly alluding to Bleak House, but evidently not without reference to it. The amount of what he said was, that the court had received a great many more hard opinions than it merited; that they had been parsimoniously obliged to perform a great amount of business by a very inadequate number of judges; but that more recently the number of judges had been increased to seven, and there was reason to hope that all business brought before it would now be performed without unnecessary delay.

In the conclusion of Mr. Dickens's speech he alluded playfully to this item of intelligence; said he was exceedingly happy to hear it, as he trusted now that a suit, in which he was greatly interested, would speedily come to an end. I heard a little by conversation between Mr. Dickens and a gentleman of the bar, who sat opposite me, in which the latter seemed to be reiterating the same assertions, and I understood him to say, that a case not extraordinarily complicated might be got through with in three months. Mr. Dickens said he was very happy to hear it; but I fancied there was a little shade of incredulity in his manner; however, the incident showed one thing, that is, that the chancery were not insensible to the representations of Dickens; but the whole tone of the thing was quite good-natured and agreeable. In this respect, I must say I think the English are quite remarkable. Every thing here meets the very freest handling; nothing is too sacred to be publicly shown up; but those who are exhibited appear to have too much good sense to recognize the force of the picture by getting angry. Mr. Dickens has gone on unmercifully exposing all sorts of weak places in the English fabric, public and private, yet nobody cries out upon him as the slanderer of his country. He serves up Lord Dedlocks to his heart's content, yet none of the nobility make wry faces about it; nobody is in a hurry to proclaim that he has recognized the picture, by getting into a passion at it. The contrast between the people of England and America, in this respect, is rather unfavorable to us, because they are by profession conservative, and we by profession radical.

For us to be annoyed when any of our institutions are commented upon, is in the highest degree absurd; it would do well enough for Naples, but it does not do for America.

There were some curious old customs observed at this dinner which interested me as peculiar. About the middle of the feast, the official who performed all the announcing made the declaration that the lord mayor and lady mayoress would pledge the guests in a loving cup. They then rose, and the official presented them with a massive gold cup, full of wine, in which they pledged the guests. It then passed down the table, and the guests rose, two and two, each tasting and presenting to the other. My fair informant told me that this was a custom which had come down from the most ancient time.

The banquet was enlivened at intervals by songs from professional singers, hired for the occasion. After the banquet was over, massive gold basins, filled with rose water, slid along down the table, into which the guests dipped their napkins—an improvement, I suppose, on the doctrine of finger glasses, or perhaps the primeval form of the custom.

We rose from table between eleven and twelve o'clock—that is, we ladies—and went into the drawing room, where I was presented to Mrs. Dickens and several other ladies. Mrs. Dickens is a good specimen of a truly English woman; tall, large, and well developed, with fine, healthy color, and an air of frankness, cheerfulness, and reliability. A friend whispered to me that she was as observing, and fond of humor, as her husband.

After a while the gentlemen came back to the drawing room, and I had a few moments of very pleasant, friendly conversation with Mr. Dickens. They are both people that one could not know a little of without desiring to know more.

I had some conversation with the lady mayoress. She said she had been invited to meet me at Stafford House on Saturday, but should be unable to attend, as she had called a meeting on the same day of the city ladies, for considering the condition of milliners and dressmakers, and to form a society for their relief to act in conjunction with that of the west end.

After a little we began to talk of separating; the lord mayor to take his seat in the House of Commons, and the rest of the party to any other engagement that might be upon their list.

"Come, let us go to the House of Commons," said one of my friends, "and make a night of it." "With all my heart," replied I, "if I only had another body to go into to-morrow."

What a convenience in sight-seeing it would be if one could have a relay of bodies, as of clothes, and go from one into the other. But we, not used to the London style of turning night into day, are full weary already; so, good night.

LETTER XIV

ROSE COTTAGE, WALWORTH, LONDON, May 2.

MY DEAR:—

This morning Mrs. Follen called, and we had quite a long chat together. We are separated by the whole city. She lives at West End, while I am down here in Walworth, which is one of the postscripts of London; for London has as many postscripts as a lady's letter—little suburban villages which have been overtaken by the growth, of the city, and embraced in its arms. I like them a great deal better than the city, for my part.

Here now, for instance, at Walworth, I can look out at a window and see a nice green meadow with sheep and lambs feeding in it, which is some relief in this smutty old place. London is as smutty as Pittsburg or Wheeling. It takes a good hour's steady riding to get from here to West End; so that my American friends, of the newspapers, who are afraid I shall be corrupted by aristocratic associations, will see that I am at safe distance.

This evening we are appointed to dine with the Earl of Carlisle. There is to be no company but his own family circle, for he, with great consideration, said in his note that he thought a little quiet would be the best thing he could offer. Lord Carlisle is a great friend to America; and so is his sister, the Duchess of Sutherland. He is the only English traveller who ever wrote notes on our country in a real spirit of appreciation. While the Halls, and Trollopes, and all the rest could see nothing but our breaking eggs on the wrong end, or such matters, he discerned and interpreted those points wherein lies the real strength of our growing country. His notes on America were not very extended, being only sketches delivered as a lyceum lecture some years after his return. It was the spirit and quality, rather than quantity, of the thing that was noticeable.

I observe that American newspapers are sneering about his preface to Uncle Tom's Cabin; but they ought at least to remember that his sentiments with regard to slavery are no sudden freak. In the first place, he comes of a family that has always been on the side of liberal and progressive principles. He himself has been a leader of reforms on the popular side. It was a temporary defeat, when run as an anti-corn-law candidate, which gave him leisure to travel in America. Afterwards he had the satisfaction to be triumphantly returned for that district, and to see the measure he had advocated fully successful.

While Lord Carlisle was in America he never disguised those antislavery sentiments which formed a part of his political and religious creed as an Englishman, and as the heir of a house always true to progress. Many cultivated English people have shrunk from acknowledging abolitionists in Boston, where the ostracism of fashion and wealth has been enforced against them. Lord Carlisle, though moving in the highest circle, honestly and openly expressed his respect for them on all occasions. He attended the Boston antislavery fair, which at that time was quite a decided step. Nor did he even in any part of our country disguise his convictions. There is, therefore, propriety and consistency in the course he has taken now.

It would seem that a warm interest in questions of a public nature has always distinguished the ladies of this family. The Duchess of Sutherland's mother is daughter of the celebrated Duchess of Devonshire, who, in her day, employed on the liberal side in politics all the power of genius, wit, beauty, and rank. It was to the electioneering talents of herself and her sister, the Lady Duncannon, that Fox, at one crisis, owed his election. We Americans should remember that it was this party who advocated our cause during our revolutionary struggle. Fox and his associates pleaded for us with much the same arguments, and with the same earnestness and warmth, that American abolitionists now plead for the slaves. They stood against all the power of the king and cabinet, as the abolitionists in America in 1850 stood against president and cabinet.

The Duchess of Devonshire was a woman of real noble impulses and generous emotions, and had a true sympathy for what is free and heroic. Coleridge has some fine lines addressed to her,—called forth by a sonnet which she composed, while in Switzerland, on William Tell's Chapel,—which begin,—

> "O lady, nursed in pomp and pleasure,
> Where learn'dst thou that heroic measure?"

The Duchess of Sutherland, in our times, has been known to be no less warmly interested on the liberal side. So great was her influence held to be, that upon a certain occasion when a tory cabinet was to be formed, a distinguished minister is reported to have said to the queen that he could not hope to succeed in his administration while such a decided influence as that of the Duchess of Sutherland stood at the head of her majesty's household. The queen's spirited refusal to surrender her favorite attendant attracted, at the time, universal admiration.

Like her brother Lord Carlisle, the Duchess of Sutherland has always professed those sentiments with regard to slavery which are the glory of the

English nation, and which are held with more particular zeal by those families who are favorable to the progress of liberal ideas.

At about seven o'clock we took our carriage to go to the Earl of Carlisle's, the dinner hour being here somewhere between eight and nine. As we rode on through the usual steady drizzling rain, from street to street and square to square, crossing Waterloo Bridge, with its avenue of lamps faintly visible in the seethy mist, plunging through the heart of the city, we began to realize something of the immense extent of London.

Altogether the most striking objects that you pass, as you ride in the evening thus, are the gin shops, flaming and flaring from the most conspicuous positions, with plate-glass windows and dazzling lights, thronged with men, and women, and children, drinking destruction. Mothers go there with babies in their arms, and take what turns the mother's milk to poison. Husbands go there, and spend the money that their children want for bread, and multitudes of boys and girls of the age of my own. In Paris and other European cities, at least the great fisher of souls baits with something attractive, but in these gin shops men bite at the bare, barbed hook. There are no garlands, no dancing, no music, no theatricals, no pretence of social exhilaration, nothing but hogsheads of spirits, and people going in to drink. The number of them that I passed seemed to me absolutely appalling.

After long driving we found ourselves coming into the precincts of the West End, and began to feel an indefinite sense that we were approaching something very grand, though I cannot say that we saw much but heavy, smoky-walled buildings, washed by the rain. At length we stopped in Grosvenor Place, and alighted.

We were shown into an anteroom adjoining the entrance hall, and from that into an adjacent apartment, where we met Lord Carlisle. The room had a pleasant, social air, warmed and enlivened by the blaze of a coal fire and wax candles.

We had never, any of us, met Lord Carlisle before; but the considerateness and cordiality of our reception obviated whatever embarrassment there might have been in this circumstance. In a few moments after we were all seated the servant announced the Duchess of Sutherland, and Lord Carlisle presented me. She is tall and stately, with a decided fulness of outline, and a most noble bearing. Her fair complexion, blond hair, and full lips speak of Saxon blood. In her early youth she might have been a Rowena. I thought of the lines of Wordsworth:—

"A perfect woman, nobly planned,

> To warn, to comfort, to command."

Her manners have a peculiar warmth and cordiality. One sees people now and then who seem to *radiate* kindness and vitality, and to have a faculty of inspiring perfect confidence in a moment. There are no airs of grandeur, no patronizing ways; but a genuine sincerity and kindliness that seem to come from a deep fountain within.

The engraving by Winterhalter, which has been somewhat familiar in America, is as just a representation of her air and bearing as could be given.

After this we were presented to the various members of the Howard family, which is a very numerous one. Among them were Lady Dover, Lady Lascelles, and Lady Labouchère, sisters of the duchess. The Earl of Burlington, who is the heir of the Duke of Devonshire, was also present. The Duke of Devonshire is the uncle of Lord Carlisle.

The only person present not of the family connection was my quondam correspondent in America, Arthur Helps. Somehow or other I had formed the impression from his writings that he was a venerable sage of very advanced years, who contemplated life as an aged hermit, from the door of his cell. Conceive my surprise to find a genial young gentleman of about twenty-five, who looked as if he might enjoy a joke as well as another man.

At dinner I found myself between him and Lord Carlisle, and perceiving, perhaps, that the nature of my reflections was of rather an amusing order, he asked me confidentially if I did not like fun, to which I assented with fervor. I like that little homely word *fun*, though I understand the dictionary says what it represents is vulgar; but I think it has a good, hearty, Saxon sound, and I like Saxon, better than Latin or French either.

When the servant offered me wine Lord Carlisle asked me if our party were all *teetotallers*, and I said yes; that in America all clergymen were teetotallers, of course.

After the ladies left the table the conversation turned on the Maine law, which seems to be considered over here as a phenomenon, in legislation, and many of the gentlemen, present inquired about it with great curiosity.

When we went into the drawing room I was presented to the venerable Countess of Carlisle, the earl's mother; a lady universally beloved and revered, not less for superior traits of mind than for great loveliness and benevolence of character. She received us with the utmost kindness; kindness evidently genuine and real.

The walls of the drawing room were beautifully adorned with works of art by the best masters. There was a Rembrandt hanging over the fireplace, which showed finely by the evening light. It was simply the portrait of a man with a broad, Flemish hat. There were one or two pictures, also, by Cuyp. I should think he must have studied in America, so perfectly does he represent the golden, hazy atmosphere of our Indian summer.

One of the ladies showed me a snuff box on which was a picture of Lady Carlisle's mother, the celebrated Duchess of Devonshire, taken when she was quite a little girl; a round, happy face, showing great vivacity and genius. On another box was an exquisitely beautiful miniature of a relative of the family.

After the gentlemen rejoined us came in the Duke and Duchess of Argyle, and Lord and Lady Blantyre. These ladies are the daughters of the Duchess of Sutherland. The Duchess of Argyle is of a slight and fairy-like figure, with flaxen hair and blue eyes, answering well enough to the description of Annot Lyle, in the Legend of Montrose. Lady Blantyre was somewhat taller, of fuller figure, with very brilliant bloom. Lord Blantyre is of the Stuart blood, a tall and slender young man, with very graceful manners.

As to the Duke of Argyle, we found that the picture drawn of him by his countrymen in Scotland was every way correct. Though slight of figure, with fair complexion and blue eyes, his whole appearance is indicative of energy and vivacity. His talents and efficiency have made him a member of the British cabinet at a much earlier age than is usual; and he has distinguished himself not only in political life, but as a writer, having given to the world a work on Presbyterianism, embracing an analysis of the ecclesiastical history of Scotland since the reformation, which is spoken of as written with great ability, in a most candid and liberal spirit.

The company soon formed themselves into little groups in different parts of the room. The Duchess of Sutherland, Lord Carlisle, and the Duke and Duchess of Argyle formed a circle, and turned the conversation upon American topics. The Duke of Argyle made many inquiries about our distinguished men; particularly of Emerson, Longfellow, and Hawthorne; also of Prescott, who appears to be a general favorite here. I felt at the moment that we never value our literary men so much as when placed in a circle of intelligent foreigners; it is particularly so with Americans, because we have nothing but our men and women to glory in—no court, no nobles, no castles, no cathedrals; except we produce distinguished specimens of humanity, we are nothing.

The quietness of this evening circle, the charm of its kind hospitality, the evident air of sincerity and good will which pervaded every thing, made the evening pass most delightfully to me. I had never felt myself more at home even among the Quakers. Such a visit is a true rest and refreshment, a thousand times better than the most brilliant and glittering entertainment.

At eleven o'clock, however, the carriage called, for our evening was drawing to its close; that of our friends, I suppose, was but just commencing, as London's liveliest hours are by gaslight, but we cannot learn the art of turning night into day.

LETTER XV

May 4.

My Dear S:—

This morning I felt too tired to go out any where; but Mr. and Mrs. Binney persuaded me to go just a little while in to the meeting of the Bible Society, for you must know that this is anniversary week, and so, besides the usual rush, and roar, and whirl of London, there is the confluence of all the religious forces in Exeter Hall. I told Mrs. B. that I was worn out, and did not think I could sit through a single speech; but she tempted me by a promise that I should withdraw at any moment. We had a nice little snug gallery near one of the doors, where I could see all over the house, and make a quick retreat in case of need.

In one point English ladies certainly do carry practical industry farther than I ever saw it in America. Every body knows that an anniversary meeting is something of a siege, and I observed many good ladies below had made regular provision therefor, by bringing knitting work, sewing, crochet, or embroidery. I thought it was an improvement, and mean to recommend it when I get home. I am sure many of our Marthas in America will be very grateful for the custom.

The Earl of Shaftesbury was in the chair, and I saw him now for the first time. He is quite a tall man, of slender figure, with a long and narrow face, dark hazel eyes, and very thick, auburn hair. His bearing was dignified and appropriate to his position. People here are somewhat amused by the vivacity with which American papers are exhorting Lord Shaftesbury to look into the factory system, and to explore the collieries, and in general to take care of the suffering lower classes, as if he had been doing any thing else for these twenty years past. To people who know how he has worked against wind and tide, in the face of opposition and obloquy, and how all the dreadful statistics that they quote against him were brought out expressly by inquiries set on foot and prosecuted by him, and how these same statistics have been by him reiterated in the ears of successive houses of Parliament till all these abuses have been reformed, as far as the most stringent and minute legislation can reform, them,—it is quite amusing to hear him exhorted to consider the situation of the working classes. One reason for this, perhaps, is that provoking facility in changing names which is incident to the English peerage. During the time that most of the researches and speeches on the factory system and collieries were made, the Earl of Shaftesbury was in the House of Commons, with the title of Lord

Ashley, and it was not till the death of his father that he entered the House of Peers as Lord Shaftesbury. The contrast which a very staid religious paper in America has drawn between Lord Ashley and Lord Shaftesbury does not strike people over here as remarkably apposite.

In the course of the speeches on this occasion, frequent and feeling allusions were made to the condition of three millions of people in America who are prevented by legislative enactments from reading for themselves the word of life. I know it is not pleasant to our ministers upon the stage to hear such things; but is the whole moral sense of the world to hush its voice, the whole missionary spirit of Christianity to be restrained, because it is disagreeable for us to be reminded of our national sins? At least, let the moral atmosphere of the world be kept pure, though it should be too stimulating for our diseased lungs. If oral instruction will do for three million slaves in America, it will do equally well in Austria, Italy, and Spain, and the powers that be, there, are just of the opinion that they are in America—that it is dangerous to have the people read the Bible for themselves. Thoughts of this kind were very ably set forth in some of the speeches. On the stage I noticed Rev. Samuel R. Ward, from Toronto in Canada, a full blooded African of fine personal presence. He was received and treated with much cordiality by the ministerial brethren who surrounded him. I was sorry that I could not stay through the speeches, for they were quite interesting. C. thought they were the best he ever heard at an anniversary. I was obliged to leave after a little. Mr. Sherman very kindly came for us in his carriage, and took us a little ride into the country.

Mrs. B. says that to-morrow morning we shall go out to see the Dulwich Gallery, a fine collection of paintings by the old masters. Now, I confess unto you that I have great suspicions of these old masters. Why, I wish to know, should none but *old* masters be thought any thing of? Is not nature ever springing, ever new? Is it not fair to conclude that all the mechanical assistants of painting are improved with the advance of society, as much as of all arts? May not the magical tints, which are said to be a secret with the old masters, be the effect of time in part? or may not modern artists have their secrets, as well, for future ages to study and admire? Then, besides, how are we to know that our admiration of old masters is genuine, since we can bring our taste to any thing, if we only know we must, and try long enough? People never like olives the first time they eat them. In fact, I must confess, I have some partialities towards young masters, and a sort of suspicion that we are passing over better paintings at our side, to get at those which, though the best of their day, are not so good as the best of ours. I certainly do not worship the old English poets. With the exception of Milton and Shakspeare, there is more poetry in the works of the writers of the last fifty years than in all the rest together. Well, these are my surmises for the present; but one thing I am determined—as my admiration is nothing to any body but myself, I will keep some likes and dislikes of my own, and will not get up any raptures that do not arise of themselves. I am entirely willing to be conquered by any picture that has the power. I will be a non-resistant, but that is all.

May 5 Well we saw the Dulwich Gallery; five rooms filled with old masters, Murillos, Claudes, Rubens, Salvator Rosas, Titians, Cuyps, Vandykes, and all the rest of them; probably not the best specimens of any one of them, but good enough to begin with. C. and I took different courses. I said to him, "Now choose nine pictures simply by your eye, and see how far its untaught guidance will bring you within the canons of criticism." When he had gone through all the rooms and marked his pictures, we found he had selected two by Rubens, two by Vandyke, one by Salvator Rosa, three by Murillo, and one by Titian. Pretty successful that, was it not, for a first essay? We then took the catalogue, and selected all the pictures of each artist one after another, in order to get an idea of the style of each. I had a great curiosity to see Claude Lorraine's, remembering the poetical things that had been said and sung of him. I thought I would see if I could distinguish them by my eye without looking at the catalogue I found I could do so. I knew them by a certain misty quality in the atmosphere. I was disappointed in them, very much. Certainly, they were good paintings; I had nothing to object to them, but I profanely thought I had seen pictures by modern landscape painters as far excelling them as a brilliant morning excels a cool, gray day. Very likely the fault was all in me, but I could not help it; so I tried the Murillos. There was a Virgin and Child, with clouds around them. The virgin was a very pretty girl, such as you may see by the dozen in any boarding school, and the child was a pretty child. Call it the young mother and son, and it is a very pretty picture; but call it Mary and the infant Jesus, and it is an utter failure. Not such was the Jewish princess, the inspired poetess and priestess, the chosen of God among all women.

It seems to me that painting is poetry expressing itself by lines and colors instead of words; therefore there are two things to be considered in every picture: first, the quality of the idea expressed, and second, the quality of the language in which it is expressed. Now, with regard to the first, I hold that every person of cultivated taste is as good a judge of painting as of poetry. The second, which relates to the mode of expressing the conception, including drawing and coloring, with all their secrets, requires more study, and here our untaught perceptions must sometimes yield to the judgment of artists. My first question, then, when I look at the work of an artist, is, What sort of a mind has this man? What has he to say? And then I consider, How does he say it?

Now, with regard to Murillo, it appeared to me that he was a man of rather a mediocre mind, with nothing very high or deep to say, but that he was gifted with an exquisite faculty of expressing what he did say; and his paintings seem to me to bear an analogy to Pope's poetry, wherein the power of expression is wrought to the highest point, but without freshness or ideality in the conception. As Pope could reproduce in most exquisite wording the fervent ideas of Eloisa, without the power to originate such, so Murillo reproduced the current and floating religious ideas of his times, with most exquisite perfection of art and color, but without ideality or vitality. The pictures of his which please me most are his beggar boys and flower girls, where he abandons the region of ideality, and simply reproduces nature. His art and coloring give an exquisite grace to such sketches.

As to Vandyke, though evidently a fine painter, he is one whose mind does not move me. He adds nothing to my stock of thoughts—awakens no emotion. I know it is a fine picture, just as I have sometimes been conscious in church that I was hearing a fine sermon, which somehow had not the slightest effect upon me.

Rubens, on the contrary, whose pictures I detested with all the energy of my soul, I knew and felt all the time, by the very pain he gave me, to be a real living artist. There was a Venus and Cupid there, as fat and as coarse as they could be, but so freely drawn, and so masterly in their expression and handling, that one must feel that they were by an artist, who could just as easily have painted them any other way if it had suited his sovereign pleasure, and therefore we are the more vexed with him. When your taste is crossed by a clever person, it always vexes you more than when it is done by a stupid one, because it is done with such power that there is less hope for you.

There were a number of pictures of Cuyp there, which satisfied my thirst for coloring, and appeared to me as I expected the Claudes would have done. Generally speaking, his objects are few in number and commonplace in their character—a bit of land and water, a few cattle and figures, in no way remarkable; but then he floods the whole with that dreamy, misty sunlight, such as fills the arches of our forests in the days of autumn. As I looked at them I fancied I could hear nuts dropping from the trees among the dry leaves, and see the goldenrods and purple asters, and hear the click of the squirrel as he whips up the tree to his nest. For this one attribute of golden, dreamy haziness, I like Cuyp. His power in shedding it over very simple objects reminds me of some of the short poems of Longfellow, when things in themselves most prosaic are flooded with a kind of poetic light from the inner soul. These are merely first ideas and impressions. Of course I do not make up my mind about any artist from what I have seen here. We must not expect a painter to put his talent into every picture, more than a poet into every verse that he writes. Like other men, he is sometimes brilliant and inspired, and at others dull and heavy. In general, however, I have this to say, that there is some kind of fascination about these old masters which I feel very sensibly. But yet, I am sorry to add that there is very little of what I consider the highest mission of art in the specimens I have thus far seen, nothing which speaks to the deepest and the highest; which would inspire a generous ardor, or a solemn religious trust. Vainly I seek for something divine, and ask of art to bring me nearer to the source of all beauty and perfection. I find wealth of coloring, freedom of design, and capability of expression wasting themselves merely in portraying trivial sensualities and commonplace ideas. So much for the first essay.

In the evening we went to dine with our old friends of the Dingle, Mr. and Mrs. Edward Cropper, who are now spending a little time in London. We were delighted to meet them once more, and to hear from our Liverpool friends. Mrs. Cropper's father, Lord Denman, has returned to England, though with no sensible improvement in his health.

At dinner we were introduced to Lord and Lady Hatherton. Lord Hatherton is a member of the whig party, and has been chief secretary for Ireland. Lady Hatherton is a person of great cultivation and intelligence, warmly interested in all the progressive movements of the day; and I gained much information in her society. There were also present Sir Charles and Lady Trevelyan; the former holds some appointment in the navy. Lady Trevelyan is a sister of Macaulay.

In the evening quite a circle came in; among others, Lady Emma Campbell, sister of the Duke of Argyle; the daughters of the Archbishop of Canterbury, who very kindly invited me to visit them, at Lambeth; and Mr. Arthur Helps, besides many others whose names I need not mention.

People here continually apologize for the weather, which, to say the least, has been rather ungracious since we have been here; as if one ever expected to find any thing but smoke, and darkness, and fog in London. The authentic air with which they lament the existence of these things *at present* would almost persuade one that *in general* London was a very clear, bright place. I, however, assured them that, having heard from my childhood of the smoke of London, its dimness and darkness, I found things much better than I had expected.

They talk here of spirit rappings and table turnings, I find, as in America. Many rumors are afloat which seem to have no other effect than merely to enliven the chitchat of an evening circle. I passed a very pleasant evening, and left about ten o'clock. The gentleman who was handing me down stairs said, "I suppose you are going to one or two other places to-night." The idea struck me as so preposterous that I could not help an exclamation of surprise.

May 6. A good many calls this morning. Among others came Miss Greenfield, the (so called) Black Swan. She appears to be a gentle, amiable, and interesting young person. She was born the slave of a kind mistress, who gave her every thing but education, and, dying, left her free with a little property. The property she lost by some legal quibble, but had, like others of her race, a passion for music, and could sing and play by ear. A young lady, discovering her taste, gave her a few lessons. She has a most astonishing voice. C. sat down to the piano and played, while she sung. Her voice runs through a compass of three octaves and a fourth. This is four notes more than Malibran's. She sings a most magnificent tenor, with such a breadth and volume of sound that, with your back turned, you could not imagine it to be a woman. While she was there, Mrs. S.C. Hall, of the Irish Sketches, was announced. She is a tall, well-proportioned woman, with a fine color, dark-brown hair, and a cheerful, cordial manner. She brought with her her only daughter, a young girl about fifteen. I told her of Miss Greenfield, and, she took great interest in her, and requested her to sing something for her. C. played the accompaniment, and she sung Old Folks at Home, first in a soprano voice, and then in a tenor or baritone. Mrs. Hall was amazed and delighted, and entered at once into her cause. She said that she would call with me and present her to Sir George Smart, who is at the head of the queen's musical establishment, and, of course, the acknowledged leader of London musical judgment.

Mrs. Hall very kindly told me that she had called to invite me to seek a retreat with her in her charming little country house near London. I do not mean that *she* called it a charming little retreat, but that every one who speaks of it gives it that character. She told me that I should there have positive and perfect quiet; and what could attract me more than that? She said, moreover, that there they had a great many nightingales. Ah, this "bower of roses by Bendemeer's stream," could I only go there! but I am tied to London by a hundred engagements. I cannot do it. Nevertheless, I have promised that I will go and spend some time yet, when Mr. S. leaves London.

In the course of the day I had a note from Mrs. Hall, saying that, as Sir George Smart was about leaving town, she had not waited for me, but had taken Miss Greenfield to him herself. She writes that he was really astonished and charmed at the wonderful weight, compass, and power of her voice. He was also as well pleased with the mind in her singing, and her quickness in doing and catching all that he told her. Should she have a public opportunity to perform, he offered to hear her rehearse beforehand.

Mrs. Hall says this is a great deal for him, whose hours are all marked with gold.

In the evening the house was opened in a general way for callers, who were coming and going all the evening. I think there must have been over two hundred people—among them Martin Farquhar Tupper, a little man, with fresh, rosy complexion, and cheery, joyous manners; and Mary Howitt, just such a cheerful, sensible, fireside companion as we find her in her books,— winning love and trust the very first few moments of the interview. The general topic of remark on meeting me seems to be, that I am not so bad looking as they were afraid I was; and I do assure you that, when I have seen the things that are put up in the shop windows here with my name under them, I have been in wondering admiration at the boundless loving-kindness of my English and Scottish friends, in keeping up such a warm heart for such a Gorgon. I should think that the Sphinx in the London Museum might have sat for most of them. I am going to make a collection of these portraits to bring home to you. There is a great variety of them, and they will be useful, like the Irishman's guideboard, which showed where the road did not go.

Before the evening was through I was talked out and worn out—there was hardly a chip of me left. To-morrow at eleven o'clock comes the meeting at Stafford House. What it will amount to I do not know; but I take no thought for the morrow.

LETTER XVI

MAY 8.

MY DEAR C.:—

In fulfilment of my agreement, I will tell you, as nearly as I can remember, all the details of the meeting at Stafford House.

At about eleven o'clock we drove under the arched carriage way of a mansion, externally, not very showy in appearance. It stands on the borders of St. James's Park, opposite to Buckingham Palace, with a street on the north side, and beautiful gardens on the south, while the park is extended on the west.

We were received at the door by two stately Highlanders in full costume; and what seemed to me an innumerable multitude of servants in livery, with powdered hair, repeated our names through the long corridors, from one to another.

I have only a confused idea of passing from passage to passage, and from hall to hall, till finally we were introduced into a large drawing room. No person was present, and I was at full leisure to survey an apartment whose arrangements more perfectly suited my eye and taste than any I had ever seen before. There was not any particular splendor of furniture, or dazzling display of upholstery, but an artistic, poetic air, resulting from the arrangement of colors, and the disposition of the works of *virtu* with which the room abounded. The great fault in many splendid rooms, is, that they are arranged without any eye to unity of impression. The things in them may be all fine in their way, but there is no harmony of result.

People do not often consider that there may be a general sentiment to be expressed in the arrangement of a room, as well as in the composition of a picture. It is this leading idea which corresponds to what painters call the ground tone, or harmonizing tint, of a picture. The presence of this often renders a very simple room extremely fascinating, and the absence of it makes the most splendid combinations of furniture powerless to please.

The walls were covered with green damask, laid on flat, and confined in its place by narrow gilt bands, which bordered it around the margin. The chairs, ottomans, and sofas were of white woodwork, varnished and gilded, covered with the same.

The carpet was of a green ground, bedropped with a small yellow leaf; and in each window a circular, standing basket contained a whole bank of primroses, growing as if in their native soil, their pale yellow blossoms and green leaves harmonizing admirably with the general tone of coloring.

Through the fall of the lace curtains I could see out into the beautiful grounds, whose clumps of blossoming white lilacs, and velvet grass, seemed so in harmony with the green interior of the room, that one would think they had been arranged as a continuation of the idea.

One of the first individual objects which attracted my attention was, over the mantel-piece, a large, splendid picture by Landseer, which I have often seen engraved. It represents the two eldest children of the Duchess of Sutherland, the Marquis of Stafford, and Lady Blantyre, at that time Lady Levison Gower, in their childhood. She is represented as feeding a fawn; a little poodle dog is holding up a rose to her; and her brother is lying on the ground, playing with an old staghound.

I had been familiar with Landseer's engravings, but this was the first of his paintings I had ever seen, and I was struck with the rich and harmonious quality of the coloring. There was also a full-length marble statue of the Marquis of Stafford, taken, I should think, at about seventeen years of age, in full Highland costume.

When the duchess appeared, I thought she looked handsomer by daylight than in the evening. She was dressed in white muslin, with a drab velvet basque slashed with satin of the same color. Her hair was confined by a gold and diamond net on the back part of her head.

She received us with the same warm and simple kindness which she had shown before. We were presented to the Duke of Sutherland. He is a tall, slender man, with rather a thin face, light brown hair, and a mild blue eye, with an air of gentleness and dignity. The delicacy of his health prevents him from moving in general society, or entering into public life. He spends much of his time in reading, and devising and executing schemes of practical benevolence for the welfare of his numerous dependants.

I sought a little private conversation with the duchess in her boudoir, in which I frankly confessed a little anxiety respecting the arrangements of the day; having lived all my life in such a shady and sequestered way, and being entirely ignorant of life as it exists in the sphere in which she moves, such apprehensions were rather natural.

She begged that I would make myself entirely easy, and consider myself as among my own friends; that she had invited a few friends to lunch, and that afterwards others would call; that there would be a short address from the ladies of England read by Lord Shaftesbury, which would require no answer.

I could not but be grateful for the consideration thus evinced. The matter being thus adjusted, we came back to the drawing room, when the party began to assemble.

The only difference, I may say, by the by, in the gathering of such a company and one with us, is in the announcing of names at the door; a, custom which I think a good one, saving a vast deal of the breath we always expend in company, by asking "Who is that? and that?" Then, too, people can fall into conversation without a formal presentation, the presumption being that nobody is invited with whom, it is not proper that you should converse. The functionary who performed the announcing was a fine, stalwart man, in full Highland costume, the duke being the head of a Highland clan.

Among the first that entered were the members of the family, the Duke and Duchess of Argyle, Lord and Lady Blantyre, the Marquis and Marchioness of Stafford, and Lady Emma Campbell. Then followed Lord Shaftesbury with his beautiful lady, and her father and mother, Lord and Lady Palmerston. Lord Palmerston is of middle height, with a keen, dark eye, and black hair streaked with gray. There is something peculiarly alert and vivacious about all his movements; in short his appearance perfectly answers to what we know of him from his public life. One has a strange mythological feeling about the existence of people of whom one hears for many years without ever seeing them. While talking with Lord Palmerston I could but remember how often I had heard father and Mr. S. exulting over his foreign despatches by our home fireside.

The Marquis of Lansdowne now entered. He is about the middle height, with gray hair, blue eyes, and a mild, quiet dignity of manner. He is one of those who, as Lord Henry Pettes, took a distinguished part with Clarkson and Wilberforce in the abolition of the slave trade. He has always been a most munificent patron of literature and art.

There were present, also, Lord John Russell, Mr. Gladstone, and Lord Grenville. The latter we all thought very strikingly resembled in his appearance the poet Longfellow. My making the remark introduced the subject of his poetry. The Duchess of Argyle appealed to her two little boys, who stood each side of her, if they remembered her reading Evangeline to them. It is a gratification to me that I find by every English fireside traces of one of our American poets. These two little boys of the Duchess of Argyle, and the youngest son of the Duchess of Sutherland, were beautiful fair-haired children, picturesquely attired in the Highland costume. There were some other charming children of the family circle present. The eldest son of the Duke of Argyle bears the title of the Lord of Lorn, which Scott has rendered so poetical a sound to our ears.

When lunch was announced, the Duke of Sutherland gave me his arm, and led me through a suite of rooms into the dining hall. Each room that we passed was rich in its pictures, statues, and artistic arrangements; a poetic eye and taste had evidently presided over all. The table was beautifully laid, ornamented by two magnificent *épergnes*, crystal vases supported by wrought silver standards, filled with the most brilliant hothouse flowers; on the edges of the vases and nestling among the flowers were silver doves of the size of life. The walls of the room were hung with gorgeous pictures, and directly opposite to me was a portrait of the Duchess of Sutherland, by Sir Thomas Lawrence, which has figured largely in our souvenirs and books of beauty. She is represented with a little child in her arms; this child, now Lady Blantyre, was sitting opposite to me at table, with a charming little girl of her own, of about the same apparent age. When one sees such things, one almost fancies this to be a fairy palace, where the cold demons of age and time have lost their power.

I was seated next to Lord Lansdowne, who conversed much with me about affairs in America. It seems to me that the great men of the old world regard our country thoughtfully. It is a new development of society, acting every day with greater and greater power on the old world; nor is it yet clearly seen what its final results will be. His observations indicated a calm, clear, thoughtful mind—an accurate observer of life and history.

Meanwhile the servants moved noiselessly to and fro, taking up the various articles on the table, and offering them to the guests in a peculiarly quiet manner. One of the dishes brought to me was a plover's nest, precisely as the plover made it, with five little blue speckled eggs in it. This mode of serving plover's eggs, as I understand it, is one of the fashions of-the-day, and has something quite sylvan and picturesque about it; but it looked so, for all the world, like a robin's nest that I used to watch out in our home orchard, that I had it not in my heart to profane the sanctity of the image by eating one of the eggs.

The *cuisine* of these West End regions appears to be entirely under French legislation, conducted by Parisian artists, skilled in all subtle and metaphysical combinations of ethereal possibilities, quite inscrutable to the eye of sense. Her grace's *chef*, I have heard it said elsewhere, bears the reputation of being the first artist of his class in England. The profession as thus sublimated bears the same proportion to the old substantial English cookery that Mozart's music does to Handel's, or Midsummer Night's Dream to Paradise Lost.

This meal, called *lunch*, is with the English quite an institution, being apparently a less elaborate and ceremonious dinner. Every thing is placed upon the table at once, and ladies sit down without removing their bonnets;

it is, I imagine, the most social and family meal of the day; one in which children are admitted to the table, even in the presence of company. It generally takes place in the middle of the day, and the dinner, which comes after it, at eight or nine in the evening, is in comparison only a ceremonial proceeding.

I could not help thinking, as I looked around on so many men whom I had heard of historically all my life, how very much less they bear the marks of age than men who have been connected a similar length of time with the movements of our country. This appearance of youthfulness and alertness has a constantly deceptive influence upon one in England. I cannot realize that people are as old as history states them to be. In the present company there were men of sixty or seventy, whom I should have pronounced at the first glance to be fifty.

Generally speaking our working minds seem to wear out their bodies faster; perhaps because our climate is more stimulating; more, perhaps, from the intenser stimulus of our political *régime*, which never leaves any thing long at rest.

The tone of manners in this distinguished circle did not obtrude itself upon my mind as different from that of highly-educated people in our own country. It appeared simple, friendly, natural, and sincere. They talked like people who thought of what they were saying, rather than how to say it. The practice of thorough culture and good breeding is substantially the same through the world, though smaller conventionalities may differ.

After lunch the whole party ascended to the picture gallery, passing on our way the grand staircase and hall, said to be the most magnificent in Europe. All that wealth could command of artistic knowledge and skill has been expended here to produce a superb result. It fills the entire centre of the building, extending up to the roof and surmounted by a splendid dome. On three sides a gallery runs round it supported by pillars. To this gallery you ascend on the fourth side by a staircase, which midway has a broad, flat landing, from which stairs ascend, on the right and left, into the gallery. The whole hall and staircase, carpeted with a scarlet footcloth, give a broad, rich mass of coloring, throwing out finely the statuary and gilded balustrades. On the landing is a marble statue of a Sibyl, by Rinaldi. The walls are adorned by gorgeous frescos from Paul Veronese. What is peculiar in the arrangements of this hall is, that although so extensive, it still wears an air of warm homelikeness and comfort, as if it might be a delightful place to lounge and enjoy life, amid the ottomans, sofas, pictures, and statuary, which are disposed here and there throughout.

All this, however, I passed rapidly by as I ascended the staircase, and passed onward to the picture gallery. This was a room about a hundred feet long by forty wide, surmounted by a dome gorgeously finished with golden palm, trees and carving. This hall is lighted in the evening by a row of gaslights placed outside the ground glass of the dome; this light is concentrated and thrown down by strong reflectors, communicating thus the most brilliant radiance without the usual heat of gas. This gallery is peculiarly rich in paintings of the Spanish school. Among them are two superb Murillos, taken from convents by Marshal Soult, during the time of his career in Spain.

There was a painting by Paul de la Roche of the Earl of Strafford led forth to execution, engravings of which we have seen in the print shops in America. It is a strong and striking picture, and has great dramatic effect. But there was a painting in one corner by a Flemish artist, whose name I do not now remember, representing Christ under examination before Caiaphas. It was a candle-light scene, and only two faces were very distinct; the downcast, calm, resolute face of Christ, in which was written a perfect knowledge of his approaching doom, and the eager, perturbed vehemence of the high priest, who was interrogating him. On the frame was engraved the lines,—

> "He was wounded for our transgressions,
>
> He was bruised for our iniquities;
>
> The chastisement of our peace was upon him,
>
> And with his stripes we are healed."

The presence of this picture here in the midst of this scene was very affecting to me.

The company now began to assemble and throng the gallery, and very soon the vast room was crowded. Among the throng I remember many presentations, but of course must have forgotten many more. Archbishop Whately was there, with Mrs. and Miss Whately; Macaulay, with two of his sisters; Milman, the poet and historian; the Bishop of Oxford, Chevalier Bunsen and lady, and many more.

When all the company were together Lord Shaftesbury read a very short, kind, and considerate address in behalf of the ladies of England, expressive of their cordial welcome. The address will be seen in the Morning Advertiser, which I send you. The company remained a while after this, walking through the rooms and conversing in different groups, and I talked with several. Archbishop Whately, I thought, seemed rather inclined to be jocose: he seems to me like some of our American divines; a man who pays little attention to forms, and does not value them. There is a kind of brusque humor in his address, a downright heartiness, which reminds one of western character. If he had been born in our latitude, in Kentucky or Wisconsin, the natives would have called him Whately, and said he was a real steamboat on an argument. This is not precisely the kind of man we look for in an archbishop. One sees traces of this humor in his Historic Doubts concerning the Existence of Napoleon. I conversed with some who knew him intimately, and they said that he delighted in puns and odd turns of language.

I was also introduced to the Bishop of Oxford, who is a son of Wilberforce. He is a short man, of very youthful appearance, with bland, graceful, courteous manners. He is much admired as a speaker. I heard him spoken of as one of the most popular preachers of the day.

I must not forget to say that many ladies of the society of Friends were here, and one came and put on to my arm a reticule, in which, she said, were carried about the very first antislavery tracts ever distributed in England. At that time the subject of antislavery was as unpopular in England as it can be at this day any where in the world, and I trust that a day will come when the subject will be as popular in South Carolina as it is now in England. People always glory in the right after they have done it.

After a while the company dispersed over the house to look at the rooms. There are all sorts of parlors and reception rooms, furnished with the same correct taste. Each room had its predominant color; among them blue was a particular favorite.

The carpets were all of those small figures I have described, the blue ones being of the same pattern with the green. The idea, I suppose, is to produce a mass of color of a certain tone, and not to distract the eye with the complicated pattern. Where so many objects of art and *virtu* are to be exhibited, without this care in regulating and simplifying the ground tints, there would be no unity in the impression. This was my philosophizing on the matter, and if it is not the reason why it is done, it ought to be. It is as good a theory as most theories, at any rate.

Before we went away I made a little call on the Lady Constance Grosvenor, and saw the future Marquis of Westminster, heir to the largest estate in England. His beautiful mother is celebrated in the annals of the court journal as one of the handsomest ladies in England. His little lordship was presented to me in all the dignity of long, embroidered clothes, being then, I believe, not quite a fortnight old, and I can assure you that he demeaned himself with a gravity becoming his rank and expectations.

There is a more than common interest attached to these children by one who watches the present state of the world. On the character and education of the princes and nobility of this generation the future history of England must greatly depend.

This Stafford House meeting, in any view of it, is a most remarkable fact. Kind and gratifying as its arrangements have been to me, I am far from appropriating it to myself individually, as a personal honor. I rather regard it as the most public expression possible of the feelings of the women of England on one of the most important questions of our day—that, of individual liberty considered in its religious bearings.

The most splendid of England's palaces has this day opened its doors to the slave. Its treasures of wealth and of art, its prestige of high name and historic memories, have been consecrated to the acknowledgment of Christianity in that form, wherein, in our day, it is most frequently denied— the recognition of the brotherhood of the human family, and the equal religious value of every human soul. A fair and noble hand by this meeting has fixed, in the most public manner, an ineffaceable seal to the beautiful sentiments of that most Christian document, the letter of the ladies of Great Britain to the ladies of America. That letter and this public attestation of it are now historic facts, which wait their time and the judgment of advancing Christianity.

Concerning that letter I have one or two things to say. Nothing can be more false than the insinuation that has been thrown out in some American papers, that it was a political movement. It had its first origin in the deep religious feelings of the man whose whole life has been devoted to the abolition of the white-labor slavery of Great Britain; the man whose eye explored the darkness of the collieries, and counted the weary steps of the cotton spinners—who penetrated the dens where the insane were tortured with darkness, and cold, and stripes; and threaded the loathsome alleys of London, haunts of fever and cholera: this man it was, whose heart was overwhelmed by the tale of American slavery, and who could find no relief from, this distress except in raising some voice to the ear of Christianity. Fearful of the jealousy of political interference, Lord Shaftesbury published an address to the ladies of England, in which he told them that he felt himself moved by an irresistible impulse to entreat them to raise their voice, in the name of a common Christianity and womanhood, to their American sisters. The abuse which has fallen upon him for this most Christian proceeding does not in the least surprise him, because it is of the kind that has always met him in every benevolent movement. When in the Parliament of England he was pleading for women in the collieries who were harnessed like beasts of burden, and made to draw heavy loads through miry and dark passages, and for children who were taken at three years old to labor where the sun never shines, he was met with determined and furious opposition and obloquy—accused of being a disorganizer, and of wishing to restore the dark ages. Very similar accusations have attended all his efforts for the laboring classes during the long course of seventeen years, which resulted at last in the triumphant passage of the factory bill.

We in America ought to remember that the gentle remonstrance of the letter of the ladies of England contains, in the mildest form, the sentiments of universal Christendom. Rebukes much more pointed are coming back to us even from, our own missionaries. A day is coming when, past all the temporary currents of worldly excitement, we shall, each of us, stand alone face to face with the perfect purity of our Redeemer. The thought of such a final interview ought certainly to modify all our judgments now, that we may strive to approve only what we shall then approve.

LETTER XVII

LETTER XVII.

MY DEAR C.:—

As to those ridiculous stories about the Duchess of Sutherland, which have found their way into many of the prints in America, one has only to be here, moving in society, to see how excessively absurd they are.

All my way through Scotland, and through England, I was associating, from day to day, with people of every religious denomination, and every rank of life. I have been with, dissenters and with churchmen; with the national Presbyterian church and the free Presbyterian; with Quakers and Baptists.

In all these circles I have heard the great and noble of the land freely spoken of and canvassed, and if there had been the least shadow of a foundation for any such accusations, I certainly should have heard it recognized in some manner. If in no other, such warm friends as I have heard speak would have alluded to the subject in the way of defence; but I have actually never heard any allusion of any sort, as if there was any thing to be explained or accounted for.

As I have before intimated, the Howard family, to which the duchess belongs, is one which has always been on the side of popular rights and popular reform. Lord Carlisle, her brother, has been a leader of the people, particularly during the time of the corn-law reformation, and *she* has been known to take a wide and generous interest in all these subjects. Every where that I have moved through Scotland and England I have heard her kindness of heart, her affability of manner, and her attention to the feelings of others spoken of as marked characteristics.

Imagine, then, what people must think when they find in respectable American prints the absurd story of her turning her tenants out into the snow, and ordering the cottages to be set on fire over their heads because they would not go out.

But, if you ask how such an absurd story could ever have been made up, whether there is the least foundation to make it on, I answer, that it is the exaggerated report of a movement made by the present Duke of Sutherland's father, in the year 1811, and which was part of a great movement that passed through, the Highlands of Scotland, when the advancing progress of civilization began to make it necessary to change the estates from military to agricultural establishments.

Soon after the union of the crowns of England and Scotland, the border chiefs found it profitable to adopt upon their estates that system, of agriculture to which their hills were adapted, rather than to continue the maintenance of military retainers. Instead of keeping garrisons, with small armies, in a district, they decided to keep only so many as could profitably cultivate the land. The effect of this, of course, was like disbanding an army. It threw many people out of employ, and forced them to seek for a home elsewhere. Like many other movements which, in their final results, are beneficial to society, this was at first vehemently resisted, and had to be carried into effect in some cases by force. As I have said, it began first in the southern counties of Scotland, soon after the union of the English and Scottish crowns, and gradually crept northward—one county after another yielding to the change. To a certain extent, as it progressed northward, the demand for labor in the great towns absorbed the surplus population; but when it came into the extreme Highlands, this refuge was wanting. Emigration to America now became the resource; and the surplus population were induced to this by means such as the Colonization Society now recommends and approves for promoting emigration to Liberia.

The first farm that was so formed on the Sutherland estate was in 1806. The great change was made in 1811-12, and completed in 1819-20.

The Sutherland estates are in the most northern portion of Scotland. The distance of this district from the more advanced parts of the kingdom, the total want of roads, the unfrequent communication by sea, and the want of towns, made it necessary to adopt a different course in regard to the location of the Sutherland population from that which circumstances had provided in other parts of Scotland, where they had been removed from the bleak and uncultivable mountains. They had lots given them near the sea, or in more fertile spots, where, by labor and industry, they might maintain themselves. They had two years allowed them for preparing for the change, without payment of rent. Timber for their houses was given, and many other facilities for assisting their change.

The general agent of the Sutherland estate is Mr. Loch. In a speech of this gentleman in the House of Commons, on the second reading of the Scotch poor-law bill, June 12, 1845, he states the following fact with regard to the management of the Sutherland estate during this period, from 1811 to 1833, which certainly can speak for itself: "I can state as from fact that, from 1811 to 1833, not one sixpence of rent has been received from that county, but, on the contrary, there has been sent there, for the benefit and improvement of the people, a sum exceeding sixty thousand pounds."

Mr. Loch goes on in the same speech to say, "There is no set of people more industrious than the people of Sutherland. Thirty years since they were engaged in illegal distillation to a very great extent; at the present moment there is not, I believe, an illegal still in the county. Their morals have improved as those habits have been abandoned; and they have added many hundreds, I believe thousands, of acres to the land in cultivation since they were placed upon the shore.

"Previous to that change to which I have referred, they exported very few cattle, and hardly any thing else. They were, also, every now and then, exposed to all the difficulties of extreme famine. In the years 1812-13, and 1816-17, so great was the misery that it was necessary to send down oatmeal for their supply to the amount of nine thousand pounds, and that was given to the people. But, since industrious habits were introduced, and they were settled within reach of fishing, no such calamity has overtaken them. Their condition was then so low that they were obliged to bleed their cattle, during the winter, and mix the blood with the remnant of meal they had, in order to save them from starvation.

"Since then the country has improved so much that the fish, in particular, which they exported, in 1815, from one village alone, Helmsdale, (which, previous to 1811, did not exist,) amounted to five thousand three hundred and eighteen barrels of herring, and in 1844 thirty-seven thousand five hundred and ninety-four barrels, giving employment to about three thousand nine hundred people. This extends over the whole of the county, in which fifty-six thousand barrels were cured.

"Do not let me be supposed to say that there are not cases requiring attention: it must be so in a large population; but there can be no means taken by a landlord, or by those under him, that are not bestowed upon that tenantry.

"It has been said that the contribution by the heritor (the duke) to one kirk session for the poor was but six pounds. Now, in the eight parishes which are called Sutherland proper, the amount of the contribution of the Duke of Sutherland to the kirk session is forty-two pounds a year. That is a very small sum but that sum merely is so given because the landlord thinks that he can distribute his charity in a more beneficial manner to the people; and the amount of charity which he gives—and which, I may say, is settled on them, for it is given regularly—is above four hundred and fifty pounds a year.

"Therefore the statements that have been made, so far from being correct, are in every way an exaggeration of what is the fact. No portion of the kingdom has advanced in prosperity so much; and if the honorable member (Mr. S. Crawford) will go down there, I will give him every facility for seeing the state of the people, and he shall judge with his own eyes whether my representation be not correct. I could go through a great many other particulars, but I will not trouble the house now with them. The statements I have made are accurate, and I am quite ready to prove them in any way that is necessary."

This same Mr. Loch has published a pamphlet, in which he has traced out the effects of the system pursued on the Sutherland estate, in many very important particulars. It appears from this that previously to 1811 the people were generally sub-tenants to middle men, who exacted high rents, and also various perquisites, such as the delivery of poultry and eggs, giving so many days' labor in harvest time, cutting and carrying peat and stones for building.

Since 1811 the people have become immediate tenants, at a greatly diminished rate of rent, and released from all these exactions. For instance, in two parishes, in 1812, the rents were one thousand five hundred and ninety-three pounds, and in 1823 they were only nine hundred and seventy-two pounds. In another parish the reduction of rents has amounted, on an average, to thirty-six per cent. Previous to 1811 the houses were turf huts of the poorest description, in many instances the cattle being kept under the same roof with the family. Since 1811 a large proportion, of their houses have been rebuilt in a superior manner—the landlord having paid them for their old timber where it could not be moved, and having also contributed the new timber, with lime.

Before 1811 all the rents of the estates were used for the personal profit of the landlord; but since that time, both by the present duke and his father, all the rents have been expended on improvements in the county, besides sixty thousand pounds more which have been remitted from. England for the purpose. This money has been spent on churches, school houses, harbors, public inns, roads, and bridges.

In 1811 there was not a carriage road in the county, and only two bridges. Since that time four hundred and thirty miles of road have been constructed on the estate, at the expense of the proprietor and tenants. There is not a turnpike gate in the county, and yet the roads are kept perfect.

Before 1811 the mail was conveyed entirely by a foot runner, and there was but one post office in the county; and there was no direct post across the county, but letters to the north and west were forwarded once a month. A mail coach has since been established, to which the late Duke of Sutherland contributed more than two thousand six hundred pounds; and since 1834 mail gigs have been established to convey letters to the north and west coast, towards which the Duke of Sutherland contributes three hundred pounds a year. There are thirteen post offices and sub-offices in the county. Before 1811 there was no inn in the county fit for the reception of strangers. Since that time there have been fourteen inns either built or enlarged by the duke.

Before 1811 there was scarcely a cart on the estate; all the carriage was done on the backs of ponies. The cultivation of the interior was generally executed with a rude kind of spade, and there was not a gig in the county. In 1845 there were one thousand one hundred and thirty carts owned on the estate, and seven hundred and eight ploughs, also forty-one gigs.

Before 1812 there was no baker, and only two shops. In 1845 there were eight bakers and forty-six grocer's shops, in nearly all of which shoe blacking was sold to some extent, an unmistakable evidence of advancing civilization.

In 1808 the cultivation of the coast side of Sutherland was so defective that it was necessary often, in a fall of snow, to cut down the young Scotch firs to feed the cattle on; and in 1808 hay had to be imported. *Now* the coast side of Sutherland exhibits an extensive district of land cultivated according to the best principles of modern agriculture; several thousand acres have been added to the arable land by these improvements.

Before 1811 there were no woodlands of any extent on the estate, and timber had to be obtained from a distance. Since that time many thousand acres of woodland have been planted, the thinnings of which, being sold to the people at a moderate rate, have greatly increased their comfort and improved their domestic arrangements.

Before 1811 there were only two blacksmiths in the county. In 1845 there were forty-two blacksmiths and sixty-three carpenters. Before 1829 the exports of the county consisted of black cattle of an inferior description, pickled salmon, and some ponies; but these were precarious sources of profit, as many died in winter for want of food; for example, in the spring of 1807 two hundred cows, five hundred cattle, and more than two hundred ponies died in the parish of Kildonan alone. Since that time the measures pursued by the Duke of Sutherland, in introducing improved breeds of cattle, pigs, and modes of agriculture, have produced results in exports which tell their own story. About forty thousand sheep and one hundred and eighty thousand fleeces of wool are exported annually, also fifty thousand barrels of herring.

The whole fishing village of Helmsdale has been built since that time. It now contains from thirteen to fifteen curing yards covered with slate, and several streets with houses similarly built. The herring fishery, which has been mentioned as so productive, has been established since the change, and affords employment to three thousand nine hundred people.

Since 1811, also, a savings bank has been established in every parish, of which the Duke of Sutherland is patron and treasurer, and the savings have been very considerable.

The education of the children of the people has been a subject of deep interest to the Duke of Sutherland. Besides the parochial schools, (which answer, I suppose, to our district schools,) of which the greater number have been rebuilt or repaired at an expense exceeding what is legally required for such purposes, the Duke of Sutherland contributes to the support of several schools for young females, at which sewing and other branches of education are taught; and in 1844 he agreed to establish twelve general assembly schools in such parts of the county as were without the sphere of the parochial schools, and to build school and schoolmasters' houses, which will, upon an average, cost two hundred pounds each; and to contribute annually two hundred pounds in aid of salaries to the teachers, besides a garden and cows' grass; and in 1845 he made an arrangement with the education committee of the Free church, whereby no child, of whatever persuasion, will be beyond the reach of moral and religious education.

There are five medical gentlemen on the estate, three of whom receive allowances from the Duke of Sutherland for attendance on the poor in the districts in which they reside.

An agricultural association, or farmers' club, has been formed under the patronage of the Duke of Sutherland, of which the other proprietors in the county, and the larger tenantry, are members, which is in a very active and flourishing state. They have recently invited Professor Johnston to visit Sutherland, and give lectures on agricultural chemistry.

The total population of the Sutherland estate is twenty-one thousand seven hundred and eighty-four. To have the charge and care of so large an estate, of course, must require very systematic arrangements; but a talent for system seems to be rather the forte of the English.

The estate is first divided into three districts, and each district is under the superintendence of a factor, who communicates with the duke through a general agent. Besides this, when the duke is on the estate, which is during a portion of every year, he receives on Monday whoever of his tenants wishes to see him. Their complaints or wishes are presented in writing; he takes them into consideration, and gives written replies.

Besides the three factors there is a ground officer, or sub-factor, in every parish, and an agriculturist in the Dunrobin district, who gives particular attention to instructing the people in the best methods of farming. The factors, the ground officers, and the agriculturists all work to one common end. They teach the advantages of draining; of ploughing deep, and forming their ridges in straight lines; of constructing tanks for saving liquid manure. The young farmers also pick up a great deal of knowledge when working as ploughmen or laborers on the more immediate grounds of the estate.

The head agent, Mr. Loch, has been kind enough to put into my hands a general report of the condition of the estate, which he drew up for the inspection of the duke, May 12, 1853, and in which he goes minutely over the condition of every part of the estate.

One anecdote of the former Duke of Sutherland will show the spirit which has influenced the family in their management of the estate. In 1817, when there was much suffering on account of bad seasons, the Duke of Sutherland sent down his chief agent to look into the condition of the people, who desired the ministers of the parishes to send in their lists of the poor. To his surprise it was found that there were located on the estate a number of people who had settled there without leave. They amounted to four hundred and eight families, or two thousand persons; and though they had no legal title to remain where they were, no hesitation was shown in supplying them with food in the same manner with those who were tenants, on the sole condition that on the first opportunity they should take cottages on the sea shore, and become industrious people. It was the constant object of the duke to keep the rents of his poorer tenants at a nominal amount.

What led me more particularly to inquire into these facts was, that I received by mail, while in London, an account containing some of these stories, which had been industriously circulated in America. There were dreadful accounts of cruelties practised in the process of inducing the tenants to change their places of residence. The following is a specimen of these stories:—

> "I was present at the pulling down and burning of the house of William Chisholm, Badinloskin, in which was lying his wife's mother, an old, bed-ridden woman of near one hundred years of age, none of the family being present. I informed the persons about to set fire to the house of this circumstance, and prevailed on them to wait till Mr. Sellar came. On his arrival I told him of the poor old woman being in a condition unfit for removal. He replied, 'Damn her, the old witch, she has lived too long; let her burn.' Fire was immediately set to the house, and the blankets in which she was carried were in flames

before she could be got out. She was placed in a little shed, and it was with great difficulty they were prevented from firing that also. The old woman's daughter arrived while the house was on fire, and assisted the neighbors in removing her mother out of the flames and smoke, presenting a picture of horror which I shall never forget, but cannot attempt to describe. She died within five days."

With regard to this story Mr. Loch, the agent, says, "I must notice the only thing like a fact stated in the newspaper extract which you sent to me, wherein Mr. Sellar is accused of acts of cruelty towards some of the people. This Mr. Sellar tested, by bringing an action against the then sheriff substitute of the county. He obtained a verdict for heavy damages. The sheriff, by whom, the slander was propagated, left the county. Both are since dead."

Having, through Lord Shaftesbury's kindness, received the benefit of Mr. Loch's corrections to this statement, I am permitted to make a little further extract from his reply. He says,—

"In addition to what I was able to say in my former paper, I can now state that the Duke of Sutherland has received, from, one of the most determined opposers of the measure, who travelled to the north of Scotland as editor of a newspaper, a letter regretting all he had written on the subject, being convinced that he was entirely misinformed. As you take so much interest in the subject, I will conclude by saying that nothing could exceed the prosperity of the county during the past year; their stock, sheep, and other things sold at high prices; their crops of grain and turnips were never so good, and the potatoes were free from all disease; rents have been paid better than was ever known. * * * As an instance of the improved habits of the farmers, no house is now built for them that they do not require a hot bath and water closets."

From this long epitome you can gather the following results; first, if the system were a bad one, the Duchess of Sutherland had nothing to do with it, since it was first introduced in 1806, the same year her grace was born; and the accusation against Mr. Sellar dates in 1811, when her grace was five or six years old. The Sutherland arrangements were completed in 1819, and her grace was not married to the duke till 1823, so that, had the arrangement been the worst in the world, it is nothing to the purpose so far as she is concerned.

As to whether the arrangement *is* a bad one, the facts which have been stated speak for themselves. To my view it is an almost sublime instance of the benevolent employment of superior wealth and power in shortening the struggles of advancing civilization, and elevating in a few years a whole community to a point of education and material prosperity, which, unassisted, they might never have obtained.

LETTER XVIII

LONDON, Sunday, May 8.

MY DEAR S.:—

Mr. S. is very unwell, in bed, worn out with, the threefold labor of making and receiving calls, visiting, and delivering public addresses. C. went to hear Dr. McNeile, of Liverpool, preach—one of the leading men of the established church evangelical party, a strong millenarian. C. said that he was as fine a looking person in canonicals as he ever saw in the pulpit. In doctrine he is what we in America should call very strong old school. I went, as I had always predetermined to do, if ever I came to London, to hear Baptist Noel, drawn thither by the melody and memory of those beautiful hymns of his[14], which must meet a response in every Christian heart. He is tall and well formed, with one of the most classical and harmonious heads I ever saw. Singularly enough, he reminded me of a bust of Achilles at the London Museum. He is indeed a swift-footed Achilles, but in another race, another warfare. Born of a noble family, naturally endowed with sensitiveness and ideality to appreciate all the amenities and suavities of that brilliant sphere, the sacrifice must have been inconceivably great for him to renounce favor and preferment, position in society,— which, here in England, means more than Americans can ever dream of,— to descend from being a court chaplain, to become a preacher in a Baptist dissenting chapel. Whatever may be thought of the correctness of the intellectual conclusions which led him to such a step, no one can fail to revere the strength and purity of principle which could prompt to such sacrifices. Many, perhaps, might have preferred that he should have chosen a less decided course. But if his judgment really led to these results, I see no way in which it was possible for him to have avoided it. It was with an emotion of reverence that I contrasted the bareness, plainness, and poverty of the little chapel with that evident air of elegance and cultivation which appeared in all that he said and did. The sermon was on the text, "Now abideth faith, hope, and charity, these three." Naturally enough, the subject divided itself into faith, hope, and charity.

His style calm, flowing, and perfectly harmonious, his delivery serene and graceful, the whole flowed over one like a calm and clear strain of music. It was a sermon after the style of Tholuck and other German sermonizers, who seem to hold that the purpose of preaching is not to rouse the soul by an antagonistic struggle with sin through the reason, but to soothe the passions, quiet the will, and bring the mind into a frame in which it shall incline to follow its own convictions of duty. They take for granted, that the reason why men sin is not because they are ignorant, but because they are distracted and tempted by passion; that they do not need so much to be told what is their duty, as persuaded to do it. To me, brought up on the very battle field of controversial theology, accustomed to hear every religious idea guarded by definitions, and thoroughly hammered on a logical anvil before the preacher thought of making any use of it for heart or conscience, though I enjoyed the discourse extremely, I could not help wondering what an American theological professor would make of such a sermon.

To preach on faith, hope, and charity all in one discourse—why, we should have six sermons on the nature of faith to begin with: on speculative faith; saving faith; practical faith, and the faith of miracles; then we should have the laws of faith, and the connection of faith with evidence, and the nature of evidence, and the different kinds of evidence, and so on. For my part I have had a suspicion since I have been here, that a touch of this kind of thing might improve English preaching; as, also, I do think that sermons of the kind I have described would be useful, by way of alterative, among us. If I could have but one of the two manners, I should prefer our own, because I think that this habit of preaching is one of the strongest educational forces that forms the mind of our country.

After the service was over I went into the vestry, and was introduced to Mr. Noel. The congregation of the established church, to which he ministered during his connection with it, are still warmly attached to him. His leaving them was a dreadful trial; some of them can scarcely mention his name without tears. C. says, with regard to the church singing, as far as he heard it, it is twenty years behind that in Boston. In the afternoon I staid at home to nurse Mr. S. A note from Lady John Russell inviting us there.

Monday, May 9. I should tell you that at the Duchess of Sutherland's an artist, named Burnard, presented me with a very fine cameo head of Wilberforce, cut from a statue in Westminster Abbey. He is from Cornwall, in the south of England, and has attained some celebrity as an artist. He wanted to take a bust of me; and though it always makes me laugh to think of having a new likeness, considering the melancholy results of all former enterprises, yet still I find myself easy to be entreated, in hopes, as Mr. Micawber says, that something may "turn up," though I fear the difficulty is radical in the subject. So I made an appointment with Mr. Burnard, and my very kind friend, Mr. B., in addition to all the other confusions I have occasioned in his mansion, consented to have his study turned into a studio. Upon the heels of this comes another sculptor, who has a bust begun, which he says is going to be finished in Parian, and published whether I sit for it or not, though, of course, he would much prefer to get a look at me now and then. Well, Mr. B. says he may come, too; so there you may imagine me in the study, perched upon a very high stool, dividing my glances between the two sculptors, one of whom, is taking one side of my face, and one the other.

To-day I went with Mr. and Mrs. B. to hear the examination of a borough-school for boys. Mrs. B. told me it was not precisely a charity school, but one where the means of education were furnished at so cheap a rate, that the poorest classes could enjoy them. Arrived at the hall, we found quite a number of *distingués*, bishops, lords, and clergy, besides numbers of others assembled to hear. The room was hung round with the drawings of the boys, and specimens of handwriting. I was quite astonished at some of them. They were executed by pen, pencil, or crayon—drawings of machinery, landscapes, heads, groups, and flowers, all in a style which any parent among us would be proud to exhibit, if done by our own children. The boys looked very bright and intelligent, and I was delighted with the system, of instruction which had evidently been pursued with them. We heard them first in the reading and recitation of poetry; after that in arithmetic and algebra, then in natural philosophy, and last, and most satisfactorily, in the Bible. It was perfectly evident from the nature of the questions and answers, that it was not a crammed examination, and that the readiness of reply proceeded not from a mere commitment of words, but from a system of intellectual training, which led to a good understanding of the subject. In arithmetic and algebra the answers were so remarkable as to induce the belief in some that the boys must have been privately prepared on their questions; but the teacher desired Lord John Russell to write down any number of questions which he wished to have given to the toys to solve, from his own mind. Lord John wrote down two or three problems, and I was amused at the zeal and avidity with which the boys seized upon and mastered them. Young England was evidently wide awake, and the prime minister himself was not to catch them, napping. The little fellows' eyes-glistened as they rattled off their solutions. As I know nothing about mathematics, I was all the more impressed; but when they came to be examined in the Bible, I was more astonished than ever. The masters had said that they would be willing any of the gentlemen should question them, and Mr. B. commenced a course of questions on the doctrines of Christianity; asking, Is there any text by which you can prove this, or that? and immediately, with great accuracy, the boys would cite text upon text, quoting not only the more obvious ones, but sometimes applying Scripture with an ingenuity and force which I had not thought of, and always quoting chapter and verse of every text. I do not know who is at the head of this teaching, nor how far it is a sample of English schools; but I know that these boys had been wonderfully well taught, and I felt all my old professional enthusiasm arising.

After the examination Lord John came forward, and gave the boys a good fatherly talk. He told them that they had the happiness to live under a free government, where all offices are alike open to industry and merit, and where any boy might hope by application and talent to rise to any station below that of the sovereign. He made some sensible, practical comments, on their Scripture lessons, and, in short, gave precisely such a kind of address as one of our New England judges or governors might to schoolboys in similar circumstances. Lord John hesitates a little in his delivery, but has a plain, common-sense way of "speaking right on," which seems to be taking. He is a very simple man in his manners, apparently not at all self-conscious, and entered into the feelings of the boys and the masters with good-natured sympathy, which was very winning. I should think he was one of the kind of men who are always perfectly easy and self-possessed let what will come, and who never could be placed in a situation in which he did not feel himself quite at home, and perfectly competent to do whatever was to be done.

To-day the Duchess of Sutherland called with the Duchess of Argyle. Miss Greenfield happened to be present, and I begged leave to present her, giving a slight sketch of her history. I was pleased with the kind and easy affability with which the Duchess of Sutherland conversed with her, betraying by no inflection of voice, and nothing in air or manner, the great lady talking with the poor girl. She asked all her questions with as much delicacy, and made her request to hear her sing with as much consideration and politeness, as if she had been addressing any one in her own circle. She seemed much pleased with her singing, and remarked that she should be happy to give her an opportunity of performing in Stafford House, so soon as she should be a little relieved of a heavy cold which seemed to oppress her at present. This, of course, will be decisive in her favor in London. The duchess is to let us know when the arrangement is completed.

I never realized so much that there really is no natural prejudice against color in the human mind. Miss Greenfield is a dark mulattress, of a pleasing and gentle face, though by no means handsome. She is short and thick set, with a chest of great amplitude, as one would think on hearing her tenor. I have never seen in any of the persons to whom I have presented her the least indications of suppressed surprise or disgust, any more than we should exhibit on the reception of a dark-complexioned Spaniard or Portuguese. Miss Greenfield bears her success with much quietness and good sense.

Tuesday, May 10. C. and I were to go to-day, with Mrs. Cropper and Lady Hatherton, to call on the poet Rogers. I was told that he was in very delicate health, but that he still received friends at his house. We found the house a perfect cabinet collection of the most rare and costly works of art—choicest marbles, vases, pictures, gems, and statuary met the eye every where. We spent the time in examining some of these while the servant went to announce us. The mild and venerable old man himself was the choicest picture of all. He has a splendid head, a benign face, and reminded me of an engraving I once saw of Titian. He seemed very glad to see us, spoke to me of the gathering at Stafford House, and asked me what I thought of the place. When I expressed my admiration, he said, "Ah, I have often said it is a fairy palace, and that the duchess is the good fairy." Again, he said, "I have seen all the palaces of Europe, but there is none that I prefer to this." Quite a large circle of friends now came in and were presented. He did not rise to receive them, but sat back in his easy chair, and conversed quietly with us all, sparkling out now and then in a little ripple of playfulness. In this room were his best beloved pictures, and it is his pleasure to show them to his friends.

By a contrivance quite new to me, the pictures are made to revolve on a pivot, so that by touching a spring they move out from the wall, and can be seen in different lights. There was a picture over the mantel-piece of a Roman Triumphal Procession, painted by Rubens, which attracted my attention by its rich coloring and spirited representation of animals.

The coloring of Rubens always satisfies my eye better than that of any other master, only a sort of want of grace in the conception disturbs me. In this case both conception and coloring are replete with beauty. Rogers seems to be carefully waited on by an attendant who has learned to interpret every motion and anticipate every desire.

I took leave of him with a touch of sadness. Of all the brilliant circle of poets, which has so delighted us, he is the last—and he so feeble! His memories, I am told, extend back to a personal knowledge of Dr. Johnson. How I should like to sit by him, and search into that cabinet of recollections! He presented me his poems, beautifully illustrated by Turner, with his own autograph on the fly leaf. He writes still a clear, firm, beautiful hand, like a lady's.

After that, we all went over to Stafford House, and the Duke and Duchess of Sutherland went with us into Lord Ellesmere's collection adjoining. Lord Ellesmere sails for America to-day, to be present at the opening of the Crystal Palace. He left us a very polite message. The Duchess of Argyle, with her two little boys, was there also. Lord Carlisle very soon came in, and with him—who do you think? Tell Hattie and Eliza if they could have seen the noble staghound that came bounding in with him, they would have turned from all the pictures on the wall to this living work of art.

Landseer thinks he does well when he paints a dog; another man chisels one in stone: what would they think of themselves if they could string the nerves and muscles, and wake up the affections and instincts, of the real, living creature? That were to be an artist indeed! The dog walked about the gallery, much at home, putting his nose up first to one and then another of the distinguished persons by whom he was surrounded; and once in a while stopping, in an easy race about the hall, would plant himself before a picture, with his head on one side, and an air of high-bred approval, much as I have seen young gentlemen do in similar circumstances. All he wanted was an eyeglass, and he would have been perfectly set up as a critic.

As for the pictures, I have purposely delayed coming to them. Imagine a botanist dropped into the middle of a blooming prairie, waving with unnumbered dyes and forms of flowers, and only an hour to examine and make acquaintance with them! Room, after room we passed, filled with Titians, Murillos, Guidos, &c. There were four Raphaels, the first I had ever seen. Must I confess the truth? Raphael had been my dream for years. I expected something which would overcome and bewilder me. I expected a divine baptism, a celestial mesmerism; and I found four very beautiful pictures—pictures which left me quite in possession of my senses, and at liberty to ask myself, am I pleased, and how much? It was not that I did not admire, for I did; but that I did not admire enough. The pictures are all holy families, cabinet size: the figures, Mary, Joseph, the infant Jesus, and John, in various attitudes. A little perverse imp in my heart suggested the questions, "If a modern artist had painted these, what would be thought of them? If I did not know it was Raphael, what should I think?" And I confess that, in that case, I should think that there was in one or two of them a certain hardness and sharpness of outline that was not pleasing to me. Neither, any more than Murillo, has he in these pictures shadowed forth, to my eye, the idea of Mary. Protestant as I am, no Catholic picture contents me. I thought to myself that I had seen among living women, and in a face not far off, a nobler and sweeter idea of womanhood.

It is too much to ask of any earthly artist, however, to gratify the aspirations and cravings of those who have dreamed of them for years unsatisfied. Perhaps no earthly canvas and brash can accomplish this marvel. I think the idealist must lay aside his highest ideal, and be satisfied he shall never meet it, and then he will begin to enjoy. With this mood and understanding I did enjoy very much an Assumption of the Virgin, by Guido, and more especially Diana and her Nymphs, by Titian: in this were that softness of outline, and that blending of light and shadow into each other, of which I felt the want in the Raphaels. I felt as if there was a perfection of cultivated art in this, a classical elegance, which, so far as it went, left the eye or mind nothing to desire. It seemed to me that Titian was a Greek painter, the painter of an etherealized sensuousness, which leaves the spiritual nature wholly unmoved, and therefore all that he attempts he attains. Raphael, on the contrary, has spiritualism; his works enter a sphere where at is more difficult to satisfy the soul; nay, perhaps from the nature of the case, impossible.

There were some glorious pieces of sunshine by Cuyp. There was a massive sea piece by Turner, in which the strong solemn swell of the green waves, and the misty wreathings of clouds, were powerfully given.

There was a highly dramatic piece, by Paul de la Roche, representing Charles I. in a guard room, insulted by the soldiery. He sits, pale, calm, and resolute, while they are puffing tobacco smoke in his face, and passing vulgar jokes. His thoughts appear to be far away, his eyes looking beyond them with an air of patient, proud weariness.

Independently of the pleasure one receives from particular pictures in these galleries, there is a general exaltation, apart from, critical considerations, an excitement of the nerves, a kind of dreamy state, which is a gain in our experience. Often in a landscape we first single out particular objects,—this old oak,—that cascade,—that ruin,—and derive from them, an individual joy; then relapsing, we view the landscape as a whole, and seem, to be surrounded by a kind of atmosphere of thought, the result of the combined influence of all. This state, too, I think is not without its influence in educating the æsthetic sense.

Even in pictures which we comparatively reject, because we see them, in the presence of superior ones, there is a wealth of beauty which would grow on us from day to day, could we see them, often. When I give a sigh to the thought that in our country we are of necessity, to a great extent, shut from the world of art, I then rejoice in the inspiring thought that Nature is ever the superior. No tree painting can compare with a splendid elm, in the plenitude of its majesty. There are colorings beyond those of Rubens poured forth around us in every autumn scene; there are Murillos smiling by our household firesides; and as for Madonnas and Venuses, I think with Byron,—

> "I've seen more splendid women, ripe and real,
> Than all the nonsense of their stone ideal."

Still, I long for the full advent of our American, day of art, already dawning auspiciously.

After finishing our inspection, we went back to Stafford House to lunch.

In the evening we went to Lord John Russell's. We found Lady Russell and her daughters sitting quietly around the evening lamp, quite by themselves. She is elegant and interesting in her personal appearance, and has the same charm of simplicity and sincerity of manner which we have found in so marry of the upper sphere. She is the daughter of the Earl of Minto, and the second wife of Lord John. We passed here an entirely quiet and domestic evening, with only the family circle. The conversation turned on various topics of practical benevolence, connected with the care and education of the poorer classes. Allusion being made to Mrs. Tyler's letter, Lady Russell expressed some concern lest the sincere and well-intended expression of the feeling of the English ladies might have done harm. I said that I did not think the spirit of Mrs. Tyler's letter was to be taken as representing the feeling of American ladies generally,—only of that class who are determined to maintain the rightfulness of slavery.

It seems to me that the better and more thinking part of the higher classes in England have conscientiously accepted the responsibility which the world has charged upon them of elevating and educating the poorer classes. In every circle since I have been here in England, I have heard the subject discussed as one of paramount importance.

One or two young gentlemen dropped in in the course of the evening, and the discourse branched out on the various topics of the day; such as the weather, literature, art, spiritual rappings, and table turnings, and all the floating et ceteras of life. Lady Russell apologized for the absence of Lord John in Parliament, and invited us to dine with, them at their residence in Richmond Park next week, when there is to be a parliamentary recess.

We left about ten o'clock, and went to pass the night with our friends Mr. and Mrs. Cropper at their hotel, being engaged to breakfast at the West End in the morning.

End of Volume I

NOTES

1.Since my return to the United States I have been informed that the Freewill Baptist denomination have adopted the same rigid principle of slavery exclusion that characterizes the Scotch Seceders and the Quakers. Let this be known to their honor.

2.This venerated, and erudite jurist, the friend and biographer of the celebrated Lord Jeffrey, has recently died.

3.This, alas! is no longer true. By the recent passage of the infamous Nebraska bill, this whole region, with the exception of two states already organized, is laid open to slavery. This faithless measure was nobly resisted by a large and able minority in Congress—honor to them.

4.This most learned and amiable judge recently died, while in the very act of charging a jury.

5.This resolution, drawn and offered, I think, by my hospitable friend, Mr. Binney, I have mislaid, and cannot find it. It was, however, in character and spirit, just what Mr. James here declares it to be.

6.I have been told since my return, that there are some slaveholding Congregational churches in the south; but they have no connection with our New England churches, and certainly are not generally known as Congregationalists distinct from the Presbyterians.

7.This has always been supposed and claimed in the United States. Now the time has come to test its truth. If there is this antislavery feeling in nine tenths of the people, the impudent iniquity of the Nebraska bill will call it forth.

8.Eight years ago I conscientiously approved and zealously defended this course of the American Board. Subsequent events have satisfied me, that, in the present circumstances of our country, making concessions to slaveholders, however slightly, and with whatever motives, even if not wrong in principle, is productive of no good. It does but strengthen slavery, and makes its demands still more exorbitant, and neutralizes the power of gospel truth.

9.This state of things is fast changing. Church members at the south now defend slavery as right. This is a new thing.

10.When your chimney has smoked as long as ours, it will, may be, need sweeping too.

11. Had I known all about New York and Boston which recent examinations have developed, I should have answered very differently. The fact is, that we in America can no longer congratulate ourselves on not having a degraded and miserable class in our cities, and it will be seen to be necessary for us to arouse to the very same efforts which, have been so successfully making in England.

12. This idea is beautifully wrought out by Mrs. Jamieson in her Characteristics of the Women of Shakspeare, to which, the author is indebted for the suggestion.

13. James Russell Lowell's "Beaver Brook."

14. The hymns beginning with, these lines, "If human, kindness meet return," and "Behold where, in a mortal form," are specimens.